Although psychologists have been relatively reticent in approaching ethical issues as a research topic, some have begun to use psychological principles, theories, and studies to understand and solve ethical dilemmas in their research. This book examines relations between ethics and psychology: the contributions that psychology can make to ethical studies and standards in all areas of human empirical science, and the specific ethics of psychological research.

The eleven contributors describe the kinds of ethical problems that arise in psychological research, review current literature with a focus on empirical studies of ethical issues in human research, and identify the theoretical and methodological tools they use to understand the ethical problems arising in their work. This book addresses important issues such as the definitions of normative and deviant groups, the discovery and neutralization of bias, sensitivity to the interests of experimental subjects, and the counterweighing factors in rules, regulations, and enforcement.

Barbara H. Stanley is a professor of psychology at City University of New York, John Jay College, and a lecturer in the Department of Psychiatry at Columbia University. Joan E. Sieber is a professor of psychology at California State University, Hayward. They are the coeditors of *Social Research on Children and Adolescents: Ethical Issues*. Gary B. Melton is a professor of neuropsychiatry, law, pediatrics, and psychology and director of the Institute for Families in Society at the University of South Carolina. He is the editor of *Adolescent Abortion: Psychological and Legal Issues* (Nebraska 1986).

Research Ethics

A PSYCHOLOGICAL APPROACH

EDITED BY BARBARA H. STANLEY,
JOAN E. SIEBER, AND GARY B. MELTON

UNIVERSITY OF NEBRASKA PRESS
LINCOLN AND LONDON

Acknowledgment for the use of previously
published material appears on page 105.

⊖ The paper in this book meets the minimum
requirements of American National Standard
for Information Sciences—Permanence of
Paper for Printed Library Materials,
ANSI Z39.48-1984.

Library of Congress Cataloging-in-
Publication Data
Stanley, Barbara, 1949–   Research ethics:
a psychological approach/Barbara H. Stanley,
Joan E. Sieber, and Gary B. Melton.
p.   cm.   Includes bibliographical
references and index.
ISBN 0-8032-4188-7 (cl: alk. paper)
1. Psychology—Research—Moral and ethical
aspects.   I. Sieber, Joan E.   II. Melton,
Gary B.   III. Title.   BF76.5.S67   1996
174'.915—dc20   95-22886   CIP

To the memory of Michael and to my children, Melissa and Thomas.—BHS

To Ric, my husband and best friend, who was always there to make dinner while I wrote, and to Ernest Fleaburger, who kept my lap warm throughout.—JES

To Julie, Jennifer, and Stephany.—GBM

Contents

Preface

This book is based on the premise that empirical investigation can play an important role in the development of ethical principles and standards that guide research on humans. The contributors to this volume review empirical research that can contribute significantly both to the development of such principles and standards and to their intelligent interpretation in the actual conduct of research.

Many investigators have criticized the development of ethical codes as insensitive to the scientific requirements of their particular kind of research. Empirical research on issues connected with such ethical problems can yield solutions that improve, rather than hinder, the ethics, validity, and practicality of scientific procedures. As the ensuing chapters illustrate, such empirical research can transform unfortunate conflicts between some general notion of "ethics" and requirements for scientific validity into win-win procedures that meet the goals of both normative ethics and scientific validity.

Ethical issues in conducting psychological research on humans have been a growing concern to psychologists, as well as to other basic and applied social scientists, to gatekeepers of social and behavioral research such as Institutional Review Boards (IRBS), and to those whose primary focus is epidemiology and biomedical research. Accordingly, ethical principles, codes, and guidelines for psychological research have been developed by the American Psychological Association (APA) and by other professional organizations and governmental agencies concerned with human research.

However, these efforts leave many relevant ethical questions unanswered and fail to provide much needed guidance to those who do research on human subjects. Although the definition of ethical conduct of research is a normative undertaking, the application of normative ethical principles often depends on untested empirical assumptions. For example, the ability of research participants to give truly informed consent depends on many factors that cognitive, personality, clinical, or social psychologists can examine empirically. Viewed from the perspective presented in the book, it becomes obvious that the ability to give informed consent may not necessarily depend on one's age or level of intellectual sophistication, for example, but on how information is presented. Such issues, which are relevant to the ethics and the validity of human research, can only be resolved through empirical research that can tell us *how* to do what is right.

This book is the product of a symposium convened by the APA Committee for the Protection of Human Participants in Research (CPHPR) at the University of Nebraska–Lincoln to examine the role of empirical study on ethical issues in research. This meeting critically reviewed studies of (1) ethical decision-making bodies, (2) privacy protection, (3) subject and experimenter bias, (4) communication in the research setting, and (5) informed consent and competency. Participants were Gary Melton, Joan Sieber and Barbara Stanley (conference organizers), Robert Boruch, Thomas Grisso, Craig Lawson, Douglas Peters, Robert Rosenthal, Michael Saks, Lawrence Tancredi, and William Thompson, with staff support from Eric Meslin of APA and Denise Herrell of the University of Nebraska. We gratefully acknowledge the support of the APA through CPHPR and APA Divisions 12 (Clinical Psychology) and 37 (Child, Youth, and Family Services), of the Interdisciplinary Applied Ethics Program of the University of Nebraska–Lincoln, and of Craig Lawson, professor of Law, for graciously facilitating, as well as participating in the conference.

It is our hope that the following reviews of ethics-relevant empirical research will demonstrate to investigators the usefulness of empirical study of ethical issues in research and that the research agendas proposed herein will inspire others to conduct useful empirical research on problems of research ethics.

Introduction / Empirical Study of Ethical Issues in Psychological Research

JOAN E. SIEBER
California State University, Hayward

Concern for ethical issues in the conduct of psychological research on humans has grown over the past two decades. The American Psychological Association (APA) has been active in developing standards for the protection of research subjects. Even though psychologists as a group have been relatively reticent in approaching ethical issues as a research topic, some psychologists have begun to use psychological principles, theories, and research findings to understand and solve ethical dilemmas in research. This book presents the work of some of these psychologists, and its authors hope to interest others in similar kinds of inquiry. It describes the kinds of ethical problems that arise in psychological research, reviews current literature on research ethics relevant to psychology, focusing especially on empirical studies of ethical issues in human research, and identifies the theoretical and methodological tools psychologists may use to solve or better understand ethical problems arising in research.

Research on Research Ethics?

This book is about an intuitively obvious idea that has remained astonishingly obscure to research psychologists: the theories and methods of social and behavioral research are uniquely suited to understanding and

Special thanks go to Mary P. diSibio, Bruce E. Trumbo, Barbara H. Stanley, Gary B. Melton, and Wendy A. Braga who read earlier drafts and provided valuable criticism; the errors that remain are my own.

solving problems of research ethics in psychology, that is, problems of figuring out *how* to conduct research ethically. Ethicists, as well as the APA
Ethical Principles, tell psychologists *what* is ethical conduct in research.
But, knowing what and knowing how are two different matters, and it remains for researchers to learn how to behave ethically in given research
settings.

What a researcher must know in order to conduct research on human
subjects ethically includes (1) what are the perspectives of the research participants, that is, their expectations, concerns, and beliefs about the research, (2) how can one communicate with participants about the research
in terms they understand, (3) how can one respect those privacies that are
important to the participants, (4) how can one conduct the most valid research possible at the least risk to participants and society, and (5) what are
the researchers' own scientific perspectives and those of other scientists?
Scientists may hold any of a number of perspectives, as shown in examples
5 and 7. One's perspective affects one's view of what comprises an ethical
concern and how such a concern may be understood and resolved. The scientist who believes in the myth that there is a single scientific perspective
can be counted on to respond naively or blindly to many ethical dilemmas.

Questions (1) through (5) are empirical ones regarding (1) beliefs and attitudes, (2) communication and comprehension, (3) personal concerns regarding control of information and exposure of self, (4) methodology and
risk assessment, and (5) socialization of scientific values, respectively.
Knowing the answers to these and other kinds of empirical questions
about ethical matters enables investigators to conduct research ethically. In
turn, ethical research leads to the ability, in most instances, to obtain valid
results, the necessary cooperation of research participants, and the societal
support needed to sustain science.

In some cases, researchers need to ask empirical questions about a *given*
research population or research procedure in order to discover the best
way to conduct a *specific* research project. In example 1, chairs of psychology departments were to be surveyed about a sensitive matter: Do they
conduct their subject pool in conformity with federal law and the APA Ethical Code? The researchers were reasonably certain that most departments
were not in total compliance with these sets of standards and wondered
how willing respondents would be to expose their noncompliance. To ensure honest responses, the researchers considered asking subjects to remain anonymous. However, anonymity would have made it impossible to
recontact respondents in order to follow up on especially interesting re-

sponses, such as voluntary information about innovative departmental subject-pool policies and procedures. To determine the candor of responses without relinquishing the opportunity to follow up some responses, the investigators conducted the survey with two experimental conditions: anonymous and identified (but confidential). The results enabled them to evaluate the candor of the responses they obtained, provided insight into respondent sensitivity to organizational privacy, and answered questions about the value of promises of confidentiality versus anonymity.

In other cases, empirical questions on research ethics can be asked generally, and the answers will enlighten research generally. Two volumes have been devoted to examination of such issues (Sieber, 1982c, 1982d). In example 6, Campbell, Boruch, Schwartz, and Steinberg asked how two or more independent investigators who wished to merge and analyze separate confidential data files could do so without releasing information on individual cases to one another. Having formulated the question, they then devised a general method for preserving the confidentiality of data in such circumstances.

So far, I have made or implied three claims, each of which will be supported later in this chapter: There are many kinds of empirical questions one may ask about the ethics of psychological research; there are many approaches to researching these various questions; and the knowledge gained from such research will benefit psychology in many ways. The reader willing to entertain these possibilities for now may still be less than ready to consider doing research on research ethics. What, indeed, would motivate a psychologist to undertake research in this area? Certainly research on these kinds of topics has been funded, and many investigators have become known for such research. The National Science Foundation currently has two programs, Ethics and Values Studies and Law and Social Science, likely to fund research in these areas. Various journals are likely to publish research on research ethics, including *American Psychologist, Law and Human Behavior, Ethics and Behavior, Science, Technology and Human Values,* and *IRB: A Review of Human Research.* However, the main reason, so far, that psychologists have conducted research on research ethics is to advance knowledge in other research areas in which they are already engaged. This may come about in a variety of ways.

The investigator may work in a substantive area of psychology that is relevant to research ethics, such as the socialization of scientists (e.g., Kimble, 1984, example 5; Mitroff & Kilmann, 1978, example 8), privacy as a behavioral phenomenon (e.g., Laufer & Wolfe, 1977, example 7), organizational research (e.g., Mirvis & Seashore, 1982), or research on children (e.g., Stanley & Sieber, 1992).

The investigator may work primarily as a methodologist and may direct attention to seeking methodological solutions to ethical problems, such as those of ensuring privacy, confidentiality, or validity of research in certain kinds of research settings (e.g., Campbell et al., 1977, example 6).

Investigators may find that their own research on sensitive topics or vulnerable populations requires that they undertake empirical study of ethical problems. Stanley (chap. 3), Melton (chap. 5), and Grisso (chap. 6) are notable examples of empirical researchers whose concern for ways to respect the autonomy of vulnerable subjects led them to conduct research on the consent process.

Investigators sometimes find themselves embroiled in an ethical or political conflict that motivates them to examine the issues that have caused turmoil in their own professional life (e.g., Peters & Ceci, 1982).

Ethical problems sometimes must be solved in order to ensure that participants will cooperate and that valid results will be obtained (e.g, examples 1 and 2).

Some new research problems pose such a complex of methodological and ethical puzzles that they call for the development of a whole new outlook on procedures and ethics. For example, how does one study crack use among gay teenage runaways who are at high risk of contracting AIDS? When, as often happens, one's "emancipated" subjects return home, what is the legal and ethical responsibility of the researcher to communicate the nature of the research to the parents, who may be unaware of many aspects of their child's behavior (Rotheram-Borus & Koopman, 1991)?

Psychologists who have found themselves troubled by ethical questions about research over the years sometimes find that research and scholarship on those concerns become the next logical direction of inquiry (e.g., Kelman, 1968, 1972).

Thus, various routes may lead psychologists to consider conducting research on research ethics. Most frequently, one begins with a pilot study, a study-within-a-study, a poststudy evaluation, or a surrogate subject study (i.e., asking people how they would feel about being a subject in a study in which such and such will occur)—any of which may be designed to inform one about the methodology or ethics of one's research. The following two examples illustrate research on research ethics performed in the service of a larger study. Example 1 is a study-within-a-study that I blush to present, being one of the investigators, but one that is the most obvious example I can recall. Example 2 comprises a pilot study and a poststudy evaluation that, in combination, were vital to the success of an elegant field experiment on the educational value of *Sesame Street*.

Example 1: The 366 psychology departments in the United States with both graduate and undergraduate departments were surveyed to learn how they conduct their subject pools and whether their procedures comply with federal law and APA standards. In designing the study, the investigators (Sieber & Saks, 1989) wondered about the following ethics-related questions: How sensitive and private would respondents consider their subject-pool practices to be, particularly if their pool did not entirely comply with federal and APA standards? Would a promise of confidentiality be sufficient to induce respondents to answer truthfully, or would anonymity produce greater honesty?

Since the survey was expected to produce about a 75% response rate (it turned out to be 89%), there were enough subjects to permit random assignment of departments to anonymous and identified (but confidential) conditions. The researchers reasoned that, if the identified respondents were to lie about any of their practices, they would lie on the nine questions that ask, in effect, whether the department complies with federal regulations and the APA code of ethics, yielding spuriously higher, that is, more ethical-appearing, scores as a group than their anonymous counterparts. Analysis of these data indicated that the identified departments had insignificantly higher scores derived from these nine questions (mean = 3.59) than the anonymous departments (mean = 3.31). Other evidence confirmed that the identified respondents were sensitive about their exposure. Nine of the departments asked to identify themselves did not do so. A review of their responses revealed that these departments were unusually far from compliance with federal and APA requirements. In response to an invitation to submit their subject-pool policy statements, only 19.4% of the anonymous respondents did so, compared with 31.4% of the identified respondents. Among those in the anonymous condition, most tore off the cover sheet or removed identifying information, and some sent their material under separate cover. However, a few departments in the anonymous condition sent unusually exemplary and complex subject pool procedures; these departments insisted on giving their name and the name of their university, even though they had been specifically requested to remain anonymous. Significantly, the identified respondents more often accompanied their admissions of violations of standards or law with defensive explanations or rationales than did the anonymous respondents.

In summary, the ethics-experiment-within-the-survey revealed that respondents were about as honest in the anonymous condition as in the identified condition, although some in the identified condition obviously felt apprehension about their disclosures. Having half of the respondents in the identified condition meant that half of the interesting surveys were available for telephone follow-up, which revealed additional useful information about subject-pool policies that work especially well.

Rather than embed the "research on research ethics" within the research it is intended to illuminate, some researchers have chosen to examine the "research ethics" question in a pilot study before the main study or in a poststudy analysis. Both approaches are exemplified in example 2:

Example 2: The researcher who evaluated the educational effects of *Sesame Street* (Conner, 1982) asked himself the following question: Is it acceptable to perform experiments in field settings that involve intrusion into the everyday lives of people? Are there conditions under which controlled field experimentation, with random assignment of subjects, is both acceptable to subjects and ethically defensible?

Most scientists and statisticians would hold that the only valid evaluation of the educational television program *Sesame Street* would be one involving random assignment of children to experimental and control conditions (e.g., Tukey, 1977), but this would mean assigning young children to conditions randomly, not on the basis of need. Would the random assignment, requisite to validity, be morally acceptable? Parents must consent to the installation of cable television and to having their children participate and be tested, but would parents consent to having their children be in the control group and undergo testing without having the benefit of the cable television? Having formulated the dilemma in this way, the investigators soon discovered a tentative solution: The experimental group subjects would be given the cable television in their homes during the first six months and would be tested over that period. The control-group subjects would be offered the cable television during the subsequent six months in return for being tested during the first six months. The investigators were then in a position to conduct some preexperimental field research on parents' perception of the situation. They found that parents were perfectly happy for their children to be in either the control or the experimental group under these conditions.

The *Sesame Street* experiment showed that some children made no educational gains. A postexperimental study examined what actually happened. It turned out that many of the experimental-group children were kept from watching *Sesame Street* by older brothers and sisters who controlled the television set and preferred to watch other programs. Parents who considered the television to be a baby-sitter rather than an educator did not bother to intervene (Cook et al., 1975), a problem that was addressed in subsequent evaluations.

Another way to begin research on research ethics is with a good idea for solving a generic ethical problem in research. For example, how can one obtain answers to "unposable" questions such as these: Have you struck your child in anger this week? Have you evaded income tax this year? Have you used illegal drugs this month? There are three reasons an investigator should not ask these kinds of questions: Data about criminal behavior may be subpoenaed, and thus investigators cannot ensure confidentiality unless they are willing to face jail sentences; persons who have committed criminal acts such as these are likely to lie to the investigator even if they are promised confidentiality; and it is mutually embarrassing for a researcher and respondent to deal with such questions. To circumvent these problems, the investigator must obtain usable data without knowing how any specific individual responded, and the subject must understand that this is so.

Example 3: Economist and algebraist Stanley Warner (1965) solved the problem by developing the randomized-response method. Since Warner's invention of this method, many variations have been developed to solve a wide range of data-gathering problems. These methods are summarized and described in Boruch and Cecil (1979, 1982), and by Boruch, Dennis, and Cecil in chapter 7. The following simplified example illustrates the basic concepts underlying the randomized-response method.

Suppose an investigator wishes to estimate the proportion of parents who have physically abused their children during the current week. He or she plans to base the estimate on a sample of 400, and therefore selects 600 subjects. The researcher fills a jar with 600 beads, 400 of which are red, 100 white, and 100 blue (or with any large number of beads, varying the color in these proportions). Each subject is asked to draw a bead, privately note its color, and replace it. The subject is then to answer the question "Have you struck your child in anger this week?" Subjects who draw a red bead are to give the true answer; those who draw a white bead are to say "yes" irrespective of the true answer; subjects who draw a blue bead are to say "no" arbitrarily. Consequently, there will be approximately 400 true answers and 100 false "yes" responses. The proportion of parents who have abused their children in the previous week is estimated by subtracting 100 from the total number of "yes" responses and dividing by 400.

The investigator does not know whether the respondent was answering the sensitive question or responding to instructions to give an arbitrary yes or no response. The proportion of persons who have struck a son or daughter in anger can be accurately estimated, but individual responses remain unknown; hence, no one's privacy is violated and the confidentiality of the data cannot be breached. Various other examples of methodological research pertaining to ways of ensuring the privacy of research participants and the confidentiality of data are discussed in chapter 7 by Boruch, Dennis, and Cecil.

As the examples are intended to convey, scientifically useful knowledge can be gained through empirical research on ethics-related questions. Yet few psychologists have ventured to investigate the ethical questions that arise in their research.

Some Misconceptions about Research Ethics

Why are more psychologists not using the conceptual and methodological tools of their trade to understand and solve ethical problems in their research? Why do some look puzzled at the mention of empirical work on research ethics? Many psychologists and other scientists would claim that science is value free and has nothing to do with ethics. Warwick (1980) has described the limited ethical perspectives of some psychologists in his description of four ways in which they deal with the tension between science and ethics:

1. By claiming that talk of values and ethics in science represents semantic confusion
2. By taking one's values from prevailing social norms and not examining the specific values of science
3. By focusing extensively on a particular ethical issue such as scientific freedom or problems of social repression and ignoring the broader matrix of ethical conflict in which science operates
4. By asserting that science inevitably contributes to human welfare without examining whether this is indeed so.

But even among those who do consider ethical issues in research, many regard ethical matters to be outside the purview of empirical investigation, seeing ethics as a normative discipline, a domain of philosophical rather than psychological study. This view obscures the fact that important ethical problems can yield to empirical inquiry. Moreover, social scientists often confuse "research ethics" with legal and professional requirements. For example, informed consent is often mistakenly treated merely as a legal procedure rather than as communication that is integral to research design. When psychologists give these matters further thought, they recognize that empirical research on problems such as consent can enhance the power and precision of psychological research. For example, research on variations in consent procedures could yield important scientific information about rapport, commitment, sampling bias due to recruitment procedures that produce a "volunteer effect," and so on. For the most part, however, psychologists have not addressed these issues, and they fail to recognize, for example, the possible induction effects that might be attributable to particular informed-consent procedures.

Social and behavioral scientists sometimes use the word *ethics* as a synonym for a professional code, a law, or professional etiquette. They may refer to an enforceable law or to a powerful public opinion as "an ethic" or may believe that law or public opinion is what gives "an ethic" its force. According to this mistaken usage, informed consent may be regarded as "an ethic" or a point of professional etiquette. The presumption is that one can be for or against informed consent without regard for broader issues such as respect for the autonomy of research participants or the validity of the research.

In contrast to this mistaken notion about "an ethic," research on research ethics is about solving ethical dilemmas, that is, conflicts between such broader issues as respect and validity. To formulate the particular dilemma that is to be resolved, one needs a more refined definition of ethics as it pertains to research on humans. To continue with our present example, one needs to understand what informed consent entails and why it is important. In addition, one must understand why informed consent, as traditionally conceived, may conflict with some other ethical principle. For example, when research requires deception, the principle of informed consent conflicts with the principle that research be valid. When the ethical dilemma is stated, then one can begin to seek ways to solve the dilemma, that is, to satisfy all or most of the ethical or methodological criteria by some creative new means.

Still another misconception about "research ethics" is that it is about refraining from the obviously unethical—fudging data, claiming credit for the work of others, stealing from one's research grant, and so on. In fact, the kinds of problems that will concern us here are problems that ensnare well-meaning researchers—problems having to do with harmful, unintended side effects of research.

Obviously we need to clarify the meaning of ethics in this context. Even before defining what we, as psychologists, mean by "ethics" here, it is useful to consider what philosophers mean by "ethics," since we build on that definition.

Philosophical Conceptions of Research Ethics

Ethics attempts to find the most general rules for judging the rightness or wrongness of conduct. Normative ethical theories are the various formulations philosophers employ to decide what is the "right thing to do." Because ordinary people and philosophers widely disagree about what is moral or right, there are various normative ethical theories. The three main theories that have been used to analyze moral choices in human research are briefly mentioned here to illustrate how ethical theories may be used to delineate ethical issues in psychological research and to decide what is right and wrong. These three theories, which we shall examine, in highly simplified form, are rule utilitarianism, act utilitarianism, and deontology. Rule utilitarians hold that one should choose the course of action that is generally likely to produce the most good. Act utilitarians hold that one should choose the course of action that would produce the most good in that particular case. And deontologists would choose the course of action that, irrespective of outcome, they believe to be right (e.g., a wrong such as lying or deceiving is never justified, even if it would produce a good outcome in a given case or set of cases).

It is not necessarily true that proponents of different ethical theories reach different conclusions about what a psychological researcher should and should not do. However, the elements they emphasize in their thinking differ, sometimes to the degree that different conclusions would follow. For example, if a rule utilitarian, an act utilitarian, and a deontologist were asked to evaluate the ethics of Milgram's research on obedience (Milgram, 1974), three different perceptions of the problem would be given, but not necessarily three different recommendations as to whether the research should have been conducted. Before considering what philosophers of dif-

ferent ethical persuasions would be likely to think about Milgram's research, it would be useful to summarize his study:

Example 4: Milgram's research was designed to discover whether
willingness to obey orders to harm or kill another can be created in ordinary people, as opposed to the common perception that such hei-
nous behavior is committed only by evil people. Stanley Milgram, a
social psychologist, advertised in local newspapers for persons to
participate in a learning experiment at Yale University. Volunteers
were told they would be divided by lot into learners and teachers.
Milgram's real aim was to study obedience, not learning, and the volunteers all found themselves in the role of teacher, where they were
instructed to teach lists of words to learners and to give learners increasingly severe electric shocks at every mistake. The "teacher" subjects did not realize that the "learners" were not really wired to the
shock apparatus and were instead paid confederates who pretended
both failure to learn and pain at being "shocked." After each subject
had either continued shocking the "student" until he appeared to
have collapsed or refused to continue shocking the "student," the
real purpose and procedure were explained.

About 65% of the subjects were willing to continue delivering shock
until they had reached levels labeled as lethal and had produced what
appeared to be grave injury or death to their subjects. Subjects who had
obediently delivered "severe shock" were assured, in the debriefing that
followed immediately, that obedience under these conditions was not unusual—that there is a human tendency to respond obediently to persons
who appear to have power and authority and to know what they are doing.
All subjects were offered the services of a skilled psychotherapist if they
wished to explore in depth their actions and feelings. A one-year follow-up
was carried out to determine whether participation in the study had had
detrimental effects. Most of the participants reported they were grateful for
the insight that their participation had provided, and only 1.3% of subjects
indicated that they wished they had not participated. Milgram's obedience
research yielded important insights into the conditions that produce
"blind obedience," and it defied both common and expert opinion on the
subject. Psychiatrists had been polled before the research and had opined
that only about 0.003 of subjects drawn from the general population would
deliver "shock" at a level known by them to be possibly lethal when ordered to do so by an authority figure.

In judging how ethical this research is, each of our three hypothetical ethicists would recognize that Milgram had selected a socially important topic and a valid research method and had taken many precautions to protect, debrief, and follow up on his research participants. Each would have noted that he used deception and had caused considerable emotional upset to participants. Utilitarian theory would emphasize the outcome—most of the participants expressed appreciation for what they had learned about themselves, immediately as well as one year after the study, and the knowledge provided to society was important and nonobvious. The rule utilitarian would have been troubled that deception was employed but may have looked to a more general rule, that the value of the research far outweighed the risk of harm or wrong to subjects. The act utilitarian may have been less troubled about the deception, since in this particular case the quality of the debriefing, the satisfaction of subjects with their participation in the research, and the importance of the research far outweighed the risk of harm to subjects; it is the particular case, not the general case, that counts for the act utilitarian. The deontologist would have emphasized the process rather than the outcome; deception was used and that is wrong, even when not harmful.

In contrast, if a college sophomore were to propose to replicate Milgram's study, with no expectation of new results or publishable replication of prior findings and with none of the resources required to debrief and follow up responsibly, ethicists of all three persuasions would probably decide that the research should not be done. Neither utilitarian would find a preponderance of good outcomes to override the harm of deception, and hence the outcome of their decision would resemble that of the deontologist.

We see that ethical theories use ethical principles. The National Commission on the Protection of Human Subjects (1978) identified three fundamental ethical principles that should govern human research: respect for the autonomy of persons; beneficence, or concern to support the best interests of human subjects in research and the best interests of society; and justice, or fairness of procedures and outcomes so that there is an equitable distribution of social benefits and costs.

From these three principles, the National Commission derived the following norms of ethical scientific research:

1. Validity of the research design. Valid research design takes account of relevant theory, methods, and prior findings, and it samples from the appropriate population only as many subjects as are needed to validly test the hypotheses that have been advanced.

The norm of validity is derived from the principles of respect and beneficence: subjects are not to be used for trivial purposes, and valid results should be obtained at minimal cost to society. Invalid research is unethical.

2. Competence of the investigator or adequate supervision. Well-designed research in the hands of incompetent or unsupervised investigators may yield invalid results and may cause harm to subjects, as in the hypothetical case of the college sophomore who sought to replicate Milgram's obedience studies. This norm derives from the principles of respect and beneficence.

3. Risk/benefit assessment. Investigators should consider the possible risks and benefits of the research. All reasonable steps should be taken to minimize the risks of harm and to maximize the benefit of the research to subjects, science, and society. As illustrated in the chapters that follow, the kinds of risk that arise in social research are typically psychological, legal, or economic rather than physical. The norm of risk/benefit assessment derives from the principle of beneficence.

4. Selection of subjects. Sampling decisions and recruitment procedures should be dictated by principles of sound science and justice. The sampling should permit adequate testing of anticipated sources of variance and appropriate generalization of findings. The population that will benefit from the research should, if possible, be the population from which the sample is drawn. Those with limited power or autonomy ordinarily should not be used as subjects. This norm derives from the principles of beneficence, respect, and justice.

5. Voluntary informed consent. Subjects should be able to consent freely without threat or undue inducement. They should be informed of and fully comprehend all that a reasonable person in that situation would want to know before giving consent. The concept of voluntary informed consent is difficult to interpret and to apply in some research settings, such as research on children, the retarded, or persons who are incarcerated or who are studied within settings where they are not free to decide without feeling pressure from others. For example, students may feel pressure from classmates or teachers, and employees from management. It is also difficult to interpret and implement the concept of voluntary informed consent when the informing is about a matter that

ordinary people tend to misunderstand, for example, probabilities of risk and benefit. The norm of voluntary informed consent derives from the principles of respect and beneficence.

6. Compensation for injury. The national commission recommended that subjects be compensated on a no-fault basis for injury in biomedical research. The Brookings Panel on Social Experimentation (Rivlin & Timpane, 1975) recommended that there be compensation in the case of social research as well. Most institutions in which social research is conducted are insured against injury through worker's compensation insurance. Physical injury in social research is rare. A more typical form of injury is psychological upset, which is usually compensated by provision of resources for counseling or psychotherapy. The norm of compensation for injury derives from all three principles.

Readers who are interested in a more detailed discussion of the nature of ethical theory or of the specific ethical principles that are considered to apply to human research are referred in general to *The Belmont Report* (National Commission for the Protection of Human Subjects of Biomedical and Behavioral Research, 1978) and in particular to Appendix Volume 1 in the report, especially the chapters "Basic Ethical Principles in the Conduct of Biomedical and Behavioral Research Involving Human Subjects," by H. Tristram Englehardt, "How to Identify Ethical Principles," by Alasdair MacIntyre, and "Some Ethical Issues in Research Involving Human Subjects," by LeRoy Walters.

Ethical Dilemmas in Psychological Research

Most research on research ethics is performed to examine or resolve an ethical dilemma. An ethical dilemma arises in human research when there is a conflict between any of the three fundamental principles of human research formulated by the national commission or between any of the six research norms that derive from them. For example, Milgram's research on obedience was beneficent; it produced valid, useful knowledge about a significant problem. However, it did not respect research participants' autonomy; it deceived them. But it appeared to Milgram and most other psychologists that valid results could not be obtained without deception. Here, the principles of beneficence and respect, as well as norms of consent and validity, are in conflict, creating an ethical dilemma. Should such research be done? Is there a valid way to conduct such research without deception? This is a methodological and empirical question—not a question that an ethicist could answer, but one for an experimental social psychologist to explore. Daniel Geller (1982), an experimental social psychologist and student of Milgram's, experimented with alternative methods using Milgram's equipment and settings. He found that subjects who were told that the shock was not real and that they were to role play as though it were replicated Milgram's results almost exactly, suggesting that role playing may reveal more about human nature than is generally believed and deserves further investigation.

In the discussion of ethical dilemmas so far, each dilemma has been stated so that it stands out in bold relief. In actual research, dilemmas do not always reveal themselves so clearly. In the hands of researchers who are not attuned to ethical issues in research, they may remain implicit. Even researchers who are attuned to ethical issues may find themselves enmeshed in dilemmas that are startling both in their subtlety and in their seriousness. The following are some ways in which ethical dilemmas may arise:[1]

An ethical problem may be unforeseen by the investigator and may even remain so after the study is completed. In example 2, Conner did not foresee that some of his young subjects in the *Sesame Street* field experiment would be placed in a situation in which they would perform poorly because they were bullied by older siblings and prevented from watching the programs on which they would be tested. Fortunately, his postexperimental investigations revealed this problem, and it was avoided in subsequent trials.

An ethical problem may be inadequately anticipated. As discussed in chapter 2 by William Thompson, it is now widely recognized in the psychological literature on decision making that the understanding of and response to statements of risk depend on the framing of the statement. For example, a 20% chance of serious harm is regarded as worse than an 80% success rate. Yet, in formulating the part of the informed-consent statement pertaining to the risks and benefits, most investigators recognize the need to consult the literature on framing of statements about risk only after they have been forced to recognize that their subjects have misunderstood what was said to them.

An ethical problem may be foreseen by the investigator, and there may be no apparent way to avoid the problem. In the Milgram obedience experiment (example 4) it was foreseen that subjects would be deceived and would experience great stress. However, there appeared to be no other valid way to test whether people would obey unjust authority and hurt others. To reduce any harm done, a thoughtful debriefing and offer of therapy were extended to subjects after their participation. Some subsequent researchers (e.g., Gamson, Fireman, & Rytina, 1982) have solved these problems by focusing on conditions that foster rebellion against unjust authority and by using a consent procedure in which the subject agrees to participate in one of various studies, some of which might involve deception.

Another version of the "foreseen problem" occurs when it is unclear what one should do because it is unclear what the consequences of one's possible actions might be. One context for foreseen problems is in the investigator's relationship with the press. Should one draw attention to one's research by sending a press release that may not be accurately conveyed, or should one not submit a press release and risk having totally misinformed journalists report unfavorably on one's research? In chapter 7, Boruch, Dennis, and Cecil cite examples of major surveys conducted in the United States, Sweden, and Norway in which the press instigated protests and disruptions of the research by publishing erroneous accounts about risks to privacy, use of people as guinea pigs, and so on when in fact the surveys were being conducted in a highly ethical way. Stocking and Dunwoody (1982) studied approaches to creating working relationships between scientists and the press and offered recommendations. More research is needed in this area.

One of the more complex kinds of dilemmas is that in which one's current moral outlook is simply inadequate to the problem and a new approach is needed. This kind of problem is exemplified in several chapters in this book: For example, chapter 3 points out that most communication between researcher and subject that has ethical and methodological implications is not part of the protocol and may even be nonverbal. Study of these nonverbal dimensions of communication in research is needed.

Psychologists' Conceptions of Research Ethics

What we mean by ethics—in the context of empirical research on research ethics—is the use of ethical theories, methods, and principles to understand what is at issue in an ethical dilemma in psychological research. We refer not to a philosopher's theorizing but to a scientist's use of psychological theory and research findings, coupled with some knowledge of ethics, perhaps gleaned from a careful reading of *The Belmont Report* and its appendix (National Commission, 1978) or from participation in a comprehensive workshop on the ethics of social research.

The psychologist who studies an ethical issue typically begins by identifying the norms or principles that are in conflict and by understanding the major philosophical arguments as to what would be the morally best course of action. The psychologist next uses the theories, methods, and skills of the social and behavioral sciences to identify questions about the nature of the value conflict and to seek insights and solutions to that conflict. Each chapter in this volume addresses research questions pertaining to the ethics of psychological research. Simplifying a bit, the following are the basic researchable questions posed by each author in this volume:

Chapter 1: William Thompson asks how the framing of risk/benefit statements affects potential research participants' perception of the research in which they are asked to participate.

Chapter 2: Joan Sieber asks whether some typically unexamined communication processes that occur in the course of research have implications for validity and ethics.

Chapter 3: Barbara Stanley and Jeannine Guido ask how informed consent can be transformed from a ritual that may be meaningless to the subject to an adequate communication and decision process.

Chapter 4: Robert Boruch, Michael Dennis, and Joe Cecil ask what problems of privacy and confidentiality tend to arise in social research, how these may affect research outcomes, and what solutions to these problems can be devised.

Chapter 5: Gary Melton and Barbara Stanley ask how one can empirically determine the competency of subjects to consent to research participation.

Chapter 6: Thomas Grisso asks how the context of organizational or institutional research affects the candor and trust of research participants.

In the conclusion, Michael Saks and Gary Melton consider how social structure could be altered through law or professional associations to "demand" ethical behavior by researchers.

To address questions such as these is to question the way science now operates. Psychologists, like other professionals, have tended to assume that doing good is simply a matter of having good intentions. Today, the press of heightened social consciousness, ethics committees, and the desire to seek solutions to problems in our troubled world force psychologists to consider broad ethical issues.

This volume is based on the premise that the quality of research and the value of psychology to society can, in the long run, be significantly improved by bringing questions of responsibility into clearer focus through thoughtful use of the tools of scientific inquiry.

Kinds and Topics of Study

Ethical issues in social and behavioral research might be described in a matrix containing three kinds of research on research ethics and 17 topics of research on research ethics (Sieber & Stanley, 1988). The following is a description of the basic kinds and topics of research. Space does not permit extensive description or examples of research within each of the 51 resulting cells. The purpose of this section is to invite the reader to consider possible areas of research on research ethics. Subsequent chapters will provide many illustrations of these various kinds and topics of research.

Parenthetically, it should be noted that, in urging research on these 51 topics, a whole new set of ethical issues in research is created; the study of some of these issues per se raises interesting ethical questions. For example, how does one test the efficacy of a design not using deception without utilizing deception as the basis of comparison? How does one investigate competency to consent in participants who may be incompetent to consent to research on this topic? Sensitivity to possible ethical issues, employment of adequate safeguards, watchfulness, and good communication with one's ethics committee are obvious requirements.

Three Approaches to Research on Research Ethics

Approaches to research on research ethics may be primarily empirical, primarily methodological, or primarily theoretical. Most empirical research uses theory and may have methodological implications; most methodological research is theoretically based and empirically tested, and most new theoretical integrations are data based. For purposes of simplicity, the following discussion is organized according to primary approach.

EMPIRICAL RESEARCH

Empirical research on ethical problems involves the use of social or behavioral research methods and provides empirical answers to ethical questions. It may focus on any aspect of the research process, from conception to dissemination, and may involve any appropriate research methods. The following four examples illustrate a few of the diverse possible approaches:

Kimble used 12 Epistemic Differential Scales to measure the epistemological orientation and scientific values of psychologists:

Example 5: Kimble (1984) examined the scientific beliefs and values of psychology undergraduates, officers of divisions of the APA, and members of APA Division 3 (Experimental), Division 9 (Society for the Psychological Study of Social Issues), Division 29 (Psychotherapy), and Division 32 (Humanistic). He found that, while psychology students differ little in their scientific values or their research and theoretical orientations, major differences exist between the various kinds of psychologists. Kimble demonstrated the existence of scientific and humanistic cultures within psychology and identified six important dimensions that define the conflicting values of these two cultures. The value dimensions he identified are scholarly values (scientific vs. humanistic), lawfulness of behavior (determinism vs. indeterminism), basic source of knowledge (observation vs. intuition), appropriate setting for discovery (laboratory vs. field study or case history), generality of laws (nomothetic vs. idiographic), and appropriate level of analysis (elementism vs. holism). Kimble notes that processes of self-selection into fields of natural science versus social, clinical, or humanistic psychology and subsequent value enhancement appear to be responsible for the establishment of these two cultures of psychologists. He comments that there appears to be little likelihood of achieving epistemological harmony between the two groups.

Goldman and Katz (1982) studied the consistency of IRB decisions by submitting identical sets of three research protocols to 32 IRBs at major universities. Each protocol posed serious ethical issues, contained flaws in scientific design, and provided an incomplete consent form. Twenty-two IRBs agreed to participate in the study, which revealed consistency in the nonapproval of the three protocols but inconsistency in the reasons offered in support of similar decisions and inconsistency in the application of standards.

Studies of typical informed consent procedures and experiments seeking ways to improve consent procedures have been performed to evaluate such elements of consent as comprehension, adequacy of decision making, willingness to volunteer, characteristics of volunteers, respect for science, and honesty of responses to subsequently administered surveys. Many empirical investigations of ways to improve the informed consent process are reviewed in subsequent chapters by Thompson (chapter 1), Sieber (chapter 2), Stanley (chapter 3), and Melton (chapter 5).

Seymour Sarason (1981) developed case studies documenting noteworthy failures to investigate the application of knowledge gained through basic research. He points to the tendency of psychologists to assume that good ideas will lead to useful and important applications; yet psychologists typically fail to engineer applications of their basic research or to study the fate of applications, resulting in sterility of theory and uselessness of research.

METHODOLOGICAL RESEARCH

Methodological research involves the development of new methods, typically followed by empirical testing of those methods. Some examples of methodological research on research ethics include the study of methods of sampling participant populations through the use of lists without invading privacy (e.g., Hartley, 1982), development of the randomized-response method (see example 3) of obtaining sensitive or private responses without invading privacy (e.g., Fox & Tracy, 1986), and development of methods of merging data sets to obtain statistical analyses or summaries without accessing the private data on which the analyses or summaries are based (e.g., Campbell et al., 1977):

Example 6: Campbell, Boruch, Schwartz, and Steinberg, along with others, have experimented with various methods for preserving confidentiality when releasing individual data for statistical analysis by outsiders. Mere deletion of unique identifiers is not sufficient to protect the identity of persons whose other demographic characteristics would permit deductive disclosure based on information publicly known. For example, if census tract, age, sex, and specialty are given for a low-frequency, visibly listed profession such as geologist, individual identification could often be made by persons who have knowledge of the demographic characteristics of geologists in the area, and thus the other information on the record could therefore be identified for a specific person (Hansen, 1971). For small populations, even birthdate and age might suffice to permit deductive identification of many persons. Some approaches to protecting confidentiality of such data include restriction of release of data that are publicly listed elsewhere, microaggregation of data, that is, creation of synthetic individuals based on the actual data (Watts, 1972), and error inoculation. Error inoculation means that most or all public variables are inoculated with enough error so that each individual record contains some imperfection on at least one of the public variables. Thus, a potential codebreaker who had a list of all names and publicly known variables would be unable to make any exact matches with the data. However, these methods of ensuring confidentiality are costly and reduce the statistical power of the data by introducing error variance. A preferable practice is for the archive containing the confidential data not to release the raw data but instead to perform on those data the statistical analyses requested by an outsider; in some cases this involves analyses that combine data from the two sources. Campbell et al., (1977) developed various approaches to interfile linkage, including the "mutually insulated file linkage" in which neither file releases individually identified data.

THEORETICAL RESEARCH

Theoretical research typically involves some methodological or empirical study as well but focuses primarily on conceptualizing and synthesizing what is already known about a given problem. Four examples are offered here to illustrate the importance of synthesizing knowledge in the service of ethics and validity, the first two in detail:

Laufer and Wolfe's (1977) behavioral theory of privacy provides the social researcher with a powerful conceptual tool for learning what a given population considers private.

Mitroff and Kilmann's (1978) taxonomy of epistemological styles of social scientists incorporates Kimble's (see example 5) two cultures, scientist and humanist, with a second dimension, divergent and convergent thinker. This produces a 2 x 2 taxonomy consisting of the analytic scientist, the conceptual theorist, the conceptual humanist, and the particular humanist. At the beginning of this chapter, we briefly considered Warwick's (1980) four reasons some social scientists dismiss ethical concerns, noting that these concerns cannot be addressed in the context of some of the dominant views within the scientific culture. Now, Mitroff and Kilmann's model of epistemological styles of social scientists demonstrates that a scientist's social attitudes, values, and actions do actually follow from scientific ideas and results and vice versa and that it is appropriate for scientists to examine how that linkage might work, to the good or detriment of society. Relatedly, the defining of a problem depends on the perspective and values of those who do the defining; hence, the willingness to view ethical problems in research from each of Mitroff and Kilmann's four epistemological models provides greater intellectual power to understand and solve the problem.

Kelman (1972) has developed a data-based theory of the power differential between researcher and subject that has important implications for the ethics of social research.

Sieber (1982a, 1983a) has developed a data-based theory or taxonomy of the nature and likely effects of deception in research, which provides the structure for the next section of this chapter.

Example 7: Laufer and Wolfe (1977) theorize about the behavioral nature of privacy and the varying ways it may be manifested in relation to age, culture, and circumstance. Their theory is data based and in turn suggests further empirical research. It also has tremendous potential value to social researchers in helping them to understand and respect the privacy needs of the participants in their research.

Laufer and Wolfe's developmental theory of privacy employs the dimensions of self-ego, environmental, interpersonal, and control-choice factors. These factors result in cultural and individual differences in the meaning of privacy and the individual's need for ways of protecting privacy.

The self-ego dimension of privacy refers to the development of autonomy and personal dignity. In infancy and early childhood, being alone is aversive. But by middle childhood, time alone is frequently sought as a context in which to establish a sense of self and autonomy and to nurture new ideas, thereby creating a basis for self-esteem, personal strength, and dignity. This means that children in middle childhood have a need and emerging right to privacy not found in infants and young children. Adults continue to need time alone and develop various means for protecting their privacy in addition to physical solitude. This means that, if researchers do not respect their privacy, they will take possibly drastic measures to protect it, such as lying to the researcher or complaining to authorities and causing the research to be halted.

The environmental dimension of privacy includes cultural, sociophysical, and life-cycle elements. Cultural elements include norms for achieving privacy; for example, one culture may permit lying while another may permit persons to have private rooms. Sociophysical elements refer to physical settings that offer privacy, such as indoor bathrooms, tree houses, automobiles, and so on. Life-cycle elements vary with age, occupation, available technology, and changing sociocultural patterns. The privacies one needs and establishes at one stage in life, under one set of responsibilities, constraints, and technological aids, may be unsatisfactory in another stage of one's life. (However, the psychological researcher's conception of privacy may not be adequate for judging what is private to others or how to arrange to protect their privacy.)

The interpersonal dimension of privacy refers to how social interaction and information are managed. One's social setting and its physical characteristics provide many options for managing social interaction; physical and social boundaries can be used to control people's access to one another.

The control/choice dimension of privacy develops out of one's dimensions of self-ego, culture, and environment. Young children have no control over their privacy, except through hiding. Later, persons learn to use personal, cultural, and physical resources to exercise subtle control over privacy. Events that would threaten one's privacy early in the development of control/choice mechanisms later become so easy to control that they are no longer considered a threat to privacy, dignity, or self-esteem. For example, many people think they have the right to question young persons about their personal habits, and many young persons feel obligated to explain or defend themselves; however, most persons would not so question a successful, educated, middle-aged person, or if they did they may quickly be put in their place with a humorous or cutting retort or a disdainful look.

I turn now to Mitroff & Kilmann's (1977) taxonomy of the beliefs and values of scientists and the value considerations that they entail:

Example 8: Drawing from the literature on the epistemology of social science, Mitroff and Kilmann present a typology of beliefs and values that suggests that there is no one real science but rather models of science, each of which is a conceptual tool from which insight and procedures can be selected to understand and solve ethical problems in research.

Mitroff and Kilmann's taxonomy is based on a Jungian typology and divides social scientists into four types.

The analytic scientist is a convergent thinker who focuses on observable facts and tests theory using classical logic. Facts are separable from values; science is disinterested, impersonal, value free, accurate, reductionistic, apolitical, and cumulative. If any values at all pertain to science, they are scientific freedom and validity of research.

The conceptual theorist is a divergent thinker whose main interest is creating interesting alternative explanations of phenomena. This ability to recast ideas makes it obvious to the conceptual theorist that what a scientist looks for and what he or she sees are highly interdependent. The conceptual theorist also considers science to be disinterested, impersonal, and value free but also holistic, imaginative, and marked by multiple causation, purposive ambiguity and uncertainty. The conceptual theorist's cognitive complexity may provide heightened ethical sensitivity to the diverse perspectives of research subjects and may engender good rapport. The major ethical values are the intellectual complexity, stimulation, and the enlightenment the research provides.

The conceptual humanist is a divergent thinker who, in addition to having alternative conceptions about the external world, thinks via the experience of self. Conceptual humanists tend to examine their own thoughts, feelings, attitudes, and intuitions and are sensitive to those of others. Research should be beneficial to human welfare. Research participants should benefit personally from participation by gaining in personal effectiveness and self-understanding. Informed consent would be a natural part of an ongoing, open communication process from which this benefit would ensue.

The particular humanist is one whose thinking converges on individuals rather than on an idea. The research orientation is largely intuitive and concerned with discovering the uniqueness of each individual. Research would probably be done by means of the in-depth case study. Objectivity consists of exposing the scientist's own interests in, or motives for, doing the study (there being no such thing as disinterested objectivity). Informed consent would be a process of mutual self-disclosure. The major ethical concerns would be to make the most responsible application of the knowledge gained and to keep secret any harmful knowledge that is gained. This taxonomy of scientific beliefs and values shows that the ethos of any single value orientation is inadequate to guide ethical sensitivity and problem solving in research.

Seventeen Topics of Research on Research Ethics

For purposes of organization, the 17 topics of study are divided into five major categories: theory, method, and design issues that precede research; risk and benefit of research; communication between researcher and participants; acquisition and use of data; and external influences on research.

THEORY, METHOD, AND DESIGN ISSUES

Values and Epistemology. This category refers to study concerned with the nature of beliefs about knowledge and reality and the effect of such beliefs on the method and product of research (see Kimble, 1984, example 5; Mitroff & Kilmann, 1978, example 8). Views on how data should be collected, used, and disseminated are closely related to one's beliefs about the nature of knowledge and reality. When knowledge per se is considered an unlimited good, issues of potentially harmful data collection or application become somewhat tangential to the research enterprise. But when knowledge is considered as a kind of power, the question of access to that power becomes a crucial ethical issue.

The way researchers define reality and their relationship to that reality influences their choice of theories and methods. When reality is believed to be something "out there" that should be studied objectively, deception may be considered the most scientific of methods. However, if reality is believed to be a construction composed of interaction between investigator and participant, scientific method consists of considering rather than ignoring such factors as trust and expectancy.

Validity. For research to be ethical, it must valid. Invalid research is disrespectful of subjects, wastes their time, and produces false information. In example 2, Conner (1982) shows that random assignment provides the most valid test of the effects of viewing *Sesame Street* on learning. Faulty designs, methods, or interpretations are not ethical. Conversely, some methods that are valid are unethical in certain contexts, for example, randomly assigning persons to risks or deprivations they would not otherwise face. In turn, subjects who perceive that they are at risk may sabotage the research; for example, AIDS patients fearing that they are being given placebos may secretly obtain treatment from an underground source while also participating in a drug trial, thus invalidating the tests of both effectiveness and toxicity (see, e.g., Melton, Levine, Koocher, Rosenthal, & Thompson, 1988).

Equitable Treatment of Participants. Issues of procedural and distributive justice arise in many parts of the process of planning, conducting, and applying research. Who sponsors and pays for the research? When is it unethical to withhold information about sponsorship from subjects? Who benefits from the research? How are participants selected? How is the power of the scientist balanced against the powerlessness of the participants (Kelman, 1972)? When is random assignment acceptable (Conner, 1982)? To continue with example 2, when Conner provided control subjects access to cable television at the end of the experiment, control subjects were ultimately deprived of nothing that the experimental subjects received.

RISK AND BENEFIT

Risk, Wrong, and Harm. What forms of harm are considered in evaluating whether a research procedure is acceptable? How does one weigh moral wrongs (e.g., lying to subjects, deceiving them) that do no obvious psychological harm? How is degree of risk assessed? How do various populations of participants perceive risk? How can procedures be made safe and how is safety judged?

Benefit and Promise of Research. One ethical justification of research is that it is beneficial to society. What the benefits of research are, how these may be estimated and maximized, and how they may be measured need to be understood. Examples include study of the factors that make research socially useful and those that make research participation beneficial to the participants themselves.

Risk/Benefit Assessment. It is recognized that the price of scientific knowledge may be some risk of harm or some wrong to an individual or group or economic cost to some sector of society. When is the price justified? How are these factors identified and weighed (e.g., Rosenthal & Rosnow, 1984)?

AGREEMENT AND COMMUNICATION BETWEEN RESEARCHER AND SUBJECT

Informed Consent. This includes studies pertinent to the understanding between the researcher and the participant about the purpose, procedure, and intended outcome of the research and pertinent to the various ways this understanding is conveyed, comprehended, and used. It is concerned with a continuum from highly informed consent to deception and concealment (e.g., see Stanley, chap. 4). It also includes agreements with larger entities such as organizations (e.g., Mirvis & Seashore, 1982) and communities (Melton et al., 1988). Apart from the issue of adequacy of consent is that of competence of participants to consent. The issue of competence to consent differs depending on whether participants are children, institutionalized persons, the mentally retarded, and so on. Legal and common-sense ideas about competence to consent can be enhanced through empirical research on the conditions that surround actual research, as described by Melton in chapter 5.

Deception. Deception is broadly defined to include concealment, intended deception, mental reservations, perceived deception, self-deception, and the use of devices intended to distract a subject from the main purpose of an activity in order to evoke spontaneous behavior (e.g., Sieber, 1982a, 1982b, 1983). It is recognized that deception in social research is a continuum from everyday management of the perceptions of others using tact and body language—forms of deception we naturally expect to encounter—to lies that may undermine a person's self-confidence and trust in others and interfere with experimental results. Once the use of deception in research begins to be examined from various theoretical and empirical perspectives, many questions arise. How does deception affect children across the span of development? How does the research assistant translate the investigator's intention that participants be deceived? What are the methodological alternatives to objectionable deception?

Relationships as a Source of Data. Qualitative social research often involves getting to know persons and then reporting on some aspect of their lives. The resulting publication typically includes a critical analysis of events that portrays the persons differently from the way they would tell their life stories (Glazer, 1982). The nature of the relationship, as perceived by the participant and the researcher, may affect how the research problem is defined, how the data are collected and organized, how the research report is framed, how the results are disseminated and used, and whether the participant is wronged or harmed by this incursion into his or her private life.

ACQUISITION AND USE OF DATA

Privacy. This refers to a person's interest in separating self from others. Privacy refers to persons, while confidentiality refers to data. Privacy is not necessarily sought or protected; participants sometimes want to tell more than a researcher wants to know. The need to establish boundaries is universal but is manifested differently depending on learning, culture, and developmental factors (e.g., Laufer & Wolfe, 1977; see example 7). Consequently, the scientist's personal views on privacy may be inadequate for judging what privacies others might want, expect, or create. For example, an investigator may fail to realize that many people (especially the elderly) do not like to answer questions about illness but may lie rather than decline to answer.

Confidentiality. This refers to limiting access to information or data. After discovering what the prospective participant population considers as private, the next step is to discover the conditions under which participants would disclose that information willingly and whether the investigator can meet those conditions. As discussed in chapter 6, there may be risks to confidentiality that are not immediately obvious to the researcher or the participant, such as subpoena of data, theft from computer files, or deductive disclosure. The researcher is obligated to seek to discover such risks and to take steps to prevent their occurrence.

Uses of Data, Obligation to Publish, and Data Sharing and Dissemination. How is scientific information disseminated? What is contained or omitted? How are the data used? Who benefits or is harmed? What misunderstanding or misinformation is conveyed? Should harmful data be suppressed? What are the likely consequences of different modes of dissemination? What is known about the dissemination process? How can social scientists participate in the dissemination process in a more responsible way? What is the role of the mass media (e.g., Stocking & Dunwoody, 1982)? What are the scientist's obligations to contribute to the scientific literacy of the layman? How should raw data be documented, archived, and shared (e.g., Feinberg, Martin, & Straf, 1985)?

EXTERNAL INFLUENCES ON RESEARCH

Government Regulations. Examples include studies by scientists that contribute to the regulatory process (e.g., Gray, Cooke, & Tannenbaum, 1978) and studies of the effect of regulations on research.

Institutional Review Boards. This includes studies of the functioning of IRBs (e.g., Tanke & Tanke, 1982), and studies of the effects on science of IRB functioning.

Questionable, Taboo, or Controversial Topics of Research. There are three kinds of research that some believe should not be done, at least not with government funding: research in which the data might cause serious or irreparable social harm, research that may produce misleading findings, that is, socially significant questions that probably are not amenable to valid research with the methods currently available, and research likely to be used in a politically harmful way. Studies in this area would focus on instances of such topics of research and surrounding circumstances. Such studies typically attempt to analyze whether more harm is done to society by the research or by suppression of the research. One kind of research deemed questionable at times for all three of the reasons given above is research on IQ.

> Example 9: Binet's creation of an intelligence test was accompanied by his warning that it is not culture free. However, many discovered the convenience of the test and ignored Binet's warning. American psychologists Goddard and Kuhlman were impressed by the convenience of the IQ test in classifying the mentally retarded. Goddard's (1928) study of the Kallikak family and the reanalysis of his data by the Harvard geneticist E. M. East (1927) appeared to prove that intellectual ability is inherited and that feeblemindedness is transmitted in accordance with Mendel's model of recessive traits—a conclusion that has since been discredited. Goddard administered IQ tests to delinquents, criminals, ethnic and racial minorities, and prostitutes and found that large numbers of these people had low IQ scores. On the basis of IQ tests administered (in English) to immigrants on Ellis Island, Goddard reported that immigrant Jews, Italians, Russians, and Poles would bring about the intellectual deterioration of the American population. Congress enacted highly restrictive immigration laws shortly thereafter (Doris, 1982).

Scientific Integrity and Responsibility. Science has been regarded as a self-correcting process in which individual investigators work for the love of knowledge. Recent events, however, suggest that pressures on scientists to publish motivate some to resort to scientific fraud (e.g., fabrication of data, plagiarism). A literature is beginning to develop that examines cases of scientific fraud (e.g., Broad & Wade, 1982; Sprague, 1987), seeks to discover the conditions likely to produce scientific dishonesty (e.g., Chubin, 1985), and theorizes about the nature of scientific fraud (e.g., List, 1985). With the increasing scientific and legislative concern over fraud, such development may be expected to accelerate.

Ethics and Politics. Charges of scientific irresponsibility or immorality often mask profound political disagreements. Scientists who investigate ethically controversial topics may be accused of scientific irresponsibility and immorality. For example, some would judge psychological research conducted for the military during World War II as morally better or scientifically more responsible than research done during the Vietnam War. The issues of whom an investigator works for and how the data are used raises ethical and political questions that are difficult to separate. Because these issues generally arise in highly partisan settings, more heat than light is usually generated in the ensuing conflict. In such cases, it is especially useful for social scientists to apply objective methods to analyze the problem so that actual facts and reasonable perspectives may become known.

Summary

Psychologists and other social scientists have been slow to recognize the range and nature of ethical problems that confront them in their scientific endeavors. Likewise, they have not recognized that the tools of social science can be used to understand, and in some cases solve, these ethical problems. The examples of research on problems of research ethics contained in the following chapters are offered as examples of what can be learned in this domain of study. Psychologists are challenged to continue the quest for a better understanding of the ethical problems that confront researchers, for better solutions to these problems, and for better science.

Notes

1. This description is adapted from Sieber (1982a).

References

Boruch, R. F., & Cecil, J. S. (1979). *Methods for assuring confidentiality of social research data*. Philadelphia: University of Pennsylvania Press.

Boruch, R. F., & Cecil, J. S. (1982). Statistical strategies for preserving privacy in direct inquiry. In J. E. Sieber (Ed.), *The ethics of social research: Surveys and experiments* (pp. 167–189). New York: Springer-Verlag.

Broad, W., & Wade, N. (1982). *Betrayers of the truth*. New York: Touchstone.

Campbell, D. T., Boruch, R. F., Schwartz, R. D., & Steinberg, J. (1977). Confidentiality-preserving modes of access to files and to interfile exchange for useful statistical analysis. *Evaluation Quarterly, 1*, 269–300.

Chubin, D. E. (1985). Misconduct in research: An issue of science policy and practice. *Minerva: Review of Science, Learning and Policy, 23*, 175–202.

Conner, R. F. (1982). Random assignment of clients in social experimentation. In Sieber, J. E. (Ed.), *The ethics of social research: Surveys and experiments* (pp. 57–77). New York: Springer-Verlag.

Cook, T. D., Appleton, H., Conner, R. F., Shaffer, A., Tamkin, G., & Weber, S. W. (1975). *Sesame Street revisited*. New York: Sage Foundation.

Doris, J. (1982). Social science and advocacy: A case study [Special issue]. *American Behavioral Scientist, 26*, 199–234.

East, E. M. (1927). *Heredity and human affairs*. New York: Scribners.

Feinberg, S. E., Martin, M. E., & Straf, M. L. (Eds.) (1985). *Sharing research data*. Washington DC: National Academy Press.

Fox, J. A., & Tracy, P. E. (1986). *Randomized response method*. Newbury Park CA: Sage.

Gamson, W. A., Fireman, B., & Rytina, S. (1982). *Encounters with unjust authority*. Homewood IL: Dorsey.

Geller, D. M. (1982). Alternatives to deception: Why, what and how? In J. E. Sieber (Ed.), *The ethics of social research: Surveys and experiments* (pp. 39–55). New York: Springer-Verlag.

Glazer, M. (1982). The threat of the stranger: Vulnerability, reciprocity and fieldwork. In J. E. Sieber (Ed.), *The ethics of social research: Fieldwork, regulation and publication* (pp. 49–70). New York: Springer-Verlag.

Goddard, H. H. (1928). Feeble-mindedness: A question of definition. *Journal of Psychoasthenics, 33*, 219–227.

Goldman, J., & Katz, M. D. (1982). Inconsistency and institutional review boards. *Journal of the American Medical Association, 248*, 197–202.

Gray, B. B., Cooke, R. A., & Tannenbaum, A. S. (1978). Research involving human subjects. *Science, 201*, 1094–1101.

Hansen, M. H. (1971). Insuring confidentiality of individual records in data storage and retrieval for statistical purposes. *Proceedings of the Fall Joint Computer Conference* (pp. 579–585). Montvale NJ: AFIPS.

Hartley, S. F. (1982). Sampling strategies and the threat to privacy. In J. E. Sieber (Ed.), *The ethics of social research: Surveys and experiments* (pp. 167–189). New York: Springer-Verlag.

Kelman, H. C. (1968). *A time to speak: On human values and social research*. San Francisco: Jossey-Bass, 1968.

Kelman, H. C. (1972). The rights of the subject in social research: An analysis in terms of relative power and legitimacy. *American Psychologist, 27*, 989–1016.

Kimble, G. A. (1984). Psychology's two cultures. *American Psychologist, 39*, 833–839.

Laufer, R. S., & Wolfe, M. (1977). Privacy as a concept and a social issue: A multidimensional developmental theory. *Journal of Social Issues, 33*, 44–87.

List, C. J. (1985). Scientific fraud: Social deviance or failure of virtue. *Science, Technology & Human Values, 10*(4), 27–36.

Melton, G. B., Levine, R. J., Koocher, G. P., Rosenthal, R., & Thompson, W. C. (1988). Community consultation in socially sensitive research: Lessons from clinical trials of treatments for AIDS. *American Psychologist, 43,* 573–581.

Milgram, S. (1974). *Obedience to authority.* New York: Harper & Row.

Mirvis, P. H., & Seashore, S. E. (1982). Creating ethical relationships in organizational research. In J. E. Sieber (Ed.), *The ethics of social research: Surveys and experiments* (pp. 79–103). New York: Springer-Verlag.

Mitroff, I. I., & Kilmann, R. H. (1978). *Methodological approaches to social science.* San Francisco: Jossey-Bass.

National Commission for the Protection of Human Subjects in Biomedical and Behavioral Research (1978). *The Belmont Report: Ethical Principles and guidelines for the protection of human subjects of research* (DHEW Publication No. OS 78–0012). Washington DC: U.S. Government Printing Office.

Peters, D. P., & Ceci, S. J. (1982). Peer-review practices of psychological journals: The fate of published articles, submitted again [Special issue]. *Behavioral and Brain Sciences, 5,* 187–255.

Rivlin, A. M., & Timpane, P. M. (1975). Introduction and summary. In A. M. Rivlin & P. M. Timpane (Eds.), *Ethical and legal issues of social experimentation* (pp. 1–19). Washington DC: Brookings Institution.

Rosenthal, R., & Rosnow, R. L. (1984). Applying Hamlet's question to the ethical conduct of research: A conceptual addendum. *American Psychologist, 39,* 561–563.

Rotheram-Borus, M. J., & Koopman, C. (1991). Protecting children's rights in AIDS research. In B. Stanley & J. E. Sieber (Eds.), *Social research on children and adolescents: Ethical issues* (pp. 143–161). Newbury Park CA: Sage.

Sarason, S. B. (1981). *Psychology misdirected.* New York: Free Press.

Sieber, J. E. (1982a). Deception in social research I: Kinds of deception and the wrongs they may involve. *IRB: A review of human subjects research, 4,* 1–2, 12.

Sieber, J. E. (1982b). Ethical dilemmas in social research. In J. E. Sieber (Ed.), *The ethics of social research: Surveys and experiments* (pp. 1–29). New York: Springer-Verlag.

Sieber, J. E. (Ed.). (1982c). *The ethics of social research: Fieldwork, regulation and publication.* New York: Springer-Verlag.

Sieber, J. E. (Ed.). (1982d). *The ethics of social research: Surveys and experiments.* New York: Springer-Verlag.

Sieber, J. E. (Ed.). (1982e). Values and Applied social science. Special issue of *American Behavioral Scientist, 26,* 147–280.

Sieber, J. E. (1983a). Deception in social research II: Factors influencing the magnitude of potential for harm or wrong. *IRB: A review of human subjects research, 5,* 1–3, 12.

Sieber, J. E. (1983b). Deception in social research III: The nature and limits of debriefing. *IRB: A review of human subjects research, 5,* 1–2, 4.

Sieber, J. & Saks, M. (1989). A census of subject pool characteristics and policies. *American Psychologist, 44,* 1051–1063.

Sieber, J. E., & Stanley, B. (1988). Ethical and professional dimensions of socially sensitive research. *American Psychologist, 43,* 49–55.

Sprague, R. L. (1987, August). *The myth of self-correcting science: Case history of reporting fraud.* Paper presented at the annual meeting of the American Psychological Association, New York.

Stocking, S. H., & Dunwoody, S. L. (1982). Social science in the mass media: Images and evidence. In J. E. Sieber (Ed.), *The ethics of social research: Surveys and experiments* (pp. 151–169). New York: Springer-Verlag.

Tanke, E. D., & Tanke, T. J. (1982). Regulation and education: The role of the institutional review board in social science research. In J. E. Sieber (Ed.), *The ethics of social research: Surveys and experiments* (pp. 131–149). New York: Springer-Verlag.

Tukey, J. W. (1977). Some thoughts on clinical trials, especially problems of multiplicity. *Science, 198,* 679–684.

Warner, S. L. (1965). Randomized response: A survey technique for eliminating evasive answer bias. *Journal of the American Statistical Association, 60,* 63–69.

Warwick, D. P. (1980). *The teaching of ethics in social sciences.* Hastings-on-Hudson NY: Hastings Center.

Watts, H. W. (1972). Microdata: Lessons from the SEO and the graduated work incentive experiment. *Economic and Social Measurement, 2,* 183–192.

Part 1 / Basic Ethical Problems

Most research involves psychologically significant relationships between members of the research staff and research participants in the course of recruitment, informed consent, and data gathering. Even nonverbal aspects of these relationships convey to participants impressions, accurate or otherwise, about the research, the investigator's integrity and expectations, and the participants' rights and obligations. Although rarely considered as part of the research per se, matters pertaining to explaining the research to prospective participants, obtaining consent, and guarding participants' privacy and the confidentiality of their data may greatly affect the ethical and scientific outcomes of the research.

Part 1 reviews some major areas of empirical research on basic issues of consent, risk/benefit assessment, rapport, privacy, and confidentiality.

In chapter 1, William Thompson draws on the work of decision theorists to show how the framing of risk/benefit statements affects people's perception of the riskiness of research in which they are asked to participate. He summarizes the literature on biases and inconsistencies in the way people use information to make decisions about risk and explores implications for decision making by potential subjects and by members of institutional review boards.

In chapter 2, Joan Sieber examines subtleties of nonverbal communication that occur in the research setting and affect strongly the rapport between investigators and research participants and the demand characteristics of the research. She reviews the pertinent literature and discusses the scientific and ethical consequences of these typically unexamined communication processes in research.

In chapter 3, Barbara Stanley and Jeannine Guido review research on several aspects of informed consent, including voluntariness, competency, disclosure, comprehension, participants' reactions to being informed, the decision-making process, and public opinion regarding informed consent, research, and the use of deception.

In chapter 4, Robert Boruch, Michael Dennis, and Joe Cecil describe problems of privacy and confidentiality that arise in research, how they affect scientific and ethical outcomes, what solutions can be devised, and the implications for communication with research participants.

As suggested by the conceptual frameworks and research agendas of these chapters, these reviews have only scratched the surface of relevant issues. Many empirical questions concerning normative and scientific issues in research remain to be investigated.

Chapter 1 / Research on Human Judgment and Decision Making: Implications for Informed Consent and Institutional Review

WILLIAM C. THOMPSON
Program in Social Ecology
University of California, Irvine

Research on human judgment and decision making has yielded some intriguing findings with far-reaching implications for research ethics. Although this research suggests that judgmental skills are often impressive, it has also identified some striking inadequacies in the way people use information to make judgments and draw inferences (Kahneman, Slovic, & Tversky, 1982; Nisbett & Ross, 1980; Slovic, Fischhoff, & Lichtenstein, 1977; Slovic, Lichtenstein, & Fischhoff, 1984a). One major review of the literature concluded that "human decisions are characterized by biases and inconsistencies that can lead to markedly non-optimal behavior" (Slovic et al., 1977). Another concluded that "people systematically violate the principles of rational decision making when judging probabilities, making predictions or otherwise attempting to cope with probabilistic tasks" (Slovic, Fischhoff, & Lichtenstein, 1976). These findings have resulted in both "an increased concern with the deficiencies of unaided human judgment" (Pitz, 1980) and in efforts to remedy these deficiencies through training (Nisbett, Krantz, Jepson, & Fong, 1982) and the use of decision aids (Dawes, 1979; Eraker & Politser, 1982).

This chapter relates this emerging knowledge of human judgment and decision making to some key ethical issues surrounding research with human subjects. The first section, which examines the doctrine of informed consent, identifies biases and inconsistencies in the way people make judgments and decisions under conditions of uncertainty, shows how these phenomena pose special problems for those seeking to "inform" potential subjects about the risks and benefits of research, and discusses the ethical implications of these problems. The second section, which examines the practice of institutional review, focuses on judgmental errors that may influence decisions by institutional review boards and discusses techniques for preventing such errors.

Judgmental Bias and Informed Consent

THE DOCTRINE OF INFORMED CONSENT

It is a fundamental principle of research ethics that human beings should be involved in research only if they have given their informed consent (Annas, Glantz, & Katz, 1977; Katz, 1972; Rosoff, 1981).[1] Informed consent is a key provision of the major codes of ethics for research involving human subjects such as the Nuremburg Code, the code of the World Medical Association, and the American Psychological Association code of ethics (Beecher, 1970). Informed consent is also required by statutory or common law for all research directly affecting the human body (Rosoff, 1981) and by federal regulations for most federally funded research involving human subjects (President's Commission, 1981; 1983).

Values Underlying Informed Consent. There are two justifications for the requirement of informed consent. First, informed consent protects subjects' welfare. Fully informed subjects are unlikely to participate in unduly risky or dangerous research and may meaningfully assess whether risks posed by a research project are acceptable in light of their own values or vulnerabilities (Annas et al., 1977). Informed consent thus helps protect subjects both from unscrupulous researchers who may expose them to patently unacceptable risks and from well-meaning researchers who believe in good faith that the risks of their research should be acceptable but whose values or perspectives in this regard differ from those of the subjects (Katz & Capron, 1975).

A second justification for informed consent is that it protects subjects' autonomy or ability to exercise self-determination. This justification is often overlooked by those with a utilitarian perspective, who may see nothing wrong with involving people in research without their informed consent so long as the benefits society gains from the research clearly outweigh any harm or inconvenience suffered by subjects. Particularly where the research poses no risks to subjects and may, indeed, benefit them, informed consent is viewed by some as dispensable. What this perspective overlooks is that protection of subjects' autonomy has an intrinsic value independent of the protection or subjects' welfare (President's Commission, 1982b, chap. 2). Western ethical traditions have long acknowledged self-determination as an essential element of human dignity (Berlin, 1969; Dworkin, 1982). If researchers are allowed to decide whether an individual will participate in a study rather than the individual's choosing for himself or herself, the individual will not have been shown proper respect as a person or given adequate protection against arbitrary domination by others. Even when researchers try to act in the best interest of subjects, they undermine their subjects' dignity as individuals by choosing for them. Domination of one individual over others is offensive even when it is done with the best of intentions (Kant, 1785/1969). A researcher who involves people in a study without their informed consent is treating them as commodities to be used for achieving his or her own goals rather than as moral equals with goals of their own that they have an equal right to pursue. Utilitarians sometimes argue that the benefits of scientific progress outweigh the harms that may result from occasionally dispensing with informed consent. But being treated with respect and dignity is an essential human right; scientific progress is not (Jonas, 1969). Hence, the utilitarian argument has few adherents among ethically sophisticated thinkers, and there is widespread support for the requirement of informed consent (President's Commission, 1982b, chap. 2).

Standards for Disclosure of Information to Subjects. Although there is general consensus that subjects should be "informed" before they agree to participate in research, there is much dispute over how much and what types of information should be disclosed. The debate centers on three standards of disclosure: the professional standard, the materiality standard, and full disclosure. Each standard provides an answer to the question "What information must researchers disclose to potential subjects in order to meet the requirements of informed consent?"

Under the professional standard, researchers are required to disclose the types of information customarily disclosed by members of their profession under the same or similar circumstances. A medical researcher, for example, has a duty to disclose to her subjects at least as much information as her professional colleagues disclose to their subjects under similar circumstances. The professional standard has been criticized for making professional custom rather than the subject's need for information the criterion for disclosure (Capron, 1974).

Under the materiality standard, the test for determining whether a given fact must be disclosed is its materiality to subjects' decision whether to participate in the research: researchers have a duty to disclose any facts likely to *make a difference* in a subject's decision. The materiality standard has two versions that differ in the test determining whether a fact is "material" (Annas et al., 1977). Under the "objective" version, a fact must be disclosed if it would make a difference to a "reasonably prudent person" in the subject's position. This is sometimes called the prudent-person test. The objective version has been criticized by some scholars for not requiring disclosure of facts that would be unimportant to a "prudent" person but might be crucial to a particular individual (Capron, 1974; Katz & Capron, 1975). These scholars favor the use of the so-called subjective test, which would require disclosure of all facts that would make a difference to the particular individual receiving the disclosure. Alexander Capron, the primary exponent of the subjective standard, argues that "adherence to what a group in the lay community believes to be 'reasonable' may rob the [subject] of the undisputed right . . . to receive information which will enable him to make a choice" (Capron, 1974). To comply with the subjective standard, a researcher would obviously need to spend some time getting to know the special concerns of potential subjects in order to ascertain what facts might be particularly important to them.

Under the full-disclosure standard, researchers are required to disclose all information bearing on subjects' decision to participate in the research. This standard incorporates both versions of the materiality standard and requires disclosure of all known risks and benefits.

The Law of Informed Consent. The researcher's duty to inform subjects is enforced through a combination of state law and federal regulation. Under state law a researcher must obtain subjects' informed consent in order to be exempted from liability for injuries suffered by subjects as a result of the research (Levine, 1981; Ludlum, 1978; Miller, 1980; Rosoff, 1981).[2] Although state laws regarding informed consent developed in connection with medical treatment (President's Commission, 1982b, pp. 18–23; Rosoff, 1981), the doctrine of informed consent is also applicable to medical research (Levine, 1981; see e.g., *Halushka v. University of Saskatchewan*, 1965) and presumably to social-science research as well, although there are no reported appellate cases in which social-science researchers have been held subject to liability for failure to obtain informed consent. Social scientists have less risk of liability, of course, because their subjects are less likely to suffer a compensable injury.

State law has traditionally imposed the professional standard of disclosure (Ludlum, 1978; Miller, 1980). In recent years, however, many states have shifted to a materiality standard as a result of two influential appellate decisions, *Canterbury v. Spence* (1972) and *Cobbs v. Grant* (1972). Both cases were medical malpractice actions in which the key issue was the adequacy of physicians' disclosures regarding the risks of surgical procedures. In both cases, the appellate court broke with tradition and held that the standard against which disclosures should be measured is their *materiality* to the patient's decision to consent. Both opinions criticized the professional standard for giving physicians too much discretion in deciding what to disclose and argued that the materiality standard is essential for protecting patients' right of self-determination. Both cases imposed the objective version of the materiality standard, however, fearing the subjective version would make recovery of damages too easy.

Federal regulations provide a more direct means of enforcing the researcher's duty to obtain informed consent. The major federal granting agencies have promulgated regulations requiring the establishment of institutional review boards (IRBS) at all grantee institutions to review funded research protocols and ensure that various ethical requirements, including informed consent, are met (Levine, 1981; President's Commission, 1982b). Current regulations of the Department of Health and Human Services (HHS), for example, require IRBs to approve proposed research only if the researcher will obtain "legally effective informed consent" (45 CFR §46.116). The regulations include an extensive list of requirements for informed consent (45 CFR §46.116), specifying the circumstances under which consent may be sought and the nature of the information that must be disclosed. Although HHS probably lacks the legal authority to require IRB review of research that is not supported by department funds (President's Commission, 1981, p. 7), most major research institutions apply the HHS mandated review procedures to all research involving human subjects.

The federal regulations appear to adopt the full-disclosure model, requiring, for example, "a description of any reasonably foreseeable risk or discomforts to the subject" (45 CFR §46.116(a)(2)). But the regulations allow the informed-consent requirement to be waived or modified under a number of circumstances (45 CFR §46.116(c)). In practice the nature of informed-consent disclosure is typically determined jointly by the researcher and IRB. The researcher composes a proposed consent form that must be reviewed by the IRB. These boards frequently "tinker" with the consent form, requiring changes in content or wording (Gray, 1978; Treat, 1977). Once the study is approved, the researcher is required to provide the written consent form to potential subjects, giving them adequate opportunity to read it and ask questions. While seeking subjects' consent, the researcher may, of course, make comments to subjects about the study, which may result in disclosure of facts not included on the consent form. Although IRBs have the authority to monitor the consent process, in practice this rarely happens (President's Commission, 1983).

LIMITATIONS AND COMPLEXITIES OF HUMAN JUDGMENT AND DECISION MAKING

The disclosure standards enforced by state law and federal regulations focus primarily on the question "What facts must be disclosed?" However, there has been relatively little discussion or concern about *how* facts are disclosed (Thompson, 1982). Indeed, some commentators have argued that the precise language and form of informed-consent disclosures is unimportant; so long as the relevant facts are made available to subjects in understandable form, subjects are assumed to be able to draw appropriate conclusions from them (Barber, 1980, p. 78).

The research discussed in this section casts doubt on this assumption. It raises the possibility that subjects may sometimes draw inappropriate conclusions from disclosures that are perfectly "understandable." It suggests that the same facts, presented in different ways, may have different effects on subjects' inferences about the risks and benefits of research and their decision to participate. It indicates, therefore, that those who design informed-consent statements should be concerned not just with *what* facts are disclosed but with *how* those facts are disclosed. It also raises questions about whether subjects' autonomy and welfare can be adequately protected by disclosure standards that focus exclusively on the *content* and ignore the *style* of disclosures.

The Role of Preconceptions. When designing informed-consent statements, researchers and IRB members must first bear in mind that potential subjects are not blank slates but bring with them a number of theories and expectations about scientists, experimentation, and the research enterprise that may complicate efforts to inform them about the risks and benefits of the research. The power of preconceptions to influence the interpretation of new information is one of the most thoroughly demonstrated phenomena in psychology—people who receive the same information may interpret it differently depending on their theories and expectations (Allport, 1954; Bruner, 1957; Chapman & Chapman, 1969; Hastorf & Cantril, 1954; Kelley, 1950; Lord, Lepper, & Ross, 1979; Nisbett & Ross, 1980; Schneider, Hastorf, & Ellsworth, 1979). Hence, subjects' preconceptions may sometimes cause them to interpret informed-consent disclosures in an unanticipated and possibly inaccurate manner. One researcher noted, for example, that medical patients who were asked to participate in a clinical trial of a "new" therapy jumped to the conclusion that the therapy was superior to traditional treatments, although no such claim was made in the informed consent disclosures. Their unwarranted interpretation probably resulted from a preconception that "new" means "improved." Had the researcher labeled the therapy "experimental" rather than "new," patients may have drawn different conclusions from the same disclosures. Yet neither label is inaccurate; either would have been acceptable under current disclosure standards and either might have received IRB approval.

The Availability Heuristic. In addition to considering people's preconceptions, those formulating informed-consent statements should bear in mind the ways people *think* about risk and uncertainty. Research suggests that people find it difficult to think clearly about probabilistic information and uncertain outcomes (Kahneman et al., 1982). These problems arise, in part, from the use of judgmental heuristics—mental strategies used to reduce complex judgments to a simpler and more manageable form (Tversky & Kahneman, 1974). Although judgmental heuristics work well in some contexts, they may lead to serious errors in judgment in others.

The availability heuristic, a strategy used to judge the frequency or likelihood of an event, is especially important to consider when informing people about risks (Covello, 1983; Slovic, Fischhoff, & Lichtenstein, 1980). People judge events as likely or frequent according to how easy it is to imagine or recall relevant examples (Tversky & Kahneman, 1973). Although this simple strategy works well when the mental "availability" of relevant instances is well correlated with the actual frequency or probability, it can lead to errors in other cases, such as when rare or unlikely events are especially vivid, memorable, or easy to imagine. Lichtenstein and her colleagues have demonstrated an availability bias in people's estimates of the frequency of various causes of death (Lichtenstein, Slovic, Fischhoff, Layman, & Combs, 1978). Dramatic and sensational causes of death, such as accidents, homicide, cancer, and natural disasters are greatly overestimated, while more mundane causes of death such as emphysema and diabetes are underestimated.

In the research context, the availability heuristic undoubtedly influences the preconceptions potential subjects bring with them to an experiment. Dramatic publicity about experimental cures may lead them to overestimate the benefits of an experimental treatment. Knowing an individual who was harmed in an experiment may lead them to overestimate the risks. More important, the availability heuristic may complicate communication of probabilistic information (Covello, 1983). Because the perceived probability of an event depends partly on the ease with which it can be imagined or with which relevant instances can be recalled, people's perception of the probability of a given outcome may be influenced by logically inconsequential factors such as the vividness of disclosures concerning the outcome. Potential subjects may overestimate the likelihood of risks and benefits that are concrete and easy to imagine and underestimate the likelihood of those that are abstract and difficult to picture. Mere mention of a highly imaginable risk or benefit may cause exaggerated concern or hope (Slovic et al., 1980).

These conclusions are supported by anecdotal evidence concerning efforts to inform people about technological hazards, such as the risks of recombinant DNA research (Rosenberg, 1978). Information designed to show people that various "disaster scenarios" are unlikely often backfires and makes people more alarmed (Slovic et al., 1980). Seeing all the possible ways something might go wrong makes a disaster more imaginable and therefore subjectively more likely, notwithstanding the experts' assurances. This process may partly explain why people who receive information supporting the safety of a technology sometimes *increase* their estimates of its hazards (see, e.g., Morgan et al., 1985). It may also explain why people sometimes place more weight on low-order risks from such things as prescription drugs than experts think they should (Keown, Slovic, & Lichtenstein, 1984).

An important implication of the availability heuristic, for present concerns, is that those framing informed-consent disclosures may be able to manipulate subjects' perceptions of the risks and benefits of a research project by varying how vividly these outcomes are described. There is much evidence that subtle and logically inconsequential changes in the way an outcome is described can influence the subjective likelihood of the outcome. Sherman, Cialdini, Schwartzman, and Reynolds (1985), for example, were able to manipulate subjects' perceptions of the likelihood of contracting a disease by describing it with either easy- or difficult-to-imagine symptoms. The easier it was to imagine the symptoms, the more likely subjects thought they were to contract the disease.

Overreliance on Case Information. A phenomenon related to availability bias is the tendency of people to give disproportionate weight to single striking examples and vivid case studies relative to more abstract statistical data (Nisbett & Ross, 1980, chap. 3). A Yiddish aphorism holds " 'For example' is not proof." Those designing informed-consent disclosures must contend with the human tendency to treat examples as if they were proof.

The power of single instances to influence judgment inappropriately has been frequently demonstrated in experimental studies (for a review see Nisbett & Ross, 1980, chap. 3). Rather than review this literature, I invite readers to participate in the following "thought experiment" which I believe will both confirm the point and relate it to present concerns.

Imagine that a medical researcher asks you to participate in an important study of heart function during anesthesia for which she needs healthy volunteers of your age. During the study, you would receive a general anesthetic and your blood circulation would be monitored by a catheter. The mortality rate for this procedure is about 0.05% and the rate of serious complications such as neurological or brain damage is 0.08%. However, the study may lead to a great reduction in the risk of general anesthesia for the thousands of people who undergo major surgery each year, thereby saving many lives. Subjects are expected to recover fully within one day and are paid $700 for participating. Based on this description, rate your willingness to participate on a scale of one to 10.

Now listen to what happened to Walter Halushka, a bright undergraduate at the University of Saskatchewan who volunteered for just such an experiment at the University Medical Center (see *Halushka v. University of Saskatchewan* 1965; also Katz, 1972, pp. 569–573). While under anesthesia, Halushka began coughing, which suggested to the experimenters that he was too lightly anesthetized. They increased the concentration of the anesthetic but may have overcompensated. A few minutes later there were changes in Halushka's cardiac rhythm that suggested the level of the anesthetic was too deep. They decreased the concentration of the anesthetic, but it was too late. He suffered an abrupt cardiac arrest. The experimenters quickly made a chest incision and pulled apart two ribs in order to begin manual massage of Halushka's heart. Within a few minutes the heart began functioning normally, but Halushka remained unconscious for four days. Thereafter, he had trouble thinking and concentrating. He failed six or seven courses before dropping out of the university and taking a menial job. He reported he had difficulty understanding instructions given to him in his work unless they were said very slowly. Neurologists concluded he had suffered permanent brain damage.

Now how inclined are you to participate in the study? A bit less than before, I imagine—perhaps considerably less. But how much weight does the information about Halushka really deserve? Assuming his case is not included among the 0.08% you previously knew about who had serious complications, his story should cause you to revise your estimate of the likelihood of complications in your case upward by a minuscule amount. If the 0.08% figure were based on 10,000 cases, you should revise the subjective probability that you will have complications from 0.0008 to 0.0009. Yet, Halushka's story probably would have considerably greater influence on most people's subjective assessments of their likelihood of being injured, for several reasons. First, people fail to appreciate sampling variability and, as a result, tend to overestimate the representativeness of small samples (Tversky & Kahneman, 1971). Second, they underestimate the effects of sampling bias and, as a result, tend to overestimate the representativeness of biased samples (Nisbett & Ross, 1980, pp. 73–89). Third, various cognitive processes act to exaggerate the impact of vivid, memorable information on inferences (Reyes, Thompson, & Bower, 1980; Bower, 1972). Fourth, striking case examples may make people think about things they previously ignored or failed to give much thought to (Nisbett & Ross, 1980). Perhaps hearing about Halushka brings home the fact that complications really do occur and that we could be among the unlucky 0.08%. Finally, his case study makes highly available a scenario in which complications could occur, which, as discussed earlier, increases the subjective likelihood of complications.

An important implication of these psychological processes is, again, that people's evaluation of the risks and benefits of a research project is malleable. By changing the presentation of a project's risks and benefits, researchers can influence potential subjects' subjective estimate of the probability of various outcomes and thereby influence their decision to participate.

The Base-Rate Fallacy. The base-rate fallacy, first identified by Kahneman and Tversky (1973), is a tendency to ignore or underutilize "base-rate information" and overutilize "diagnostic information." Base-rate information concerns the incidence rate of a given event among members of some group (e.g., the rate of injuries among all subjects exposed to a particular procedure). Diagnostic information is any information relevant to the likelihood of an event for the specific entity with which we are concerned (e.g., information relevant to the likelihood that a subject will be injured in *this* study). A number of studies show that, when judging the likelihood of an event, people tend to give less weight than warranted to the base-rate statistics and, correspondingly, more weight than warranted to the diagnostic information (for reviews see Bar-Hillel, 1980; Borgida & Brekke, 1981). These findings suggest that members of an IRB may, for example, give more weight than warranted to testimony about safety precautions in a specific study and less weight than warranted to the base rate of injuries associated with the experimental procedures when assessing the study's risks. This judgmental bias could cause them to misestimate significantly the risks of a study in cases in which the base rates and diagnostic information point to different conclusions about risk.

Conjunctive and Disjunctive Probabilities. Informed-consent disclosures often present information about the risks of a study in the form of long lists of possible negative outcomes. A subject in a drug trial, for example, may read a long list of risks that include possible serious side effects (e.g., liver cancer, stroke, heart disease) as well as less serious side effects (e.g., depression, fluid retention, weight gain). Sometimes the risk associated with each side effect (or with certain side effects) is quantified; more often there is *only* a rough indication of the likelihood of various outcomes. In either case, this method of presentation may fail to tell subjects what they most want to know. Subjects are less likely to want to know about the separate probabilities of a number of separate risks than about disjunctive probabilities (the likelihood that one of several events will occur) and conjunctive probabilities (the likelihood that each of several events will occur). The subject in the drug trial, for example, will probably want to know the likelihood that any serious side effect will occur (a disjunctive probability). Or he may wonder about the likelihood that some of the less serious side effects will all occur (a conjunctive probability).

If information about disjunctive and conjunctive probabilities is not provided, subjects themselves are likely to try to estimate these probabilities, which may lead to serious misperceptions of research risks because people do a poor job of making such estimates (Pitz, 1980). People typically overestimate conjunctive probabilities and underestimate disjunctive probabilities. If a person learns the probability of event *A* is 0.2 and the probability of event B is 0.1 and knows the two events are independent, he or she will typically estimate the likelihood that both A and B will occur to be higher than 0.02 and the likelihood that one of the two will occur to be lower than 0.28. (The specified figures are the correct ones according to the law of probability.) This phenomenon may lead the subject in the drug trial to underestimate the likelihood of having one of the several serious side effects and overestimate the likelihood of having several of the less serious side effects.

Interpreting Qualitative Expressions of Probability. Yet another difficulty in communicating information about risk is finding a good way to convey information about probabilities. The lack of good data about the probability of outcomes, as well as skepticism about subjects' ability to deal with probabilistic information, has led researchers to rely heavily on qualitative descriptions of probability, using terms such as *likely, probable, expected, moderate risk, low risk,* and so on in informed-consent disclosures (Annas et al., 1977; Thompson, 1982). Unfortunately, research raises doubts about whether people can extract from these terms an accurate or consistent impression of the probabilities to which they refer. One study of physicians, for example, found that doctors ascribe wildly divergent meanings to words commonly used in medical practice to refer to probability (Bryant & Norman, 1980). When asked to give a numerical probability equivalent to the term *moderate risk,* for example, doctors' answers ranged from 0.20 to 0.80; for *probable,* answers ranged from 0.30 to 0.95; and for *sometimes,* answers ranged from 0.10 to 0.80. If physicians cannot understand each other when using nonnumerical terms to describe probability we can hardly expect lay subjects to understand such terms. Moreover, the wide range of meanings compatible with such terms leaves open the possibility that researchers can shade meanings in various ways to convey an inaccurate impression of risks without saying anything demonstrably incorrect in their informed-consent disclosures. This research does not prove, of course, that the use of probabilities is a better way to convey information about likelihood. The question of how best to convey information about probability to a lay person remains open and invites research.

Framing Effects. The way in which information about risks is presented or "framed" is another important consideration in designing informed-consent disclosures. People's perceptions of risk and their subsequent choices are sometimes dramatically altered by subtle and logically inconsequential changes in the presentation of risks. (Kahneman & Tversky, 1979; Tversky & Kahneman, 1981). Framing effects are important to psychological theory because they reveal inconsistencies in people's choices that violate norms of rationality. More important for present purposes, however, is the practical consequence of framing effects: because information about a given risk can often be framed in various ways, those doing the framing may greatly influence perceptions of risks and the decision to accept those risks.

To understand the operation of framing effects, one must first appreciate some basic patterns in the way choices are made among risky alternatives. People do not always choose the option they believe to have the greatest expected utility or value. Moreover, their departures from the norms of expected-utility theory are systematic and predictable. One important pattern noted by Kahneman and Tversky (1979) is a tendency to respond differently to risk when facing a prospective gain than when facing a prospective loss. Faced with a prospective gain, people tend to be risk averse. In one study, the great majority of subjects said they would prefer to accept $3,000 with certainty than to take a gamble in which they have a probability of 0.8 of winning $4,000 and 0.2 of winning nothing, even though the expected value of the gamble is obviously greater than $3,000 (Kahneman & Tversky, 1979). Faced with a prospective loss, however, people are much more willing to gamble. Rather than accept a certain loss of $3,000, the great majority of Kahneman and Tversky's subjects would accept a gamble in which they have a probability of 0.8 of losing $4,000 and 0.2 of losing nothing.

This pattern of risk aversion in the face of prospective gains and risk taking in the face of prospective losses has been demonstrated for a number of choices (Tversky & Kahneman, 1981; Kahneman et al., 1982). In one study, medical patients were asked which of two drugs they would choose for various medical problems (Eraker & Sox, 1981). The patients were provided hypothetical data about the effect of the drugs. In each scenario one drug was certain to produce a moderate effect while the other drug's effects were uncertain and could, by chance, be either much stronger or much weaker than those produced by the first drug. When the effects of the drug were positive, most patients showed aversion to risk and chose the drug with the certain effects. Most, for example, preferred a drug producing one hour of pain relief with certainty to a drug that had a 50% chance of relieving pain for two hours and a 50% chance of not relieving the pain. When the effects of the drug were negative, however, this pattern of preferences reversed. Given a choice between a drug that produced a moderate adverse reaction with certainty and one that produced either a doubly serious reaction or no reaction, most people preferred to gamble on the latter drug.

A willingness to gamble to avoid losses but not to achieve gains is neither wrong nor irrational in itself; it is simply a set of tastes regarding risk taking. This pattern of risk preferences can lead to irrational inconsistencies in people's choices, however, under two circumstances: where the same option can be framed as either a gain or a loss and where the same option may be framed as either a sure bet or a gamble.

As an example of the way in which a given option can be framed as either a gain or a loss, consider the following problem from Tversky and Kahneman (1981):

Problem 1: Imagine that the U.S. is preparing for the outbreak of an unusual Asian disease, which is expected to kill 600 people. Two alternative programs to combat the disease have been proposed. Assume that the consequences of the programs are as follows: If Program A is adopted, 200 people will be saved. If Program B is adopted, there is ⅓ probability that 600 people will be saved, and ⅔ probability that no people will be saved. Which of the two programs would you favor?

When Tversky and Kahneman presented this problem to a group of physicians, 75% chose Program A—preferring a certain "gain" of 200 lives to a gamble. The results were different, however, when the description of risks in the problem was reframed as follows:

Problem 2: [Same cover story as Problem 1.] If Program C is adopted, 400 people will die. If Program D is adopted, there is ⅓ probability that nobody will die, and ⅔ probability that 600 people will die. Which of the two programs would you favor?

Among physicians who read Problem 2, 67% chose Program D, preferring the gamble to a certain loss of 400 lives. Notice, however, that Program A and C are identical options, as are B and D. A subtle rewording of the description of the situation, shifting the emphasis from prospective lives saved to prospective lives lost, produced a dramatic reversal of preferences.

This reversal of preferences is important for present purposes because it suggests that choices can be manipulated, either intentionally or inadvertently, by those who "frame" the options among which people must choose. Suppose, for example, that a medical researcher wishes to recruit cancer patients for a clinical trial of a risky new therapy that is potentially far more effective than the traditional treatment but has more dangerous side effects for some patients. The patients must choose between the traditional treatment, which is safe but only moderately effective, and the experimental treatment, which is riskier but potentially more effective. The framing literature suggests that patients facing this choice are more likely to opt for the risky experimental treatment if the informed-consent disclosures describe the alternative therapy in terms of its prospects for preventing the patient's current state from deteriorating than if the disclosures describe the new therapy in terms of its prospects for improving an otherwise-dismal prognosis (Thompson, 1982, p. 95).

A second circumstance under which risk preferences can lead to irrational inconsistencies is where the same option can be framed as either certain or merely probable. According to Kahneman and Tversky's prospect theory (1979; Tversky & Kahneman, 1981), people give disproportionate weight to outcomes that will occur with certainty relative to those that are merely probable. Thus, as noted earlier, sure gains are more attractive and sure losses are more aversive than probable gains and losses of equivalent expected value. Whether a particular outcome is viewed as certain or merely probable may depend, however, on the way it is framed. An insurance policy that covers only fire may be described either as certain protection against the risk of fire or as a reduction in the overall probability of property loss (Tversky & Kahneman, 1981, p. 456).

The impact of such a manipulation on people's choices is illustrated nicely by Slovic, Fischhoff, and Lichtenstein (1982). Health-policy professionals were asked whether they would get vaccinated to protect themselves from a disease likely to afflict 20% of the population. Among subjects told the vaccine would, on a random basis, protect half the people who receive it, 40% said they would be vaccinated. Among subjects told the vaccine would provide complete protection against one strain of the disease likely to affect 10% of the population but no protection against a second strain of the disease likely to affect another 10% of the population, 56% said they would be vaccinated. The first group may have found the vaccine less attractive because of the apparent uncertainty about whether it would provide any benefit. The latter group presumably found the vaccine more attractive because it was certain to protect them, albeit from only half the threat. Of course the difference in apparent certainty of outcome is illusory; in both cases the vaccine would reduce one's chances of getting a disease from 20% to 10%. Hence, Tversky and Kahneman (1981) call this phenomenon the pseudocertainty effect.

A researcher wishing to influence subjects' choices may induce the pseudocertainty effect in a number of ways. One way is to vary the time frame when describing the probability of various outcomes. An outcome that is certain to occur at some point during a lengthy period is often merely probable during any particular unit of time. In such a case, adopting a longer time frame will emphasize the certainty of the outcome, while adopting a shorter time frame will emphasize its uncertainty. Another way to induce pseudocertainty is to vary the level of analysis when describing outcomes. Often an intervention is certain to produce one of several outcomes but merely likely to produce a particular outcome. In such a case, a detailed analysis of outcomes, describing each separately, will make the effects of the intervention sound probabilistic, while a more global analysis, describing several outcomes as a group, will make the effects of the intervention sound certain. To induce subjects to choose a given option, the researcher would frame disclosures to emphasize the certainty of positive outcomes and the uncertainty of negative outcomes. The framing of decisions has also been shown to influence people's choices in a number of ways beyond those described here (see Tversky & Kahneman, 1981).

ETHICAL IMPLICATIONS

The findings discussed in the previous section suggest that researchers may be able to influence subjects' perceptions of the risks and benefits of research, and in turn their decision to participate, by making subtle changes in the presentation of information. Logically inconsequential changes in disclosures may make a big difference in subjects' perceptions. Two disclosures, both of which contain essentially the same information and meet the traditional requirements of informed consent, may give subjects very different perceptions of the risks and benefits of a study.

The Inadequacy of Current Disclosure Standards. These findings raise doubts about the adequacy of traditional disclosure standards. The primary concern underlying current informed-consent requirements is that subjects will misperceive the risks and benefits of a study because they are told too little. Consequently there is widespread support for requiring researchers to disclose all facts likely to have any bearing on a subject's decision to participate in a study (President's Commission, 1981, 1983). The research suggests, however, that people are often strongly influenced by logically inconsequential information. In other words, some facts have a bearing on subjects' decisions when they logically and normatively should not. These facts are likely to mislead subjects and leave them with an inaccurate impression of the risks and benefits of the research. Indeed, they may have a bearing on subjects' decision precisely because they create an incorrect impression. Hence, requiring disclosure of all facts that have a bearing on subjects' decision may require disclosure of misleading information.

This point has important implications for the goals of informed consent: protecting subjects' autonomy and welfare. Subjects' autonomy is arguably only protected if they are given all information that would make a difference to their decision to participate (see Beauchamp & Childress, 1979, chap. 3). But if certain pieces of information induce an inaccurate picture of the risks and benefits of an experiment, disclosing such information may lead people to act in a manner contrary to their best interests. In other words, fully preserving subjects' autonomy may require sacrificing their welfare and vice versa (Thompson, 1982).

The following example illustrates the trade-off between autonomy and accurate perception. A researcher wishes to inject live cancer cells subcutaneously into human subjects as part of a study of the ability to reject foreign cells.[3] For argument's sake, let us assume the injection poses no risk to subjects other than minor discomfort but that learning the injections contain cancer cells will cause subjects to greatly overestimate the dangers posed by the experiment. The researcher wants to tell subjects only that the injections contain "foreign tissue." Should the IRB require that potential subjects be told the injections contain cancer cells? This disclosure is one that will make a difference to the decision of many subjects; hence, disclosure is essential to protect their autonomy (and is required under the materiality standard). But this disclosure may protect their autonomy at the price of their objectivity. Subjects' assessment of the risk of physical injury posed by the experiment may be more accurate if they are not told about the cancer.

In this case, most people may feel protecting subjects' autonomy is more important than ensuring that subjects assess accurately risks and benefits. But it is possible to imagine cases in which accurate risk assessment will be seen as more important than protecting autonomy. Suppose, for example, that a researcher wishes to recruit cancer patients for a dangerous experiment in which they will be injected with a substance that has no known therapeutic value. Suppose further that if subjects learn the name of the substance they will, despite disclosures to the contrary, tend to view it as therapeutic (which might happen if its name sounded something like laetrile or interferon). Should the researcher disclose the name of the substance? This disclosure will make a difference to subjects' decision about whether to participate and is therefore necessary to fully protect their autonomy (as well as being required by the materiality standard). But in this case "protecting" subjects' autonomy may result in their participating in a dangerous experiment—one they would have refused had they not been misled about its possible benefits by "full" disclosure.

These two examples illustrate that the quality of an informed-consent disclosure does not necessarily depend on the amount of information disclosed. More is not necessarily better. In this light, federal regulations requiring "full disclosure" and state law requiring disclosure of all material facts may be viewed as mixed blessings. Institutional review boards should take care that in their efforts to protect subjects' autonomy they do not require information to be disclosed in such a way that it misleads subjects into making nonoptimal decisions.

New Standards for Evaluating Disclosures. Identifying inadequacies in current disclosure standards is far easier than coming up with new standards to replace them. Given that the same information can have a wide range of effects depending on its presentation, however, new disclosure standards must deal with the *manner* as well as the *scope* of disclosures. The new standards must address two ethical questions: What information should be presented in informed consent disclosures? How should that information be formulated, given that its formulation may have considerable impact on subjects' decisions apart from the content of the disclosures?

The major goal of informed consent is to give potential subjects an accurate impression of the risks and benefits of a study so they may intelligently evaluate whether participation is consistent with their values. Accordingly, one might propose accuracy of communication as a standard, that is, the best disclosures are those that leave subjects with the most accurate perception of the risks and benefits of the study. The problem with using *accuracy of risk perception* as an ethical standard is that risk perception has two components, only one of which may be measured for "accuracy." The degree to which a particular outcome is perceived as a risk depends on both the perceived probability of the outcome and the perceived consequences of the outcome, that is, how likely and how bad it is.

In theory, one could evaluate the accuracy of probability perceptions by testing whether subjects' perceptions are consistent with those of knowledgeable experts, such as the researcher or perhaps IRB members. Although it may be difficult to measure subjective probabilities, it is possible in principle to assess whether a subject's perception of the probability of a given outcome is right or wrong. For example, if disclosure A gives subjects the impression they have one chance in 1,000 of being injured and disclosure B gives them the impression that they have one chance in 100 of being injured, one can assess whether A or B is better by comparing the impression created by each disclosure to experts' assessments of the probability of injury. Evaluating the "accuracy" of a subject's perception of the consequences of an outcome, however, is more problematic. A disagreement between the subject and experts about the "badness" of a particular outcome does not prove that the subject's evaluation is wrong. For example, if disclosure C leads subjects to conclude a particular risk is acceptable and disclosure D leads subjects to conclude the identical risk is not acceptable, although the risks are equal, determining which disclosure is "better" (more protective of autonomy) is more problematic.

There are normative standards for evaluating such choices, but these seem ill suited in the context of informed consent. One normative approach would require second-guessing subjects' moral judgment, asking which choice (i.e., to accept or not accept a particular risk) is more consistent with the general moral principles to which subjects subscribe. Since the whole point of informed consent is to allow subjects to apply their own values, however, this norm seems less than satisfactory. The theory of rational choice offers two other normative criteria for evaluating choice. One criterion is coherence, which holds that the most rational choice is the one that is most consistent with other choices the subject makes. As Tversky and Kahneman (1981) note, however, "The susceptibility of preferences to variations of framing raises doubt about the feasibility and adequacy of the coherence criterion." A final normative criterion is utility maximization, that is, whether the subject's choice will maximize his or her utility in the long run. While this criterion seems appealing, it is unlikely to provide much practical guidance to researchers and IRBS, given the difficulty of knowing exactly what values subjects are trying to maximize.

Perhaps the best a conscientious researcher can hope to do, as a practical matter, is to avoid giving subjects an inaccurate impression of the probability of various outcomes. But achieving even this goal may be trickier than most people imagine. A number of commentators have argued that creating adequate informed-consent disclosures is simple (e.g., Barber, 1980, p. 78). All that is necessary, they suggest, is to provide a straightforward, jargon-free explanation of the risks, and accurate comprehension will follow. The research reviewed in the previous section suggests, how-

ever, that the matter is not so simple. Clear, easy-to-understand disclosures may convey an inaccurate impression of the probability of an outcome in a number of ways, such as playing on subjects' preconceptions,
making the outcome particularly vivid and imaginable (or nonvivid and
hard to imagine), presenting (or not presenting) examples that illustrate
the outcome, and so on. All of this suggests that to adequately inform subjects, and thereby protect their autonomy, researchers and IRBs must do
more than assure that disclosures are clearly written. They must be sensitive to subtle psychological factors that may lead subjects to form inaccurate impressions of the likelihood of various outcomes.

Several steps might be taken to help ensure the adequacy of disclosures.
First, IRB members should be made aware of the subtle psychological factors that may influence subjects' impressions of probability. This knowledge will not necessarily enable IRB members to identify misleading disclosures—even the most sophisticated students of risk perception
sometimes find it difficult to predict the conclusions people draw from
communications about risk (Slovic, Fischhoff, & Lichtenstein, 1982)—but
it is a step in the right direction. There is also a need for additional research
on the conclusions people generally draw from various types of informed-
consent disclosures. Research along this line could seek to identify those
formulations or techniques for describing probabilities that promote accurate subjective impressions and misleading ones. What is needed, in other
words, is work on the psychometrics of risk perception. The work of
Slovic, Lichtenstein, Fischhoff, and their colleagues on the perception of
technological hazards (Fischhoff, Slovic, Lichtenstein, Layman, & Combs,
1978; Slovic, et al., 1984a) provides a fine model that could easily be extended to study informed consent to experimental research. A third step
toward protecting subjects' autonomy would be for IRBs to require researchers to demonstrate the effectiveness of their disclosures in cases in
which IRB members are particularly concerned that subjects might be misled. An IRB might require, for example, that a researcher administer a questionnaire to subjects after obtaining their "informed" consent to check
whether their understanding of likelihood of various outcomes is accurate.
Under current HHS regulations, IRBs have broad authority to monitor the
consent process (see especially 45 CFR §46.109(e)), which would almost
certainly extend to monitoring of this type.

It is worth noting that some of the psychological factors discussed above
influence choices mainly by influencing the perceived probability of good
and bad outcomes, while others may work by influencing the perceived

desirability of outcomes. Availability effects are an example of the former, and framing effects of the latter. Some factors may influence both perceived likelihood and perceived desirability. The story of Walter Halushka, for example, probably made being left brain damaged as a result of participating in the medical experiment seem both more likely and more terrible.

Judgmental Bias and Institutional Review

It is also a fundamental principle of research ethics that human subjects be protected from needless risks and that the risks they are exposed to be reasonable in relation to the potential benefits of the research (Beecher, 1970; President's Commission, 1981; Katz, 1972). Nevertheless, recent history provides many examples of research violating this principle. The Nazi atrocities documented in the Nuremburg trials (e.g., *United States v. Brandt*, 1947) and the U.S. Public Health Service's Tuskegee syphilis experiment (Gray, 1978) are leading examples, but many other instances of abuse or alleged abuse of human subjects have been documented (Barber, 1976; Beecher, 1966; Katz, 1972; Katz & Capron, 1975; Pappworth, 1967; President's Commission, 1982a, chap. 2).

Two major mechanisms have evolved to help protect subjects from excessive risk. First, there is the doctrine of informed consent, which was discussed in the previous section. Immediately after the Nuremburg trials it was thought that a researcher could fully discharge his or her obligation to subjects by completely and accurately disclosing risks (President's Commission, 1982a, p. 25). Since that time, however, a number of instances have come to light in which "informed" subjects were exposed to needless or excessive risks (President's Commission, 1982a, chap. 2). Publicity surrounding these instances helped create a widespread consensus that "informed consent should not be the sole mechanism by which societal decisions are made regarding whether the risks of a research investigation are justified by its expected results" (Gray, 1978). Concerns about the quality of informed-consent disclosures (Lidz et al., 1984), the ability of subjects to comprehend information about risks (Meisel & Roth, 1981), and the vulnerability of subjects to subtle coercive pressure (Thompson, 1982) have also contributed to support for a second mechanism to protect subjects from undue risk. The second mechanism is prior review of research protocols to control or limit the amount of risk to which subjects might be exposed. Federal regulations now require IRBs to exercise prior review of all funded projects involving human subjects (President's Commission, 1981). Current HHS regulations, among other things, require IRBS to approve proposed research only if "risks to subjects are minimized" and "risks to subjects are reasonable in relation to anticipated benefits" (45 CFR §46.111(a)).

Researchers and IRBS may take two approaches to assessing the risks of a research project. First, they may look at empirical data on the risks of research. There is surprisingly little data available on the overall rate of injuries in research involving human subjects. The President's Commission for the Study of Ethical Problems in Medicine and Biomedical and Behavioral Research attempted to compile data on research injuries in 1980 in order to evaluate proposals for a system to compensate injured research subjects, but it found only two institutions that had collected such data (President's Commission, 1982a, chap. 4). Both institutions had relatively low rates of injury and death among research subjects, although it is unclear whether the research risks at these institutions are comparable to the risks at other institutions, nor is it clear whether the risks that produced injuries and deaths were "reasonable in relation to anticipated benefits." At the University of Washington, where 356,000 subjects had participated in biomedical and behavioral research over eight years, only 144 had been temporarily disabled, none had been permanently disabled, and only two had died. At the Quincy Research Center in Kansas City, a drug-testing facility, risks were a bit higher. Among healthy subjects participating in Class I drug trials, 0.2% needed hospitalization and 0.24% died. Among sick patients participating in Class II drug trials, 1.43% required hospitalization and none died.

Such data may, of course, be unhelpful for assessing the risks of a specific new study using different procedures than those employed in the past. Nevertheless, these historical data provide some clues regarding the general level of risk associated with biomedical and behavioral research. These data may also provide insights into specific things that can go wrong in such research. At the University of Washington, for example, one common source of injuries was infection caused by contaminated experimental materials. Without such data, this is a source of risk that a researcher or IRB might overlook in assessing the overall risks of a study.

Another source of data on research risks concerns the rate of injuries associated with specific clinical procedures. Such data exist for a number of procedures commonly used in biomedical research (for a review, see Harvey & Levine, 1982). Existing studies indicate, for example, that lumbar puncture produces morbidity rates ranging from 0.4% to 47% and cardiac catheterization produces morbidity rates ranging from 2.3% to 10.1% and a mortality rate of 0.44%. Although data of this type are sometimes unreliable (Harvey & Levine, 1982) and may not offer a generalization from one clinical situation to another, they provide a starting point for risk assessment. To assess the risk of a particular study, the IRB members would need to consider both the *base rate* of injuries and deaths generally associated with the research procedures and more specific information about the way the procedures would be carried out in the study under review.

A second approach researchers and IRBs may take to assess risk is simply to rely on informed judgment. Given the paucity of relevant data on research risks and the uncertainties about its applicability in a given case, it seems likely that in most cases risk assessment is mainly a matter of educated guessing. Evaluating the risks of a complex experiment may, however, be an intricate and difficult task. The researcher and IRB members presumably must consider all possible outcomes of the research, estimate the likelihood and importance of each of those outcomes, integrate these considerations into a global evaluation of the risks and benefits of the research, and then decide whether the benefits outweigh the risks sufficiently to justify the study. In the following section I consider whether, in making these risk assessments, researchers and IRB members may fall victim to judgmental fallacies or errors of reasoning that lead to bad decisions. Although there is no evidence that researchers or IRB members actually make such errors, research on human judgment and decision making identifies a number of inferential pitfalls that might affect these important decisions.

Pitfalls in Risk Assessment and Evaluation

Many of the judgmental phenomena discussed with respect to informed consent may also affect the judgments and decisions of researchers and IRB members. When evaluating the riskiness of a proposal these individuals are likely influenced by preconceptions, the base-rate fallacy, striking examples, and availability and framing effects. These effects have been demonstrated in both lay and expert populations (Kahneman et al., 1982), so it is unlikely that the superior knowledge and education of researchers and IRB members render them immune. Furthermore, because of the nature of the judgments they must make, these individuals may be susceptible to certain judgmental errors in addition to those already discussed.

Illusion of Immunity. As noted above, researchers sometimes have information available on the base rate of injury and death associated with specific procedures (see, e.g., Harvey & Levine, 1982). Research on the base-rate fallacy suggests, of course, that such information is likely to be underutilized relative to "diagnostic" information. To disregard base rates is not always an error, however. A researcher may have good reason to believe that base-rate statistics are inapplicable to his or her own research. The relatively high rate of injuries associated with cardiac catheterization, for example, may be due to the use of the technique by inexperienced technicians. A researcher with superior clinical skills may justifiably believe these base rates are uninformative with respect to his or her own subjects. Members of an IRB may well agree. Research on human judgment suggests, however, that people tend to jump too quickly to the conclusion that a given instance is a "special case" for which the general odds do not apply (Slovic et al., 1980). People are unrealistically optimistic when estimating the chances that a wide variety of bad events will affect them personally, particularly where the hazards are partly under their own control; 97% of respondents to one survey judged themselves "above average" in their likelihood of avoiding bicycle and power-mower accidents. Hazardous activities such as driving have such a low incidence rate of injury that even the most negligent person may engage in the activity many times without ill effect, which may lead to the unwarranted conclusion that accidents are more likely to happen to someone else. These processes may cause researchers to be overly optimistic about the likelihood of a serious injury in their research. Institutional review board members should be careful not to be persuaded by researchers' unwarranted sense of personal immunity.

Overconfidence. Both experts and laypeople are often overconfident about the accuracy of their judgments (Alpert & Raiffa, 1982; Fischhoff, 1982; Lichtenstein, Fischhoff, & Phillips, 1982; Oskamp, 1982). Once people make a judgment, they tend to dramatically underestimate the likelihood that they could be mistaken. In one study, participants were given pairs of lethal events (e.g., drowning and suicide) and asked to judge which occurred more frequently. They were also asked to estimate the odds of their judgment being wrong. Most subjects estimated their chances of being wrong were 1:100 or less; in fact, their judgments were wrong about one time in eight (Slovic et al., 1980). Similar findings are quite common (Lichtenstein et al., 1982). Hence, researchers and IRB members likely tend to be overconfident when judging the probability of research injuries.

One important aspect of overconfidence is that people overestimate the likelihood they have fully considered a problem and, correspondingly, underestimate the likelihood there are important factors they have failed to consider. For example, people tend to overestimate the likelihood they have considered all possible reasons for an automobile's failure to start. When they are given a list of reasons an automobile might fail to start and are asked to judge the completeness of the list, the judgments of both laypeople (Fischhoff, Slovic, & Lichtenstein, 1978) and expert mechanics are insensitive to how complete the list actually is. Incomplete lists that omit major, commonly known sources of problems, such as fuel-system failure and ignition failure, are judged nearly as complete as far more comprehensive lists. These findings suggest people jump too readily to the conclusion they have considered all possible things that might go wrong or, put differently, underestimate the likelihood that a factor they have not considered could be a problem. This tendency might lead IRB members to seriously miscalculate when they rely on informed judgment to estimate research risks.

Integrating Multiple Judgments. Another problem with relying on informed judgment to evaluate research risks arises from the sheer complexity of many risk-assessment problems. An experimental intervention may have a multitude of risks and benefits of varying likelihood and importance. Institutional review board members not only must estimate the likelihood and importance of each possible outcome, they must integrate all these considerations into a global evaluation of the acceptability of the intervention. Research suggests that the process of integration is fraught with problems (Gettys, Kelly, & Peterson, 1982; Pitz & McKillip, 1984, chap. 3; Thompson, 1984). Pitz, Heerboth, and Sachs (1980) found that when people made global judgments about complex options they sometimes used inappropriate simplifying strategies that created systematic biases in the global judgments and reduced the sensitivity of those judgments to important features of the problem. One simplifying strategy, for example, is to ignore uncertainty about the underlying judgments when integrating them into a global evaluation. This strategy renders the global judgments insensitive to important variations in the reliability of the underlying judgments and may also bias the global judgment toward unwarranted certainty (Thompson, 1984). Global evaluations may also be biased by inappropriate integration strategies (Pitz & McKillip, 1984). Where the occurrence of a given outcome depends on the joint occurrence of several independent but uncertain events, for example, people's tendency to over-estimate joint probabilities leads them to overestimate the probability of that outcome (Pitz, 1980). Thus, IRB members may greatly overestimate the likelihood of a research injury in cases in which the injury will only occur if several independent but unlikely events occur simultaneously.

Improving Decisions about Research Risks

One approach to improving decisions about research risks is through a quantitative method called decision analysis. Decision analysis is a tech-nique for decomposing complex decisions into their constituent elements (Howard, 1980; Pitz & McKillip, 1984; Raiffa, 1968). Rather than make a global assessment of whether the benefits of a study outweigh its risks, for example, the decision maker might make a number of separate judgments concerning the probability and desirability of all possible outcomes. These separate judgments would then be integrated using formal mathematical techniques derived from expected-utility theory (Keeney & Raiffa, 1976; Von Neumann & Morgenstern, 1947). The result of this integration would be a rating of the overall utility or desirability of each option open to the de-cision maker. In theory, these ratings reflect the decision maker's own values and judgments of likelihood. Advocates claim the results of deci-sion analysis are less susceptible to the sorts of judgmental biases that af-fect global judgments and therefore can help improve decision making (Howard, 1980; Pitz & McKillip, 1984; Schwartz, Gorry, Kassirer, & Essig, 1973).

Decision analysis has been used for a number of years to help make de-cisions about complex technologies such as nuclear power (Brown, Kahn, & Peterson, 1974). More recently it has been applied extensively in medical decision making (Albert, 1978; Krischer, 1980; Politser, 1981). For example, decision analysis has been used to help establish the relative utility of med-ical and surgical therapy for coronary artery disease for patients with var-ious goals and values (Pauker, 1976) and to evaluate treatment options for lung cancer and laryngeal cancer (McNeil, Weichselbaum & Pauker, 1981).

The use of decision analysis to help IRBs decide whether to approve risky research has a number of advantages. First, it may help remedy er-rors of judgment that result from people's limited ability to process and in-tegrate complex information. Although the benefits of decision analysis are controversal (Eraker & Politser, 1982), a number of studies suggest decisions made with the help of decision analysis are more consistent and more sensitive to variations in important features of the problem than unaided global judgments (Gardiner & Edwards, 1975; Pitz 1980; Pitz et al., 1980). Decision analysis is particularly useful on problems requiring assessment and integration of the probabilities of a number of independent events. Misaggregation of probabilistic data tends to bias unaided judgments on such problems (Pitz & McKillip, 1984); decision analysis remedies this tendency by using a formal model to perform the integration.

A second advantage of decision analysis is that it would force IRBs to be explicit about the assumptions and values underlying their decisions. To decompose decisions into meaningful constituent judgments, IRB members would be forced to identify all outcomes they thought might flow from the research and specify their assumptions about the probability and utility of each outcome (Pitz & McKillip, 1984). This process would not only force IRB members to examine assumptions in a particularly searching manner, it would also reveal which assumptions about probability and utility are most crucial to the overall decision. Decision-analysis models allow explicit tests of the sensitivity of the overall decision to variations in constituent elements of the model. This sensitivity analysis could help IRB members identify those assumptions about facts or assessments of value that are most crucial and therefore might require additional research or consideration. The explicit listing of assumptions and values might also help reduce the influence of improper considerations. The IRB members' personal feelings of affection or animosity for the researcher, for example, would not be among the constituent elements integrated by the decision analysis. These feelings could only influence the analysis by influencing a number of discrete judgments of probability and utility that would be open to examination, perhaps leaving less room for the operation of personal bias. Finally, the explicit listing of assumptions and values might help the IRB justify its decision to approve or disapprove a proposal.

These advantages of decision analysis must be weighed against its disadvantages. First, the technique can be costly and time-consuming. To begin implementing the technique, members of an IRB would either need to invest the time necessary to learn it themselves or hire a consultant to help them apply it. Using decision analysis would undoubtedly take more time and effort than simply making a global judgment. According to Pitz and McKillip (1984), "Typically it takes at least two or three hours to complete even a very simple analysis; sometimes several days of effort might be required from several different people." Obviously an IRB could afford such efforts only for research raising the most serious ethical issues.

Second, although decision analysis may improve the consistency and sensitivity of judgments, it might not remedy many other types of judgmental biases (Eraker & Politser, 1982). Certain judgmental errors could seriously skew the results of a decision analysis by affecting the decision maker's assessment of constituent probabilities and values. Decomposing a judgment into its constituent elements would not necessarily prevent availability effects from influencing assessments of constituent probabilities or framing effects from influencing assessments of the desirability of outcomes (see, e.g., McNeil, Pauker, Sox, & Tversky, 1982). Since the results of a decision analysis depend on the accuracy of these constituent judgments, these judgmental errors could affect the outcome of an analysis as seriously as they affect unaided global judgments. Practitioners of decision analysis are aware of judgmental bias and are able to draw on a number of techniques to reduce its effects on constituent judgments (Fischhoff, Slovic, & Lichtenstein, 1980; Pitz & McKillip, 1984; Sirken, 1986). Nevertheless, decision analysis is best viewed as only a partial solution to problems posed by the limitations of unaided human judgment. Whether the benefits of this partial solution outweigh its considerable costs is a question that warrants further consideration and research.

Conclusion

This chapter raises challenging questions for scholars in a number of areas. For legal professionals and regulators it raises questions about the adequacy of current laws and regulations for protecting the autonomy and welfare of human subjects. Current laws and regulations regarding informed consent focus on the content rather than the style of disclosures. Yet research suggests that the way a disclosure is formulated may considerably influence subjects' perceptions of the risks involved and their decision to participate in research, quite apart from the content of the disclosure. Thus, two disclosures about the risks and benefits of a given study may both meet the requirements of current laws and regulations yet convey different impressions to subjects and induce different rates of participation. In light of this research, those concerned with protecting subjects' welfare and autonomy should consider whether current disclosure standards are adequate and, if not, whether better standards can be devised.

The same research raises questions about the adequacy of IRB review that also deserve consideration.

For ethicists and moral philosophers this chapter raises questions about the meaning of autonomy and about the normative status of judgmental "bias." Whether current laws and regulations adequately protect subjects' autonomy, for example, is a question that may ultimately turn on what we mean by autonomy. The research discussed in this chapter raises a number of questions on this issue that have not been explicitly addressed by experts in the field of research ethics. Is a choice based on mistaken preconceptions less autonomous than one based on more veridical preconceptions? Does it undermine subjects' autonomy when a researcher "frames" disclosures in a way likely to maximize participation (and does it matter whether the researcher's choice of a "frame" was inadvertent or intentionally manipulative)? Is it sensible even to talk about autonomous choice when logically inconsequential changes in the information subjects receive can induce dramatic reversals in their preferences? General theoretical treatments of the concept of autonomy (e.g., Beauchamp & Childress, 1979, chap. 2) suggest no clear or obvious answers to such questions. Additional scholarly work is therefore needed on these issues.

More generally, ethicists might contribute to our understanding of the normative status of judgments and choices that are subject to psychological influence. Suppose, for example, that two informed-consent disclosures contain essentially the same information but induce different perceptions of the desirability of a given outcome. Is there any good way to decide which perception, and, in turn, which disclosure, is better? Because framing effects may exert considerable influence on subjects' decision to participate, the choice of a frame is an ethically significant act. What principle or theories may we look to for guidance in making such choices?

For psychologists, especially those interested in human judgment, risk communication, risk perception, and social cognition, this chapter suggests a variety of hypotheses for applied and theoretical research. Research is needed to test whether the judgmental biases demonstrated in other areas actually influence the decisions of human subjects and IRB members in the ways suggested here and, if so, how these biases might be prevented or remedied. More generally, research is needed on the psychophysics of risk perception—on how human subjects draw conclusions from informed-consent disclosures and how information regarding the likelihood of various outcomes of a research project may be most accurately conveyed to subjects.

Finally, for researchers and IRB members this chapter raises the practical question of how to deal with the limitations of human judgment when designing informed-consent disclosures and assessing the risks of research. Recognizing some of the pitfalls of human judgment may be a first step toward avoiding them. But to find a satisfactory answer to this question, researchers and IRB members will need to draw on new scholarship in psychology, ethics, and law. Let us hope that this scholarship is forthcoming.

Notes

1. The term "informed consent," however, is of relatively recent origin. It did not appear until 1957, when it was used in an appellate court opinion (*Salgo v. Stanford University Bd. of Trustees*), although the concept of informed consent is implicit in the Nuremburg Codes (Annas, Glantz, & Katz, 1977, p. 6).

2. All fifty states have either statutes or common law rules that require physicians to disclose a certain amount of information to patients and subjects before obtaining their consent (Rosoff, 1981; Miller, 1980; Ludlum, 1978). In some states, injured subjects may recover damages under a theory of battery (unconsented touching) by proving merely that they were inadequately informed and that they were harmed. In most states, however, injured subjects may recover only under a theory of negligence, which requires subjects not only to prove they were inadequately informed and injured, but also to prove that a reasonably prudent person would not have consented to the intervention *but for* the physician's failure to make adequate disclosures (see, e. g., *Cobbs v. Grant*, 1972).

3. Such an experiment was actually conducted at the Jewish Chronic Disease Hospital in Brooklyn in the early 1960s (see Katz, 1972, pp. 9–65).

References

Albert, D. A. (1978). Decision theory in medicine: A review and critique. *Milbank Memorial Fund Quarterly, 56*, 362–401.

Allport, G. W. (1954). *The nature of prejudice*. Reading MA: Addison Wesley.

Alpert, M., & Raiffa, H. (1982). A progress report on the training of probability assessors. In D. Kahneman, T. Slovic, & A. Tversky (Eds.), *Judgment under uncertainty: Heuristics and biases* (pp. 294–305). Cambridge: Cambridge University Press.

Annas, G. J., Glantz, L. H., & Katz, B. F. (1977). *Informed consent to human experimentation: The subject's dilemma*. Cambridge MA: Ballinger.

Barber, B. (1976). The ethics of experimentation with human subjects. *Scientific American, 234,* 25–31.

Barber, B. (1980). *Informed consent in medical therapy and research.* New Brunswick NJ: Rutgers University Press.

Bar-Hillel, M. (1980). Base-rate fallacy in probability judgments. *Acta Psychologica, 44,* 211–233.

Beauchamp, T. L., & Childress, J. F. (1979). *Principles of biomedical ethics.* New York: Oxford University Press.

Beecher, H. K. (1966). Ethics and clinical research. *New England Journal of Medicine, 274,* 1354.

Beecher, H. K. (1970). *Research and the individual: Human studies.* Boston: Little Brown.

Berlin, I. (1969). *Two concepts of liberty.* Oxford: Clarendon.

Borgida, E., & Brekke, N. (1981). The base-rate fallacy in attribution and prediction . In J. Harvey, W. Ickes, & R. Kidd (Eds.), *New directions in attribution research* (Vol. 3, pp. 63–95). Hillsdale NJ: Erlbaum.

Bower, G. H. (1972). Mental imagery and associative learning. In L. Gregg (Ed.), *Cognition in learning and memory* (pp. 51–88). New York: Wiley.

Brown, R. V., Kahn, A. S., & Peterson, C. (1974). *Decision analysis: An overview.* New York: Holt, Rinehart & Winston.

Bruner, J. S. (1957). Going beyond the information given. In H. Gruber, K. Hammond, & R. Jessor (Eds.), *Contemporary approaches to cognition* (pp. 41–69). Cambridge MA: Harvard University Press.

Bryant, G. D., & Norman, G. R. (1980). Expressions of probability: Words and numbers [Letter to the Editor]. *New England Journal of Medicine, 302,* 411.

Canterbury v. Spence, 464 F.2d 772 (D.C. Cir. 1972).

Capron, A. M. (1974). Informed consent in catastrophic disease research and treatment. *University of Pennsylvania Law Review, 123,* 340–420.

Chapman, L. J., & Chapman, J. P. (1969). Illusory correlation as an obstacle to the use of valid psychodiagnostic signs. *Journal of Abnormal Psychology, 74,* 271–280.

Cobbs v. Grant, 8 Cal.3d 229, 502 P.2d 1 (1972).

Covello, V. T. (1983). The perception of technological risks: A literature review. *Technological Forecasting and Social Change, 23,* 285–297.

Dawes, R. M. (1979). The robust beauty of improper linear models in decision making. *American Psychologist, 34,* 571–582.

Dworkin, G. (1982). Autonomy and informed consent. In President's Commission for the Study of Ethical Problems in Medicine and Biomedical and Behavioral Research (Eds.), *Making health care decisions: Appendices: Studies on the foundations of informed consent* (Vol. 3, pp. 63–81). Washington DC: U.S. Government Printing Office.

Eraker, S. A., & Politser, P. (1982). How decisions are reached: Physician and patient. *Annals of Internal Medicine, 97,* 262–268.

Eraker, S. A., & Sox, H. C. (1981). Assessment of patients' preferences for therapeutic outcomes. *Medical Decision Making, 1,* 29–39.

Fischhoff, B. (1982). Debiasing. In D. Kahneman, P. Slovic, & A. Tversky (Eds.), *Judgment under uncertainty: Heuristics and biases* (pp. 422–444). Cambridge: Cambridge University Press.

Fischhoff, B., Slovic, P., & Lichtenstein, S. (1978). Fault trees: Sensitivity of estimated failure probabilities to problem representation. *Journal of Experimental Psychology: Human Perception and Performance, 4,* 330–344.

Fischhoff, B., Slovic, P., & Lichtenstein, S. (1980). Knowing what you want: Measuring labile values. In T. Wallsten (Ed.), *Cognitive processes in choice and decision behavior* (pp. 117–141). Hillsdale NJ: Erlbaum.

Fischhoff, B., Slovic, P., Lichtenstein, S., Layman, M., & Combs, B. (1978). Judged frequency of lethal events. *Journal of Experimental Psychology: Human Learning and Memory, 4,* 551–578.

Gardiner, P. C., & Edwards, W. (1975). Public values: Multiattribute utility measurement for social decision making. In M. F. Kaplan & S. Schwartz (Eds.), *Human judgment in decision making.* New York: Academic Press.

Gettys, C. F., Kelly, C., & Peterson, C. R. (1982). The best-guess hypothesis in multistage inference. In D. Kahneman, T. Slovic, & A. Tversky (Eds.), *Judgment under uncertainty: Heuristics and biases* (pp. 370–377). Cambridge: Cambridge University Press.

Gray, B. H. (1978). Complexities of informed consent. *Annals of the American Academy of Political and Social Sciences, 437,* 37–48.

Halushka v. University of Saskatchewan, 52 W.W.R. 608 (Sask. 1965).

Harvey, M., & Levine, R. J. (1982). Risk of injury associated with twenty invasive procedures used in human experimentation and assessment of reliability of risk estimates. In President's Commission for the Study of Ethical Problems in Medicine and Biomedical and Behavioral Research (Eds.), *Compensating for research injuries: Appendices* (Vol. 2, pp. 73–171). Washington DC: U.S. Government Printing Office.

Hastorf, A. H., & Cantril, H. (1954). They saw a game: A case study. *Journal of Abnormal and Social Psychology, 49,* 129–134.

Howard, R. (1980). An assessment of decision analysis. *Operations Research, 28,* 4–27.

Jonas, H. (1969). *Ethical aspects of experimentation with human subjects.* Boston: Daedalus.

Kahneman, D., Slovic, P., & Tversky, A. (Eds.). (1982). *Judgment under uncertainty: Heuristics and biases.* Cambridge: Cambridge University Press.

Kahneman, D., & Tversky, A. (1973). On the psychology of prediction. *Psychological Review, 80,* 237–251.

Kahneman, D., & Tversky, A. (1979). Prospect theory: An analysis of decisions under risk. *Econometrica, 47,* 263–291.

Kant, I. (1969). *Foundations of the metaphysics of morals.* New York: Bobbs Merrill. (Original work published 1785)

Katz, J. (1972). *Experimentation with human beings.* New York: Russell Sage.

Katz, J., & Capron, A. M. (1975). *Catastrophic disease: Who decides what? A psychosocial and legal analysis of the problems posed by hemodialysis and organ transplantation.* New York: Sage.

Keeney, R. L., & Raiffa, H. (1976). *Decisions with multiple objectives: Preferences and value tradeoffs.* New York: Wiley.

Kelley, H. H. (1950). The warm-cold variable in first impressions of persons. *Journal of Personality, 18,* 431–439.

Keown, C., Slovic, P., & Lichtenstein, S. (1984). Attitudes of physicians, pharmacists, and lay persons toward seriousness and need for disclosure of prescription drug side effects. *Health Psychology, 3,* 1–11.

Krischer, J. P. (1980). An annotated bibliography of decision analytic applications to health care. *Operations Research, 28,* 97–113.

Levine, R. J. (1981). *Ethics and regulation of clinical research.* Baltimore: Urban & Schwarzenberg.

Lichtenstein, S., Fischhoff, B., & Phillips, L. D. (1982). Calibration of probabilities: The state of the art to 1980. In D. Kahneman, P. Slovic, & A. Tversky (Eds.), *Judgment under uncertainty: Heuristics and biases* (pp. 306–334). Cambridge: Cambridge University Press.

Lichtenstein, S., Slovic, P., Fischhoff, B., Layman, M., & Combs, B. (1978). Judged frequency of lethal events. *Journal of Experimental Psychology: Human Learning and Memory, 4,* 551–578.

Lidz, C. W., Meisel, A., Zerubavel, E., Carter, M., Sestak, R., & Roth, L. H. (1984). *Informed consent: A study of decision making in psychiatry.* New York: Guilford.

Lord, C., Lepper, M. R., & Ross, L. (1979). Biased assimilation and attitude polarization: The effects of prior theories on subsequently considered evidence. *Journal of Personality and Social Psychology, 37,* 2098–2109.

Ludlum, R. (1978). *Informed consent.* Chicago: American Hospital Association.

McNeil, B. J., Pauker, S. J., Sox, H. C., & Tversky, A. (1982). On the elicitation of preferences for alternative therapies. *New England Journal of Medicine, 306,* 1259–1262.

McNeil, B. J., Weichselbaum, R., & Pauker, S. J. (1981). Speech and survival: Trade-offs between quality and quantity of life in laryngeal cancer. *New England Journal of Medicine, 305,* 982–987.

Meisel, A., & Roth, L. H. (1981). What we do and do not know about informed consent: An overview of the empirical studies. *Journal of the American Medical Association, 246,* 2473–2477.

Miller, L. J. (1980). Informed consent. *Journal of the American Medical Association, 244,* 2100–2103, 2347–2350, 2556–2558.

Morgan, M. G., Slovic, P., Nair, I., Geisler, D., MacGregor, D., Fischhoff, B., Lincoln, D., & Florig, K. (1985). Powerline frequency electric and magnetic fields: A pilot study of risk perception. *Risk Analysis, 5,* 139–149.

Nisbett, R. E., Krantz, D. H., Jepson, C., & Fong, G. T. (1982). Improving inductive inference. In D. Kahneman, P. Slovic, & A. Tversky (Eds.), *Judgment under uncertainty: Heuristics and biases* (pp. 445–462). Cambridge: Cambridge University Press.

Nisbett, R. E., & Ross, L. (1980). *Human inference: Strategies and shortcomings of social judgment.* Englewood Cliffs NJ: Prentice-Hall.

Oskamp, S. (1982). Overconfidence in case-study judgments. In D. Kahneman, P. Slovic, & A. Tversky (Eds.), *Judgment under uncertainty: Heuristics and biases* (pp. 287–293). Cambridge: Cambridge University Press.

Pappworth, M. H. (1967). *Human guinea pigs.* Boston: Beacon.

Pauker, S. J. (1976). Coronary artery surgery: The use of decision analysis. *Annals of Internal Medicine, 85,* 8–18.

Pitz, G. F. (1980). Sensitivity of direct and derived judgments to probabilistic information. *Journal of Applied Psychology, 65,* 164–171.

Pitz, G. F., Heerboth, J., & Sachs, N. J. (1980). Assessing the utility of multiattribute utility assessments. *Organizational Behavior and Human Performance, 26,* 65–80.

Pitz, G. F., & McKillip, J. (1984). *Decision analysis for program evaluators.* Beverly Hills CA: Sage.

Politser, P. E. (1981). Decision analysis and clinical judgment: A reevaluation. *Medical Decision Making, 1,* 361–389.

President's Commission for the Study of Ethical Problems in Medicine and Biomedical and Behavioral Research. (1981). *Protecting human subjects: The adequacy and uniformity of federal rules and their implementation.* Washington DC: U.S. Government Printing Office.

President's Commission for the Study of Ethical Problems in Medicine and Biomedical and Behavioral Research. (1982a). *Compensating for research injuries: The ethical and legal implications of programs to redress injured subjects.* Washington DC: U.S. Government Printing Office.

President's Commission for the Study of Ethical Problems in Medicine and Biomedical and Behavioral Research. (1982b). *Making health care decisions: The ethical and legal implications of informed consent in the patient-practitioner relationship.* Washington DC: U.S. Government Printing Office.

President's Commission for the Study of Ethical Problems in Medicine and Biomedical and Behavioral Research. (1983). *Implementing human research regulations: The adequacy and the uniformity of federal rules and their implementation.* Washington DC: U.S. Government Printing Office.

Raiffa, H. (1968). *Decision analysis: Introductory lectures on choices under uncertainty.* Reading MA: Addison-Wesley.

Reyes, R. M., Thompson, W. C., & Bower, G. H. (1980). Judgmental biases resulting from differing availabilities of arguments. *Journal of Personality and Social Psychology, 39,* 2–12.

Rosenberg, J. (1978). A question of ethics: The DNA controversy. *American Educator, 2,* 27.

Rosoff, A. J. (1981). *Informed consent: A guide for health care providers.* Rockville MD: Aspen Systems.

Schneider, D. J., Hastorf, A. H., & Ellsworth, P. C. (1979). *Person perception.* Reading MA: Addison-Wesley.

Schwartz, W. B., Gorry, G. A., Kassirer, J. P., & Essig, A. (1973). Decision analysis and clinical judgment. *American Journal of Medicine, 55,* 459–472.

Sherman, S. J., Cialdini, R. B., Schwartzman, D. F., & Reynolds, K. D. (1985). Imagining can heighten or lower the perceived likelihood of contracting a disease: The mediating effect of ease of imagery. *Personality and Social Psychology Bulletin, 11,* 118–127.

Sirken, M. G. (1986). Error effects of survey questionnaires on the public's assessments of health risks. *American Journal of Public Health, 76,* 367–368.

Slovic, P., Fischhoff, B., & Lichtenstein, S. (1976). Cognitive processes and societal risk taking. In J. S. Carroll & J. W. Payne (Eds.), *Cognition and social behavior* (pp. 165–184). Hillsdale NJ: Erlbaum.

Slovic, P., Fischhoff, B., & Lichtenstein, S. (1977). Behavioral decision theory. *Annual Review of Psychology, 28,* 1–39.

Slovic, P., Fischhoff, B., & Lichtenstein, S. (1978). Accident probabilities and seat belt usage: A psychological perspective. *Accident Analysis and Prevention, 10,* 281–285.

Slovic, P., Fischhoff, B., & Lichtenstein, S. (1980). Informing people about risk. In L. Morris, M. Mazis, & B. Barofsky (Eds.), *Product labeling and health risks: Banbury Report 6* (pp. 165–181). Cold Spring Harbor NY: Cold Spring Harbor Laboratory.

Slovic, P., Fischhoff, B., & Lichtenstein, S. (1982). Response mode, framing and information processing effects in risk assessment. In R. M. Hogarth (Ed.), *New directions for methodology of social and behavioral science: Question framing and response consistency* (pp. 21–36). San Francisco: Jossey-Bass.

Slovic, P., Lichtenstein, S., & Fischhoff, B. (1984a). Decision making. In R. C. Atkinson, R. J. Herrnstein, G. Lindsey, & R. D. Luce (Eds.), *Stevens' Handbook of Experimental Psychology* (2nd ed., Vol. 2, pp. 673–738). New York: Wiley.

Slovic, P., Lichtenstein, S., & Fischhoff, B. (1984b). Modeling the societal impact of fatal accidents. *Management Science, 30,* 464–474.

Thompson, W. C. (1982). Psychological issues in informed consent. In President's Commission for the Study of Ethical Problems in Medicine and Biomedical and Behavioral Research (Eds.), *Making health care decisions* (Vol. 3, pp. 83–115). Washington DC: U.S. Government Printing Office.

Thompson, W. C. (1984). *Integration of judgments in cascaded inference: Intuitive and Bayesian assessments of circumstantial evidence*. Unpublished doctoral dissertation, Stanford University, Palo Alto CA.

Treat, D. A. (1977). Proposed changes for obtaining informed consent from experimental subjects. *Law and Human Behavior, 1,* 403–422.

Tversky, A., & Kahneman, D. (1971). The belief in the "law of small numbers." *Psychological Bulletin, 76,* 105–110.

Tversky, A., & Kahneman, D. (1973). Availability: A heuristic for judging frequency and probability. *Cognitive Psychology, 5,* 207–232.

Tversky, A., & Kahneman, D. (1974). Judgment under uncertainty: Heuristics and biases. *Science, 185,* 1124–1131.

Tversky, A., & Kahneman, D. (1981). The framing of decisions and the psychology of choice. *Science, 211,* 453–458.

United States v. Brandt, 1948 (reprinted in 1–2 Trials of War Criminals Before the Nuremburg Military Tribunals).

Von Neumann, J., & Morgenstern, O. (1947). *Theory of games and economic behavior*. Princeton NJ: Princeton University Press.

Chapter 2 / Typically Unexamined Communication Processes in Research

JOAN E. SIEBER

California State University, Hayward

Conducting research on human beings is analogous to producing and directing a play. What is communicated by the setting, the research assistants, the way subjects are recruited, and so on has a major impact on the validity of the research findings and on the ethical dimension of the research. However, research is often conducted with insufficient attention to these subtleties of communication and to their implications for the outcome of the research.

When we read a play, we notice that there are a few instructions in parentheses. For example, in *King Henry VI*, William Shakespeare offers such instructions as: (Enter soldiers bearing the body of John Talbot.) (Drums sound from afar.) (Enter fiends.) (They hang their heads.) (Exit the Bastard of Orleans, Reignier, and others.) But any director knows that more than a few instructions in parentheses are required to orchestrate an effective performance. Each actor's position on stage, body language, and voice tone must communicate at least as effectively and appropriately as his or her words. Costumes must convey the intended message: a rumpled gown on the queen conveys a different message than a well-ironed one. The stage and props must also "work" to convey the intended message; an elegant ballroom scene is hard to convey on a tiny stage with beat-up props.

The literature search on which this chapter is based was conducted by Joan Thornton, whose conscientious work is deeply appreciated. This chapter benefitted greatly from critical comments on prior drafts by Robert Rosenthal, Barbara Stanley, Gary Melton, and Wendy Braga. The shortcomings that remain are of my own doing.

Similarly, much more takes place among the "cast of characters" and in the "staging" of a research project than is documented in the institutional review board protocol or in the method section of the resulting publication. Some of the communication between researcher and subject is official or authorized in the sense that it is precisely what is supposed to be communicated, such as the informed-consent statement and the specific instructions given to participants. Some of the communication is unofficial and perhaps incidental to the research process, for example, statements made to subjects when they are being recruited or directed to the laboratory. Much of the informal communication is nonverbal, such as the investigator's body language and style of dress, the room configuration, and the prestige of the research setting. The official communication is documented and the unofficial communication typically is not. But unlike professional play directors, most investigators give little or no thought to the unofficial communication; it simply occurs in the process of doing the research and is regarded as inconsequential since it is considered incidental to getting the research done. This has unfortunate consequences for research, for, as in a play, the undocumented or unofficial communication can give emphasis to what has been communicated officially, contradict what has been communicated officially, or convey a different message altogether.

The purpose of this chapter is to raise consciousness about the ways in which consequential communication can occur without awareness on the part of the investigator, to review research on these processes, and to indicate future directions for research.

Are Unexamined Communication Processes an Ethical Issue?

The unofficial communication in the recruitment, consent, and debriefing process may raise any of a variety of solely ethical concerns. It may coerce, convey disrespect, confuse or worry subjects, limit rapport, reduce willingness of subjects to ask questions pertinent to their decision whether to participate, or otherwise limit their autonomy. Implicit or unexamined communication may set up demand characteristics that pressure potential subjects to participate against their will, as when a course instructor urges students to participate in "optional" research in the same breath in which the course requirements and grading standards are discussed. The researcher's body language, intonation, or choice of words may convey disrespect; for example, the official informed-consent statement may say that participants are entitled to have their questions answered, but the posture, facial expression, or voice tone of the researcher may convey that the subject's feelings are unimportant and that only an idiot would have any questions.

The unexamined messages conveyed in research may also have methodological consequences. They may affect the research conditions and thus the outcome of the study. Stated another way, the unexamined communication may confound the design by causing the subjects to behave differently than they would if the intended or assumed communication processes had occurred. This validity issue, in turn, is an ethical issue. The ethical justification for taking subjects' time is that the research design be valid. To produce invalid results is to waste subjects' time and to produce erroneous conclusions.

There are a host of other ways in which "experimenter effects" may influence the outcome of the research. The experimenter's own biases may cause erroneous observation of behavior or interpretation of the data. Carelessness, poor judgment, wishful thinking, and outright fraud may occur. These kinds of experimenter effects, which have been discussed elsewhere (e.g., Chubin, 1985; Rosenthal, 1966), are not engendered by the communication between researcher and subject and are beyond the purview of this chapter.

What Communication Processes Should Concern Researchers?

The research act is surrounded by communication: communication about the research when recruiting participants, communication during the consent process, instructions to participants, debriefing, and communication about the research after it has been analyzed. This communication occurs through various channels: visual, postural, tonal, verbal, written, and so on.

The effects of communication in research are mediated by many factors, such as the congruence of the researcher's messages across communication channels, the personality characteristics of the subject and the researcher, the status differential between the parties to the communication, the number of researchers in relation to the number of subjects, the proximity of the parties to the communication, the timing of the communication, and the attitudes of those who serve some gatekeeping function but are not strictly part of the research relationship. Moreover, the personality and background of the subject and researcher may cause one or both to bring implicit expectations to the research setting that, in turn, affect the results of the study.

Finally, the context of the research probably plays an important role in determining the impact of the communication. For example, participants in a laboratory experiment at a prestigious laboratory are likely to be more attentive to behavioral cues from the investigator than are participants in a field study where they are being interviewed on their home turf. As another example, Grisso (in this volume) points out that communication by researchers with juvenile offenders in prison is probably more affected by what the subjects believe the warden thinks of the research than by what the researcher says.

In this chapter, the following topics are examined: channels of communication, mirroring, congruence, personality and background characteristics of the communicators, the volunteer effect, experimenter and subject expectancy, factors that make subjects vulnerable to untoward communication effects, and causes of untoward communication processes in research. Currently, there is no adequate taxonomy of the aspects of communication that should concern researchers or guide this review. It is hoped that this discussion will stimulate further investigation of communication processes in research.

Channels of Communication

Communication may occur through many channels besides words, such as paralanguage (voice tone, mumbling, stuttering), physical characteristics (body odor, skin color and tone, beauty), kinesic cues or body language (gestures, postures, facial expressions, gaze, touch), proxemics (distance between people, seat selections), room arrangement, and so on. Understanding of the effects of nonverbal communication on the research process comes from several sources, including general research on person perception, research on the perception of authority figures such as physicians and psychiatrists, and research on the actual behavioral research process.

There is now a large body of literature on channels of nonverbal communication in contexts other than research (e.g., Ekman & Friesen, 1975; Heslin & Patterson, 1982; Knapp, 1978). This literature provides a background for understanding how nonverbal communication might operate in the research process. The very brief summary of research that follows is in no way intended to summarize that vast literature but is only intended to demonstrate some findings that seem likely to be generalizable to the research setting.

That at least some nonverbal communication is an important and meaningful "language" is shown by two kinds of findings. First, there is considerable agreement as to the meaning of many nonverbal cues. In some cases the meanings are universally shared. For example, extending Darwin's notion that some facial expressions of emotion are universally understood, Ekman has demonstrated the people of various cultures easily identify photographs of faces as happy, fearful, surprised, angry, disgusted or sad (Ekman & Friesen, 1975). Second, nonverbal cues are taken seriously by perceivers. Persons tend to believe, that since many actions (e.g., kinesic and proxemic cues) are displayed unintentionally, they are more valid sources of information than verbal behavior (Heslin & Patterson, 1982). Moreover, even physical characteristics that we tell ourselves to ignore ("Don't judge a book by its cover" "Beauty is only skin deep") overwhelmingly affect our perceptions. Attractive people are seen as more confident, happy, assertive, active, candid, serious, and outspoken than people with average looks (Knapp, 1978). We tend to assume that attractive people possess a range of positive attributes (Dion, Berscheid, & Walster, 1972).

Kinesic cues such as those an experimenter might provide when giving instructions are read with considerable agreement as to meaning. Basic research in person perception, done with drawings or role playing, indicates that persons who lean forward when interacting are perceived as warm (Reece & Whitman, 1962), intimate (Breed, 1972), empathic (Haase & Tepper, 1972; Tepper & Haase, 1978; Trout & Rosenfeld, 1980), and attentive (Genthner & Moughan, 1977). Open positions of the arms and legs are considered to communicate a more positive attitude than closed postures (Machotka, 1965; Mehrabian, 1968), especially when the person leans backward (McGinley, Nicholas, & McGinley, 1978). Folded arms and crossed legs (ankle on knee) are rated as negative (Smith-Hanen, 1977). Head nodding is regarded as a gesture of approval or agreement (Argyle, 1975; Eibl-Eibesfeldt, 1975) and is associated with liking, affiliation, persuasiveness, attraction (LaCrosse, 1975; Mehrabian & Williams, 1969; Sobelman, 1974), warmth, understanding, and effectiveness (D'Augelli, 1974).

Can these results, based on stick figures and role playing, be generalized to the relationship between the researcher and research participant, the clinician and patient, and other related contexts of concern to psychologists? Studies by Harrigan and her associates on the perception of rapport between physician and patient seem more relevant to the research setting, and their results suggest that the above findings may indeed be broadly generalizable. In one study (Harrigan & Rosenthal, 1983), physicians' non-verbal behavior was varied so that there were three levels of trunk angle (forward, straight, and backward), two levels of arm position (open and folded), two levels of leg position (open and crossed), and two levels of head attitude (nodding and not nodding). Undergraduate students rated videotapes of these physicians and judged most positively physicians who leaned forward with open arm positions and who nodded their heads. In a second study (Harrigan, Oxman, & Rosenthal, 1985) in which psychiatric nurses rated actual videotapes of family-medicine residents in interviews with patients, physicians were rated more highly when they sat directly facing the patient with uncrossed legs and arms in symmetrical side-by-side positions and engaged in moderate eye contact.

The few studies conducted on the effects of nonverbal communication in the research setting confirm the relevancy of findings in other contexts to the research setting, but not necessarily in obvious ways. Vrolijk (1966) examined the effects of periodic verbal reinforcement ("um hum") on the verbalizations of 36 subjects in an association task, in conjunction with a posture of either avoidance or approach. Verbal reinforcement ("um hum") affected subjects' verbalizations only when combined with a posture of avoidance; when combined with an approach posture, saying "um hum" had no effect. Tang (1987) varied the attentiveness of experimenters to Taiwanese undergraduates engaged in an anagram-solving task. Subjects had previously been tested and classified as Type A, Intermediate, or Type B. In the high experimenter attentiveness condition, all three groups of subjects spent significantly more time on the task than in the low experimenter attentiveness condition, and the three groups did not differ in time spent on the task. However, only the Type A students in the high experimenter attentiveness group solved significantly more anagrams. Burkhart (1976) tested the notion that vocal paralinguistic cues in the researcher's instructions, coupled with subjects' evaluation apprehension, are critical to the transmission of experimenter bias effects. Using the Rosenthal picture-rating task, strongly positive, strongly negative, and neutral vocal paralinguistic cues were used, in connection with high and low evaluation apprehension. No main effects were observed. Contrary to expectation, only the subjects high in evaluation apprehension failed to conform to the vocal paralinguistic cues provided by the experimenter.

There is clear evidence, however, that subjects form definite impressions about subjects on the basis of nonverbal cues. In a series of experiments, Rosenthal and his associates found that subjects show significant agreement in their ratings of experimenters on attributes such as professional, important, business-like; expressive voice, slow speech; enthusiastic, relaxed manner; and body gestures. Moreover, they found that experimenters who were perceived as having these attributes were the experimenters most likely to produce the expectancy effect. That is, they were the most likely to obtain the data they were led to expect (Rosenthal, Persinger, Vikan-Kline, & Mulry, 1963b). Rosenthal (1966) summarizes the effects of four dimensions of nonverbal behavior as follows:

1. Professional status. Experimenters who are perceived as more important, professional, business-like, and consistent exert greater expectancy effects on their subjects.
2. Interpersonal style. Those who are more relaxed, interested, enthusiastic, and personal exert greater expectancy effects, but probably only as long as they maintain a professional manner and do not lapse into a "social hour."
3. Kinesic communication. Subtle body movements exert expectancy effects, but more overt movements are likely to be perceived as unprofessional.
4. Paralinguistic communication. Slow, expressive speech exerts expectancy effects.

In our discussion thus far of nonverbal communication in the research process, no mention has been made of research in which the actual *process* of communication was observed. How, exactly, do experimenters signal to subjects what they expect? Rosenthal (1966, chap. 16) reports an extensive series of studies that uncovered no well-specifiable system of unintentional signaling, yet they repeatedly found experimenter expectancy effects. If these cues are so elusive, how then do experimenters know what cues to use and how to use them? How do they learn this? A clue to the answer comes from data showing that subjects run later in the study show greater expectancy effects than those run earlier (Vikan-Kline, 1962). Rosenthal (1966) interprets this to mean that experimenters are learning to increase their unintended influence in the course of running the experiment. And who is their teacher? Apparently it is the subject. It must be rewarding to have one's expectations confirmed. Thus, whenever the subject responds according to the experimenter's expectations, the probability that the experimenter will repeat those covert communication behaviors that preceded the subjects' response is increased.

How significant are these findings for understanding communication in the research process? These may be some of the cues by which subjects evaluate investigators when they are face to face, as in the consent or debriefing process. But are these the key contexts in which critical communication occurs between subject and researcher? Are there not other contexts and other cues that may be crucial to the research participants' perception of the researcher? The significance of such cues cannot be evaluated until more analysis of communication processes within actual research settings is performed.

Mirroring and Congruence of Communication

Within the last decade, pioneers in neurolinguistic programming (e.g., Bandler & Grinder, 1975) have discovered that it is not simply factors such as the postural position, breathing pattern, rate of speech, eye contact, voice tone, and an individual's choice of words that matter. Also critical is whether the elements of communication used by one party *mirror* those of the other party and whether communication is *congruent*, that is, whether what is said verbally is consistent with what is signaled nonverbally.

Mirroring can occur in a variety of ways. Postural mirroring means assuming a posture similar to that of the person with whom one is communicating (e.g., sitting in a posture that is a mirror image of that of the other party). Verbal mirroring means using the terminology that the other party seems to find meaningful rather than imposing a different terminology. For example, in survey research on early perception of parents, the respondent may say, "I remember my father coming home and ranting at me." In seeking elaboration, if the interviewer mirrored the respondent, he or she might say, "What kinds of things would he say when he ranted at you?" rather than impose his own meaning and terminology, for example, "What did he say when he verbally abused you?" Similarly, one may mirror the rate of speech (e.g., Matarazzo & Wiens, 1967, 1977), the breathing pattern, and other elements of the other party's communication.

The role of mirroring in creating trust and rapport is readily apparent. Rather than set oneself apart from the other, the communicator who mirrors sends a message of a peer relationship or acceptance and comfort with the style of the other party. It is also apparent that exact mirroring is not always desirable. For example, the communicator may not wish to mirror the anxiety or hostility of the other person. Rather than mirror dysfunctional aspects of the other person's communication, the effective communicator uses vocabulary the other person can comprehend, speaks in gentle direct tones at about the same rate of speech as that used by the other person, breathes deeply and calmly, stands or sits straight and relaxed, and is accessible to eye contact. Moreover, to communicate effectively and with empathy, the communicator's mind must be relatively clear of distracting thoughts, and he or she must have positive regard for the other person and say what is appropriate to the circumstances.

Incongruity comes about when the communicator's mind is not clear of distraction. Consider the likely behavior of a researcher who entertains thoughts and feelings that are incompatible with respect and desire to communicate. Perhaps the researcher has just run his or her 100th subject since the research assistant quit without notice last week and is also upset about a disagreement he or she is having with a dean. This person is likely to engage, unwittingly, in nonverbal communication that is incongruent with the spoken words. He or she is likely to:

- Shake his or her head "no" while saying something positive.
- Speak in a high or harsh voice.
- Tense his or her neck and facial muscles.
- Breathe quickly and shallowly.
- Avoid eye contact when the subject seeks it.
- Omit details the subject wants to hear.
- Speak too rapidly.
- Assume a posture different from that of the subject when it would be appropriate to mirror the subject's posture.
- Laugh inappropriately, express hostility, or make distracting movements.
- Give the subject no graceful opportunity to formulate and ask questions.

According to specialists in psycholinguistic programming (e.g., Bandler & Grinder, 1975), *incongruence* between the ostensible content of communication and the actual communication is perceived by the listener, even if only at an unconscious level, and may produce stress, anxiety, and doubt. Stanley (in this volume) contends that consent issues in biomedical and psychological research differ little; the following actual case (Sieber, 1979a) coupled with the research reported in this chapter on incongruence in consent to psychological research bear out that contention.

Ms. Z, who sought a relatively safe optional surgical treatment, was recruited to participate in a study comparing a new variation of the operation with the standard operation. She had learned about the known advantages and disadvantages of both procedures and understood the rather minimal risks quite well. On arrival at the medical center, she was shown to an office by a receptionist. An anxious-looking young physician arrived, propped himself in a half-sitting, half-standing position in the doorway, and ascertained that she was indeed the woman whose name was in his appointment book. He informed her that this was unnecessary surgery and asked whether she knew that. She attempted to explain her rationale in a sentence or two, but he appeared not to hear her. He read off a long list of possible causes of death and disablement associated with the operation, with probability values attached to each. The probability values were low and were already known to Ms. Z, and yet she began to experience fear. She tried to assuage the fear by telling herself that the physician was socially immature and unable to communicate effectively and that this was no measure of his competence as a surgeon. She tried to dismiss the significance of the informed-consent procedure by telling herself that it was a formality she could ignore since she already knew everything necessary about the operation to make an informed decision. However, her attempts to console herself were unsuccessful. Prior knowledge and the physician's spoken words were not nearly as powerful as the impact of his nonverbal communication and his failure to treat her respectfully. She felt that, once she signed the form, the physician would not care whether she lived or died; he had done his duty by reading the consent statement. Her sympathy for the physician turned to anger. She fantasized about suing him for malpractice and experienced a sense of control over her malaise as she did so. Hardly unable to keep her composure, she told the physician she would make up her mind later and left. She had arrived to have a simple operation. She had been willing to be assigned to the experimental procedure. But now she did not want to have any procedure performed, at least not by that physician.

This example, while compelling and believable, nevertheless leads one to wonder what effect incongruent consent procedures have in social research in which life and limb are not in jeopardy. A pilot study of consent procedures with congruent and incongruent nonverbal cues, and with a congruent versus incongruent decision procedure (J. Sieber, 1979b), suggests that the effects of congruency and incongruency may be quite high. Subjects were recruited from an introductory psychology subject pool for participation in a study of health habits that would require them to keep a diary (checklist of health-related activities) over a period of six weeks. They were randomly assigned to one of four experimental conditions. In each condition, participants received an adequate consent statement that informed them of the purpose of the study, the advantages of participation (heightened awareness of own health practices) and the risks of participation (possible invasion of privacy and inconvenience), the confidentiality of participation (storage of the data without unique identifiers), and the voluntary nature of participation and freedom to withdraw with impunity at any time.

The rest of the informed-consent procedure was varied in a 2 x 2 design in which subjects received either congruent nonverbal cues and a balance-sheet decision procedure, congruent nonverbal cues and a traditional decision procedure, incongruent nonverbal cues and a balance-sheet decision procedure, or incongruent nonverbal cues and a traditional decision procedure.

In the *congruent* nonverbal cue condition, the room ecology and the grooming and body language of the researcher were congruent with an equal-status, respectful professional relationship in which the subject's autonomy is acknowledged. The chairs in the room were arranged in a circle to suggest open, equal status discussion, the researcher dressed and groomed in a way that was orderly, respectful, and dignified but not overly formal, and the researcher graciously rose to greet participants, was warm and friendly, engaged in a comfortably high level of eye contact, was available to eye contact initiated by the participants, had open body language (i.e., sat facing participants squarely, arms and legs uncrossed, breathing deeply, with voice and body relaxed), and was comfortably open to comment, question, or discussion.

In the *incongruent* nonverbal cue condition, the room ecology and the grooming and body language of the researcher were incongruent with an equal-status, respectful relationship. Participants were seated in rows, and the investigator was dressed in jeans and a tie-dyed T-shirt, and lectured subjects from behind a podium, was tense, maintained little eye contact, did not face participants squarely, and acted slightly preoccupied.

In the *balance-sheet* decision condition, participants were assisted in making a carefully considered decision using a technique developed by Janis and Mann (1977); they were given a balance sheet on which to formulate the consequences of participating in terms of the likely utilitarian gains for oneself, gains for significant others in one's life, one's values or moral

TABLE 1

Body Language and Behavior of Subjects by Condition

Condition	Percent of Time			Number of Subjects	
	Body Open	Looking at Speaker	Restless	Made Appt.	Kept Appt.
1 Cong./Bal.	98	97	0	18	18
2 Congruent	83	98	6	14	9
3 Incong./Bal.	50	68	22	16	13
4 Incongruent	76	52	25	6	3

Note: N = 18 subjects per group, 72 subjects total.

standards, and what others would think of one for making the decision. Subjects were first given the informed-consent statement and an opportunity to ask questions. The balance sheet was then introduced as follows: "We are going to ask a lot of you in this study, but we will also give you an opportunity to learn about your own health care habits and possibly to become healthier and more satisfied with your life. We want you to consider carefully the kinds of difficulties this study might involve for you. We are concerned that if you decide to participate just to be a good sport or to please us, you may find that your participation is far more work and inconvenience than it is worth, that parts of it are objectionable, that you are getting nothing out of it except irritation, or perhaps guilt for not participating exactly as asked, and that you regret having signed up."

Students were then given a detailed description of the tasks they would be asked to perform in the study and attendant advantages and disadvantages. They were asked to discuss among themselves the pros and cons as they perceived them and how they felt with respect to each part of the balance sheet. Finally, they were to make an individual decision as to whether to participate.

In the *traditional decision procedure*, subjects were given no special instructions to make a carefully considered decision and given no balance-sheet decision procedure. They were simply asked to make a decision.

In each condition, a member of the research team sat near the investigator and used a time-sampling procedure to observe each participant for 10 seconds at two-minute intervals, during the times when participants were not supposed to be reading or writing. They observed whether each was looking at the researcher, whether each had open body language (arms at sides facing forward), and whether each was restless (doodling, squirming). After subjects had made their decision, the researcher tabulated the number of subjects who decided to participate and made an appointment for their first session the next week and the number of subjects who kept their appointment the next week. The results are quite dramatic, as shown in table 1.

In addition to these formal observations, it was informally observed that subjects in the incongruent conditions tended to apologize and demean themselves for asking questions. Although it is unlikely that subjects in this study experienced anything approaching the negative experience of Ms. Z in the preceding case study, it is evident that incongruent consent procedures are mirrored in the behavior of subjects, result in inattention, affect volunteering to participate, and, more dramatically, affect willingness to actually participate after volunteering.

This pilot study of the effects of congruent versus incongruent and balance-sheet versus traditional consent procedures on attention, volunteering, and actual participation in the research suggests that the nature of the communication in the consent process may be highly consequential for the outcome of the study itself. Coupled with the findings reported elsewhere in this volume by Thompson, Stanley and Guido, Melton and Stanley, and Grisso, it is apparent that the psychology of communication in the consent process merits more research and consideration than it has received so far. Obviously, informed-consent cannot usefully be administered without careful consideration of the cognitive, perceptual, and social stimuli that the consent process provides to subjects, the nature of the subjects, the context of the research setting, and the nature of the research, itself. However, psychologists have as yet only a rudimentary understanding of what factors require careful consideration. The ecology of informed consent— how various kinds of subjects respond depending on the kinds of environments in which informed consent occurs—is still a relatively unexamined topic.

Background and Personality of the Subject and Researcher

The background and personality of the subject or of the researcher may produce certain behavior tendencies or expectations that are brought to the research setting and may affect the results of the study. In this section some background and personality factors are examined. Expectancy effects are discussed subsequently.

CULTURAL DIFFERENCES

Some of the kinds of nonverbal communication that may affect rapport are subject to cultural norms and local customs. For example, Hawaiian researchers have been quick to observe that Caucasian research participants are more likely to trust a researcher who makes eye contact, while Asian research participants may find such intimacy offensive. Because such cultural norms of nonverbal communication are ingrained, it is difficult for researchers to perceive when they are behaving inappropriately or to "read" accurately the nonverbal behavior of members of other cultures. For example, Katz, Robinson, Epps, and Waly (1964) and Williams (1964) found that the responses of African-American subjects to questions depended on the interviewer's racial background and that the interviewer's racial background, in turn, affected his or her interpretation of the respondents' behavior. However, Kadushin (1972) notes that sometimes subjects feel more comfortable discussing personal information with a researcher who is not a member of their own ethnic community.

Freeman, Gonzalez, and Montgomery (1983) examined the effects of Mexican-American and Anglo-American status of the experimenter on the electromyograph (EMG) biofeedback performance of Mexican-American and Anglo-American subjects. Although the Anglo-American experimenter initially obtained higher EMG responses from the Mexican-American subjects, this effect diminished over sessions.

AGE DIFFERENCES

Ethnic differences are not the only basis for differences in style, perception, and interpretation on the part of the experimenter or the subject. Levine (1982) reviewed many studies of the elderly in which researchers have demonstrated considerable naivete in interpreting the behavior of the elderly and have assumed they could generalize from their sample of elderly to all elderly. Typically, the researchers have been unaware of the demography of their subject population, which tended to be poor and uneducated. Levine notes that the kinds of nonverbal behavior that have sometimes been interpreted to mean that the aged are egocentric and childlike could as well be explained by their lack of formal education. Many elderly research participants are difficult to assemble as an audience: they seem inattentive, talk to their neighbors, and ask irrelevant questions. One interpretation is that they are unable to concentrate or that their minds wander. Another is that classroom behavior is a skill they have not learned or have forgotten. Still another is that such behavior is a response to the freedom of retirement; as one 71-year-old man said, "One of the best things about be-ing older and retired is that you don't have to listen to or take orders from anyone else. You can finally do whatever you want" (Levine, 1982, p. 136). Levine's review of her own and other's research readily suggests that many researchers' stereotypes about the elderly interfere with their ability to de-sign and interpret research on the elderly. Much remains to be learned about overcoming these problems.

SEX DIFFERENCES

A number of studies have been conducted to learn the role of experimenter and subject sex in experimenter expectancy effects. Sex differences, be-tween researchers and subjects have rather consistently been found to af-fect subject responses to the research (e.g., Barnes & Rosenthal, 1985; Etaugh, Houtler, & Ptasnik, 1988; Thompson & Connelly, 1988). However, only one general principle has emerged from this body of research, based on the studies conducted by Rosenthal and his associates (Persinger, 1962; Rosenthal & Fode, 1963a, 1963b; Rosenthal, Persinger, Mulry, Vikan-Kline, & Grothe, 1964a, 1964b; Rosenthal, Persinger, Vikan-Kline, & Fode, 1962) and supporting literature on the role of sex in interpersonal influence. A number of studies showed no differences between male and female sub-jects in their susceptibility to experimenter expectancy effects, but no study has ever shown a situation in which male subjects were significantly more susceptible than females. Rosenthal (1966) postulates that cultural sanctions operate to approve women's influenceability and to disapprove of men's. Rosenthal and Fode (1963b) provide interesting data to support this assertion. In a study in which a biased experimenter is the source of in-fluence, more influenceable female subjects were better liked by their in-fluencing experimenters (rho = +.59); however, more influenceable male subjects were less liked by their influencing experimenters (rho = -.54). (For a more detailed discussion of these effects, see Rosenthal, 1966.)

EXPERIMENTER AND SUBJECT ANXIETY

A number of studies have examined the influence of anxiety of experimen-ters and subjects on research outcomes. Although the general literature on influenceability by persuasion indicates that more anxious subjects are more conforming or influenceable, studies of the research setting have produced less clear-cut evidence. Some of the most instructive studies in this area are those of Fode (1965). In the first study, he found that subjects at a medium level of anxiety showed the greatest susceptibility to experimenter expectancy effects; in subsequent studies in this series, he found the strongest expectancy effects in highly anxious subjects in three studies, in those medium in anxiety in two studies, and in those low in anxiety in two studies. Rosenthal (1966) reviewed a number of studies that might clarify this finding. He concluded that a wide range of factors may be mediating these complex processes, ranging from differential researcher treatment of anxious and nonanxious subjects to the greater influenceability of researchers who are similar in anxiety level to their subjects.

CONTROLLING FOR PERSONALITY FACTORS

The kinds of personality factors that should concern researchers most are not personality variations underlying interindividual variance but the unidentified factors that systematically bias the results of research or the interpretation of results. The findings of research that has controlled for experimenter effects illustrates the potential for erroneous conclusions created by such variations. In Rorschach research, Cleveland (1951) and Sanders and Cleveland (1953) found that experimenters with more covert anxiety obtained from subjects more hostile content responses, more passive trends, more fantasies, and more self-awareness than did less covertly anxious experimenters. Similar results were obtained by Turner and Coleman (1962) and Masling (1960). Mulry (1962) found that, in a pursuit rotor task, experimenters with a high need for social approval obtained better performance from their subjects than experimenters low in need for social approval. Sarason (1962) had 10 male experimenters and 10 female experimenters reinforce the choice of mildly hostile verbs in sentence-construction tasks. More hostile experimenters elicited more hostile verbs, especially if they were running more hostile subjects and if the experimenters were male.

In some cases, experimenter bias effects, especially bias in interpretation of results, can also be gleaned from a review of the literature. For example, Nikelly (1971) reviewed research on student protest and found that some researchers viewed dissenting students as sick, while others viewed society and its institutions as culpable and drew conclusions accordingly.

Unless researchers are systematically varied, the researcher becomes an uncontrolled part of the stimulus presentation and of the measurement and inference process. The design implications, once one has identified experimenter characteristics likely to influence results, are considerable. First, if only one experimenter is to be used, one should consider whether that individual's personality will cause the results to be misleading, provide adequate training and monitoring of experimenter performance, consider an experimenter-blind design in the experimental conditions or limiting experimenter contact with subjects, and consider using more than one experimenter. Second, if more than one experimenter is to be used, the assignment of experimenters to treatments should be stratified so that experimenter and treatment effects are not confounded. Third, and preferrable to the previous two, researcher effects as well as treatment effects may be analyzed. Fourth, and last of all, researcher-by-subject interaction effects may be examined. For a detailed discussion of ways to control experimenter expectancy effects, see Rosenthal (1966, chap. 19–24).

Consideration of the findings of research that has controlled for experimenter effects would lead one to wonder why the role of experimenter characteristics is so lacking in research training and handbooks. Controlling for experimenter characteristics in the design of the research is excellent but costly. Better science and more self-aware investigators might result from more emphasis on methods of "calibrating and monitoring the experimenter."

THE VOLUNTEER EFFECT

The most obvious and well-studied personality factor systematically affecting results is the "volunteer" personality—the predisposition to volunteer for research.

As Rosenthal and Rosnow (1975) have shown, the person most likely to volunteer to participate in research is young, female, and married, receives high grades, is well educated and religious (especially Jewish or Protestant but not Catholic), comes from a small community, believes in science and in helping others, and tends to be sociable. Rosenthal and Rosnow present many studies of differences between volunteers and nonvolunteers. Generally, volunteers have been found to have a greater need for social approval and achievement. They tend to have more unconventional personalities, to be firstborns, and to be not as well adjusted. In addition, volunteers, especially males, tend to be more intelligent. Clearly, research that attracts such volunteers cannot be generalized with confidence to the general public. However, preliminary research (Sieber, 1979b) suggests that the informed-consent procedure can be arranged so that the *volunteer effect* does not occur, that is, so that a more representative sample of the population will volunteer. While replication with larger samples and in various research contexts is needed before these results can be generalized with confidence, the following study is representative of possible approaches to solving some problems connected with the volunteer effect.

TABLE 2

Characteristics of Volunteers

Characteristic	Balance Sheet	Traditional
Number married	3	5
Mean age	24.3	21.7
Number of females	4	5
Number of Jews and Protestants	2	5
Number of agnostics or atheists	1	0
Interest in religion*	2.9	4.6
Size of community of birth*	2.8	3.2
Sociability*	3.4	4.6
Helpfulness to others*	3.4	4.8

*On Likert scale of five points.

Evidence suggests that the volunteer effect occurs not because volunteers truly want to participate but because they think they should and want to please or impress the experimenter. Consequently, it was hypothesized that the balance-sheet decision procedure (as described earlier), which requests that people decide what is best for themselves, would negate this effect.

Potential subjects were asked to complete a personal information sheet that inquired into their status on each of the demographic and attitudinal characteristics of the "volunteer." Each of the 28 subjects was then randomly assigned to one of two groups. One group received the informed consent described earlier with the balance-sheet decision procedure, and the other received only the consent.

The formal results support the prediction that persons often volunteer as a result of a personal predisposition to volunteer, not as a considered decision. Five of the 14 persons in each group volunteered. However, the only persons who volunteered in the group not employing a balance sheet were archetypical volunteers, while the members of the balance-sheet group tended to be more randomly demographically selected as shown in table 2.

Informal observation of student behavior in this study was at least as interesting as the formal findings and provided a useful context for understanding these findings. Despite assurances to the contrary, some subjects indicated they felt obligated to volunteer. In the traditional decision group, the leader's high level of eye contact and friendly manner obviously induced a high level of guilt in those who did not wish to volunteer. In the discussion that ensued, students who were not inclined to participate apologized for their unwillingness. Toward the end of the discussion, one of the students lectured the others on how they could make time for partici- pation in a worthwhile study. That student was a married 22-year-old woman; she maintained a 4.00 grade point average, was employed full- time, was Protestant, active in her church, and interested in religion, be- lieved in helping others, and was raised in a small town.

In the balance-sheet group, initial indications of guilt and feelings of obligation gave way to statements about the inappropriateness of partici- pation by those who apparently found themselves too busy to participate. This pilot study suggests that the so-called volunteer effect, and perhaps other self-selection versus random-selection effects that worry research methodologists, may be better understood and controlled through further research on the processes of subject recruitment and administration of consent.

Investigator and Participant Expectancy Effects

It has been amply demonstrated that researchers in a wide range of disci- plines have tended to "discover" what they expect to discover (Boring, 1950; Chubin, 1985; Fisher, 1947; Hanson, 1958; Wilson, 1952). Is this a result of deliberate fraud, self-deception, or some subtle process of unconscious interpersonal communication? As the ensuing discussion will show, a number of processes may account for these lapses of objectivity in re- search.

The understanding of these processes may have important implications for those who wish to control for unintentional interpersonal processes that bias research (Rosenthal, 1981), to use such processes in teaching and other professional relationships (e.g., to create the expectancy of desirable behavior and consequently cause others to live up to that expectancy) (Rosenthal & Jacobson, 1968), to examine so-called psi phenomena (Pinch, 1979), and to understand how premature ideas in science can mislead large numbers of scientists for a considerable period of time, how scientists may deceive themselves (Chubin, 1985), and why honest scientists may tolerate colleagues whose data are suspect (Kamin, 1974; Wynne, 1979).[1] Basic to all these phenomena is the desire or expectancy that results will turn out a cer- tain way and a vision of what such an outcome would look like or how it would occur, if indeed it occurred. In addition, expectancy effects in research assume an ethic of professional autonomy and respect for science, some failure to value and use replication (and especially nonreplication) as a basic tool, ambiguity concerning scientific standards of research design, data collection, and analysis, ambiguous professional and ethical norms, and inadequacy of transmission of these norms in scientific training (Chubin, 1985). Thus, some of the conditions that typically surround expectancy effects may in extreme cases also account for scientific misbehavior. However, this section is limited to consideration of expectancy phenomena within an investigation as a process of nonverbal communication and does not further consider misbehavior-related phenomena.

Rosenthal and his colleagues (Rosenthal, 1963, 1966; Rosenthal & Fode, 1963a, 1963b; Rosenthal & Lawson, 1964) have demonstrated that an investigator's expectation about the outcome of a study can influence both animal and human performance. For example, Rosenthal and Fode (1963a) performed an experiment in which students assisted in a maze-learning experiment on rats. Each student was told either that the assigned rat was "maze bright" or "maze dull." Although these labels were applied randomly, experimenter expectancy somehow prevailed: the performance of "maze bright" rats was found to be superior to that of "maze dull" rats. Apparently the expectancies conveyed by the labels influenced the students' behavior, which in turn influenced the rats' behavior. A variety of mechanisms may account for these findings.

The horse Clever Hans and the various other animals who have ostensibly displayed humanlike cognitive abilities such as the ability to add and subtract have turned out to be responding not to the stimulus problem but to subtle cues from their trainers (Pfungst, 1911, reported in Rosenthal, 1981). In other cases, the observation of expected differences in behavior between groups was the result of selective attention ("I wouldn't have seen it if I didn't believe it") or conformity, as when ostensibly independent coders who can see one another code behavior with remarkable interrater reliability. While these processes are important to psychology, they are beyond the purview of this section. We turn now to those expectancy effects that result from subtle communication processes between the investigator and the human subject.

Interpersonal expectancies may be mediated through a complex of variables as follows (Rosenthal, 1981):

A. *Distal independent variables*. These variables include personality, ethnicity, gender, status, age, ability, or any other stable attributes of either party to the communication. As a hypothetical example, a researcher conducting a longitudinal study of achievement also happens to have a complex of false stereotypes about the disabled, including the assumption that physically disabled children are not achievement oriented.

B. *Proximal independent variables.* These variables include specific expectations that happen to arise in the research (or other) setting or hypotheses that the researcher has set out to test (i.e., that the researcher hopes to prove). To continue with our hypothetical example, the investigator finds that there is a disabled child among the children he or she is observing and automatically assumes that the child will find it too taxing to try hard and will readily give up on difficult tasks.

C. *Process variables.* These variables are the processes by which the investigator's expectation is communicated to the subject. To continue with our hypothetical example, the investigator presents problems to the disabled child as though the problems are unengaging and as though the child would surely find them uninteresting and too difficult.

D. *Proximal dependent variables.* These variables are responses that immediately result from the interaction. In the hypothetical example, the disabled child senses the investigator's disinterest in his or her performance and desire to complete the testing as soon as possible and complies by quickly indicating that he or she is ready to stop.

E. *Distal dependent variables.* These variables are the long-term outcome responses to the interaction. To conclude with our hypothetical example, the disabled child comes to recognize that the annual testing situation to which his parents have committed him for the next 10 years is a strange one in which quick compliance to the investigator's directives is probably the best policy. Unlike the other participants in the study who have learned to anticipate and practice for the research tasks, this child has learned to be as inconspicuous and non–task oriented as possible in the researcher's laboratory.

Rosenthal (1981) has devised a model for the study of these five classes of variables.

The following 10 relationships can be investigated to understand communication and expectancy effects in research. Rosenthal's model provides a useful way to conceptualize research on the phenomena discussed in this chapter. For those who simply want to identify and control for (or train out) unwanted communication effects, this model provides a useful conceptual tool to direct one's arm-chair analysis, observation of pilot-study behavior, research assistant training program, or planning of design and analyses that control for experimenter effects.

AB. These relationships may loom large when the researcher or subject brings some generalized attribute (appearance, style, preconception, personality characteristic, or attitude) to the research setting in the form of a specific attribute or expectancy that has some stimulus value for the subject. Interestingly, while it is recognized that investigators and subjects may bring such generalized or long-term tendencies to the research setting in the form of specific, identifiable attributes or expectancies, research on experimenter bias has rarely examined *AB* relationships. For example, in major surveys in which many interviewers are employed, how do the interviewers' personality and demographic characteristics influence their attitudes toward the specific topic of the interview and their expectancies of the persons they will interview? How are characteristics of the respondents (e.g., their ethnicity or socioeconomic class) manifested in their specific expectancies in the interview?

AC. These are the relationships between the background characteristics of the parties to the communication and the (typically nonverbal) communication processes that occur in the interaction. For example, how is the background of the interviewers or respondents manifested in their body language? Does the Anglo-Saxon interviewer try to establish eye contact while the Asian respondent tries to avoid it? Does the hostile interviewer systematically engage in incongruent communication and "unmirror" whenever the respondent seeks to mirror?

AD. These are the relationships between the expecter's characteristics and the behavior induced in the research setting. Does the Anglo-Saxon interviewer cause the Asian respondent to be upset with the interview and to fail to respond to some probes? Does the hostile interviewer fail to get the initially cooperative respondent to answer the sensitive question at the end of the interview?

AE. This is the relationship between the expecter's generalized characteristics and the expectee's eventual behavior. Does either respondent in the example agree to be interviewed a second time? If so, how candid is each in the follow-up interview?

BC. This is the effect of the expecter's specific beliefs or expectations on the interaction process. Because personality characteristics of persons are not consistently or predictably manifested in specific settings, it may be more appropriate, or at least more reliable, to measure proximal variables, that is, specific expectations relevant to the research interaction, rather than *AC* variables. One might ask parties to the interviews to indicate, perhaps on a checklist or true-false inventory, specifically how one ought to conduct oneself (e.g., one ought always look the other party in the eye; to establish one's position as the researcher, one should hold oneself in a dignified manner; etc.). The relation of these specific beliefs to subsequent interaction processes could then be observed.

BD. This is the effect of a specific expectancy on behavior in the research setting. Because process variables often are difficult to monitor, the study of the relation between expectancies established before the research process and subject behavior may be a more valid indication that an expectancy effect has occurred. However, this leaves unspecified exactly what happened in the interaction. Placebo studies are instances of *BD* studies. For example, in a 2 x 2 factorial design, subjects may receive the experimental treatment or not and may believe they have received it or not. Because of the power of experimenter expectancy, this design may be expanded to a 2 x 2 x 2 design in which the experimenter may believe that the subjects receive the experimental treatment or are control subjects (Rosenthal, 1985).

BE. This relationship defines the longer-term effects of specific expectations. In longitudinal research or long-term intervention research, *BE* studies are crucial to understanding how experimenter and subject expectancies influenced the ultimate conclusions of the project.

CD. This is the relationship between a specific interaction process and outcome. Studies of *CD* would be useful adjuncts to attempts to train investigators in specific skills and to evaluate the effectiveness of the training. For example, interviewers often are uncomfortable probing and have ineffective probing skills. Research on the effectiveness of various approaches to teaching the use of verbal mirroring when probing would be useful to determining the most effective ways to teach interviewers skills of verbal mirroring, recording and observing actual processes of verbal mirroring as they occur in the interview process, and evaluating the role of verbal mirroring in producing probes which evoke appropriate interview responses. In short, given an understanding of the possible nature of some nonverbal communication processes that affect research, *CD* research is the next step necessary to gain a better understanding of those processes and how to control them.

CE. This is the relationship between a process and a long-term outcome. The concern over training researchers in effective interaction processes would seem, on the face of it, to be most appropriate in research containing a long-term relationship between researcher and subjects. But is this concern appropriate? Does the interaction skill of the researcher matter in the long run, or do subjects get used to the idiosyncrasies of the researcher and come to ignore them? There is anecdotal evidence that respondents to repeated interviews develop a relationship with the interviewer that makes follow-up interviews easier to obtain if the same interviewer returns. Does this depend on the interaction skills of the interviewer or does it occur despite poor interaction skills?

DE. This effect describes the predictability of the immediate response to the later response (of the researcher or of the subject). Is the respondent's comfort or candor with the interviewer in the first interview predictive of willingness to respond or candor in a subsequent mail follow-up survey? Is the interviewer-in-training's response to a successful mirroring experience predictive of continued development and use of mirroring skills?

While Rosenthal's model is useful in directing attention to the way unintended communication may affect research processes and results, it omits specific mention of what makes a *B* variable salient enough to affect the process (*C*) or outcomes (*D* and *E*). Some research settings seem more conducive to powerful expectancy effects than others. While little is known about this matter, the following speculation may point to useful directions for future research.

Subject Vulnerability to Untoward Communication

Some of the factors that mediate the impact of communication in the research process have been studied and are perhaps best summarized by the theory of social impact (Latane, 1981) and demonstrated by the famous Milgram (1963) studies of obedience and the Gamson (1975) studies of rebellion. In these studies, nonverbal aspects of the researcher's communication were deliberately varied to determine under which conditions subjects could be coerced to act against their better judgment. According to the theory of social impact, the effect of any communication is mediated by three factors: the relative status of the parties involved, the proximity or availability of the recipient of the communication, and the relative number of persons on each side of the communication process. As the Milgram and

Gamson studies vividly illustrate, researchers are in a powerful position to command obedience when they are perceived as prestigious, when they stand near the subject as opposed to giving instructions from elsewhere, when only one subject interacts with the researcher at a time, and when subjects have little opportunity to seek support and consensus from their peers.

Generalizing from Milgram's research on obedience, the Gamson studies, and the theory of social impact, it is plausible to infer that the context of the research apparently has an important bearing on the communication processes in the research. The following are conjectures that deserve further testing.

In laboratory settings, the subject is on the researcher's turf. As Milgram's research indicates, it may be difficult for the subject to decline to participate and difficult to resist obeying instructions in this setting, especially under the kinds of conditions Milgram created in the high-obedience condition. In contrast, in most survey research the researcher is either not physically present or meets the respondent in neutral territory (e.g., a shopping mall) or on the subject's turf. In such settings, the subject is in a more powerful position to resist the researcher's authority, if indeed the subject perceives the researcher to have any authority at all. The subject may decline to participate by hanging up the phone, throwing away the mailed survey, or closing the door. He or she may have heard about the survey from neighbors and discussed with them whether participation would be worthwhile. Pilot studies by the Bureau of Census indicate that ethnic minorities, in particular, are likely to be suspicious of any researcher who comes to the door and likely to have made prior arrangements in collaboration with neighbors to avoid the encounter altogether (Turner, 1982).

Organizational settings differ markedly from either the laboratory or the subject's home. In organizations, neither the researcher nor the subject has much power relative to that of the executive officers of the organization and other forces such as a union. These more powerful forces serve as gatekeepers and may also seek to use the research information for their own purposes (contrary to any assurances of confidentiality by the researcher). In this context, the subject is probably attuned to the apparent attitudes of those gatekeepers toward the research, as well as to the apparent attitudes of the researcher. The researcher would be wise to be attentive to the attitudes of the gatekeepers and to keep communication lines open with them if things are to go well (Grisso, in this vol.; Mirvis & Seashore, 1982).

Causes of Untoward Communication Processes in Research

I have examined various communication processes that may invalidate research or reduce the autonomy and comfort of the research participant. However, it is at least as important to know what is likely to cause these events and hence how one might avoid them as it is to identify the processes as they occur or to study them. Several general kinds of causes seem apparent.

First, incongruent or untoward nonverbal communication sometimes results from the researcher's preoccupation. While the subject enters expecting a respectful relationship, the researcher (or research assistant) may be thinking of other things, may have run too many subjects that day and be on "automatic pilot" or exhausted, or may unfortunately not be in the habit of treating subjects with respect. These are proximal (B) factors that may be highly situational (unless the experimenter is always preoccupied or disrespectful), which might be overcome by heightened awareness and better management of the research process.

Second, the nature of one's nonverbal communication is heavily determined by cultural factors (A variables). Hence, cultural differences between subject and researcher may underlie the perception (B variables) by one party that the nonverbal communication is negative in character. An understanding of operative cultural factors and amelioration of undesirable factors should be part of the methodology and planning of any research on human beings.

Third, the epistemology and the attitudes of the scientist may influence the treatment of subjects. Those subscribing to an extreme determinist view in which subjects are manipulated without reference to interpersonal factors may express this through an authoritarian or detached attitude toward individual subjects. Those espousing a more humanistic theoretical framework may express this perspective through a warm, caring relationship with their subjects. In other respects as well, the researcher's beliefs, attitudes, stereotypes, and prejudices need to be taken into account as they may influence the subjects or the interpretation of the results. Sensitivity to the range of AB, AC, and AD relationships likely to occur and careful observation of the pilot-study process may enable the investigator to "train out" those specific expectancies (B variables) associated with the enduring qualities of the experimenters.

Fourth, insensitivity to methodology and data may underlie some untoward communication processes in research. For example, an unreflecting researcher may fail to note that the subjects' baseline data change from time to time during an experiment, but a more astute researcher may notice both that systematic changes in baseline responses occur throughout the study and that they coincide with personnel changes of research assistant. Even without knowing what differences are operative, one can observe occurrences of unexplained differences in the data and take appropriate measures to control for them. That is, *BD* relationships may be observed without observing *C*.

Finally, the context of the research seems to be critical in determining the power relationship between researcher and subject and hence the impact of the communication. This is yet another dimension that the researcher must take into account in the design of research.

As these five points suggest, there is much that the thoughtful researcher might do to improve communication in the research process without performing further research on the communication process. However, there are limits to the adequacy of armchair speculation. The understanding of communication processes in research depends as well on the continued development of empirical research and theory in this domain.

Summary

Nonverbal communication within the research setting may have serious methodological and ethical implications. While a literature in this area already exists, it is sparse and notably lacks any overarching taxonomy of the kinds of nonverbal communication that may be operative, and the ways in which these may be operative depending on context, personality factors, and operational aspects of the research itself. A taxonomy of *effects* of nonverbal communication in the research process is also needed. For example, the response of a subject depends on a range of cognitive and affective processes: perception, comprehension, trust, decision making, liking, comfort, and so on. Each of these processes may serve as mediators between the nonverbal communication and the behavioral response. Although the range of independent variables, communication processes, and effects of nonverbal or unplanned communication processes in research has not been adequately conceptualized, a model for examining these (as yet not fully specified) variables exists. Rosenthal's (1981) model of expectancy effects may be used to conceptualize both how to detect and cure unwanted effects as well as how to investigate such effects.

Notes

1. The designation of fraud or misconduct is generally reserved for those who intentionally deviate from main tenets of the scientific code of conduct, for example, those who "dry lab" their data, rather than those who are careless, incompetent, or self-deceiving about the objectivity of their findings. However, it is difficult to discern intentions reliably, especially since many of the same conditions that surround intentional dishonesty also surround nonfraudulent failures of objectivity. Moreover, it is doubtful that budding scientists ever embark on their research career with fraud in mind; rather, one suspects that those who have engaged in fraud first engaged in unintentional experimenter biasing of results, followed by more obvious forms of self-deception, and then finally engaged in intentional dishonesty to avoid admitting that their conclusions were based on invalid data.

References

Argyle, M. (1975). *Bodily communication*. New York: International Universities Press.

Bandler, R., & Grinder, J. (1975). *The structure of magic, Volumes I and II*. Palo Alto CA: Science and Behavior.

Barnes, M. L., & Rosenthal, R. (1985). Interpersonal effects of experimenter attractiveness, attire, and gender. *Journal of Personality and Social Psychology, 48,* 435–446.

Bellotti v. Baird, 443 U.S. 662 (1979).

Boring, E. G. (1950). *A history of experimental psychology* (2nd ed.). New York: Appleton-Century-Crofts.

Breed, G. R. (1972). The effect of intimacy: Reciprocity or retreat? *British Journal of Social and Clinical Psychology, 11,* 135–142.

Burkhart, B. R. (1976). Apprehension about evaluation, paralanguage cues and the experimenter-bias effect. *Psychological Reports, 39,* 15–23.

Chubin, D. E. (1985). Misconduct in research: An issue of science policy and practice. *Minerva: A review of science, learning and policy, 23,* 175–201.

Cleveland, S. (1951). The relationship between examiner anxiety and subjects' Rorschach scores. *Microfilm Abstracts, 11,* 415–416.

D'Augelli, A. R. (1974). Nonverbal behavior of helpers in initial helping interactions. *Journal of Counseling Psychology, 21,* 360–363.

Dion, K. L., Berscheid, E., & Walster, E. (1972). What is beautiful is good. *Journal of Personality and Social Psychology, 24,* 285–290.

Eibl-Eibesfeldt, I. (1975). *Ethnology: The biology of behavior* (2nd ed.). New York: Holt, Rinehart, & Winston.

Ekman, P., & Friesen, W. V. (1975). *Unmasking the face*. Englewood Cliffs NJ: Prentice Hall.

Etaugh, C., Houtler, B. D., & Ptasnik, P. (1988). Evaluating competence of women and men: Effects of experimenter gender and group gender composition. *Psychology of Women Quarterly, 12,* 191–200.

Fisher, R. A. (1947). *The design of experiments* (4th ed.). Edinburgh and London: Oliver & Boyd.

Fode, K. L. (1965). *The effect of experimenters' and subjects' anxiety and social desirability on experimenter outcome-bias*. Unpublished doctoral dissertation, University of North Dakota, Grand Forks.

Freeman, F. E., Gonzalez, D., & Montgomery, G. T. (1983). *Journal of Social Psychology, 119,* 119–123.

Gamson, W. A. (1975). *The strategy of social protest*. Homewood IL: Dorsey.

Genthner, R., & Moughan, H. (1971). Perception of affect in interpersonal contexts. *Small Group Behavior, 24,* 249–256.

Haase, R. F., & Tepper, D. T. (1972). Nonverbal components of empathic communication. *Journal of Counseling Psychology, 19,* 417–424.

Hanson, N. R. (1958). *Patterns of discovery*. Cambridge: Cambridge University Press.

Harrigan, J. A., Oxman, T. E., & Rosenthal, R. (1985). Rapport expressed through nonverbal behavior. *Journal of Nonverbal Behavior, 21,* 95–110.

Harrigan, J. A., & Rosenthal, R. (1983). Physicians' head and body positions as determinants of perceived rapport. *Journal of Applied Social Psychology, 13,* 496–509.

Heslin, R., & Patterson, M. L. (1982). *Nonverbal behavior and social psychology*. New York: Plenum.

Janis, I. L., & Mann, L. (1977). *Decision making: A psychological analysis of conflict, choice and commitment*. New York: Free Press.

Kadushin, A. (1972). The social factor in the interview. *Social Work, 17,* 98.

Kamin, L. (1974). *The science and politics of IQ*. Potomac MD: Erlbaum.

Katz, I., Robinson, J. M., Epps, E. G., & Waly, P. (1964). The influence of race of the experimenter and instructions upon the expression of hostility by Negro boys. *Journal of Social Issues, 20,* 54–59.

Knapp, M. L. (1978). *Nonverbal communication in human interaction* (2nd ed.). New York: Holt, Rinehart, & Winston.

LaCrosse, M. B. (1975). Nonverbal behavior and perceived counselor attractiveness and persuasiveness. *Journal of Counseling Psychology, 22,* 563–566.

Latane, B. (1981). The psychology of social impact. *American Psychologist, 36,* 343–356.

Levine, E. K. (1982). Old people are not all alike: Social class, ethnicity/race, and sex are bases for important differences. In J. E. Sieber (Ed.), *The ethics of social research: Surveys and experiments* (pp. 126–143). New York: Springer-Verlag.

McGinley, H., Nicholas, K., & McGinley, P. (1978). Effects of body position and attitude similarity on interpersonal attraction and opinion change. *Psychological Reports, 42*, 127–138.

Machotka, P. (1965). Body movement as communication. *Dialogues: Behavioral Science Research, 2*, 33–66.

Masling, J. (1960). The influence of situational and interpersonal variables in projective testing. *Psychological Bulletin, 57*, 65–85.

Matarazzo, J. D., & Wiens, A. N. (1967). Interviewer influence on durations of interviewee silence. *Journal of Experimental Research in Personality, 2*, 56–69.

Matarazzo, J. D., & Wiens, A. N. (1977). Speech behavior as an objective correlate of empathy and outcome in interview and psychotherapy research. *Behavior Modification, 1*, 453–480.

Mehrabian, A. (1968). Inference of attitudes from posture, orientation and distance of a communicator. *Journal of Consulting and Clinical Psychology, 32*, 296–308.

Mehrabian, A., & Williams, M. (1969). Nonverbal concomitants of perceived and intended persuasiveness. *Journal of Personality and Social Psychology, 13*, 37–58.

Milgram, S. (1963). Behavioral study of obedience. *Journal of Abnormal and Social Psychology, 67*, 371–378.

Mirvis, P. H., & Seashore, S. (1982). Creating ethical relationships in organizational research. In J. E. Sieber (Ed.), *The ethics of social research: Surveys and experiments* (pp. 79–104). New York: Springer-Verlag.

Mulry, R. C. (1962). *The effects of the experimenter's perception of his own performance on subject performance in a pursuit rotor task.* Unpublished master's thesis, University of North Dakota, Grand Forks.

Nikelly, A. G. (1971). Ethical issues in research on student protest. *American Psychologist, 23*, 475–478.

Persinger, G. W. (1962). *The effect of acquaintanceship on the mediation of experimenter bias.* Unpublished master's thesis, University of North Dakota, Grand Forks.

Pinch, T. J. (1979). Normal explanations of the paranormal: The demarcation problem and fraud in parapsychology. *Social Studies of Science, 9*, 329–348.

Reece, M. M., & Whitman, R. N. (1962). Expressive movements, warmth, and verbal reinforcement. *Journal of Abnormal and Social Psychology, 64*, 234–236.

Rosenthal, R. (1963). On the social psychology of the psychological experiment: The experimenter's hypothesis as unintended determinant of experimental results. *American Scientist, 51*, 268–283.

Rosenthal, R. (1966). *Experimenter effects in behavioral research.* New York: Appleton Century Crofts.

Rosenthal, R. (1981). Pavlov's mice, Pfungst's horse, and Pygmalion's PONS: Some models for the study of interpersonal expectancy effects. In T. A. Sebeok and R. Rosenthal (Eds.), *The Clever Hans phenomenon: Communication with horses, whales, apes and people* (pp. 182–198). *Annals of the New York Academy of Sciences*, No. 364.

Rosenthal, R. (1985). Designing, analyzing, interpreting and summarizing placebo studies. In L. White, B. Tursky, and G. E. Schwartz (Eds.), *Placebo: Theory, research, and mechanisms* (pp. 110–136). New York: Guilford.

Rosenthal, R., & Fode, K. L. (1963a). The effect of experimenter bias on the performance of the albino rat. *Behavioral Science, 8,* 183–189.

Rosenthal, R., & Fode, K. L. (1963b). Three experiments in experimenter bias. *Psychological Reports, 11,* 491–511.

Rosenthal, R., & Jacobson, L. (1968). *Pygmalion in the classroom.* New York: Holt, Rinehart, & Winston.

Rosenthal, R., & Lawson, L. (1964). A longitudinal study of the effects of experimenter bias on the operant learning of laboratory rats. *Journal of Psychiatric Research, 2,* 61–72.

Rosenthal, R., Persinger, G. W., Mulry, R. C., Vikan-Kline, L., & Grothe, M. (1964a). Changes in experimental hypotheses as determinants of experimental results. *Journal of Projective Techniques and Personality Assessment, 28,* 465–469.

Rosenthal, R., Persinger, G. W., Mulry, R. C., Vikan-Kline, L., & Grothe, M. (1964b). Emphasis on experimental procedure, sex of subjects, and the biasing effects of experimental hypotheses. *Journal of Projective Techniques and Personality Assessment, 28,* 470–473.

Rosenthal, R., Persinger, G. W., Vikan-Kline, L., & Fode, K. L. (1962). The effect of early data returns on data subsequently obtained by outcome-biased experimenters. *Sociometry, 26,* 487–498.

Rosenthal, R., Persinger, G. W., Vikan-Kline, L., & Fode, K. L. (1963). The effect of experimenter outcome-bias and subject set on awareness in verbal conditioning experiments. *Journal of Verbal Learning and Verbal Behavior, 2,* 275–283.

Rosenthal, R., Persinger, G. W., Vikan-Kline, L., & Mulry, R. C. (1963). The role of the research assistant in the mediation of experimenter bias. *Journal of Personality, 31,* 313–335.

Rosenthal, R., & Rosnow, R. L. (1975). *The volunteer subject.* New York: Wiley-Interscience.

Sanders, R., & Cleveland, S. E. (1953). The relationship between certain examiner personality variables and subjects' Rorschach scores. *Journal of Projective Techniques, 17,* 34–50.

Sarason, I. G. (1962). Individual differences, situational variables and personality research. *Journal of Abnormal and Social Psychology, 65,* 376–380.

Sieber, J. E. (1979a). Informed consent as respectful communication. *Forum on Medicine*, 2, 484–87.

Sieber, J. E. (1979b). *The effects of experimenter nonverbal behavior and suggested decision procedures on subjects' decision behavior and commitment to participate in a longitudinal study of health habits.* Unpublished manuscript.

Smith-Hanen, S. (1977). Effects of nonverbal behaviors on judged levels of counselor warmth and empathy. *Journal of Counseling Psychology*, 24, 87–91.

Sobelman, S. A. (1974). The effects of verbal and nonverbal components on the judged level of counselor warmth. *Dissertation Abstracts International*, 35, 273A. (University Microfilms No. 74–14, 199).

Stanley, B., & Sieber, J. E. (Eds.). (1992). *Social research on children and adolescents.* Newbury Park CA: Sage.

Tang, T. L. (1987). Effects of Type A personality on experimenter interest on behavior. *Journal of Social Psychology*, 127(6), 619–627.

Tepper, D. T., & Haase, R. F. (1978). Verbal and nonverbal communication of facilitative conditions. *Journal of Counseling Psychology*, 25, 35–44.

Thompson, J. K., & Connelly, J. J. (1988). Experimenter gender and size estimation accuracy. *International Journal of Eating Disorders*, 7(5), 723–725.

Trout, D., & Rosenfeld, H. M. (1980). The effect of postural lean and body congruence on the judgment of psychotherapeutic rapport. *Journal of Nonverbal Behavior*, 4, 176–190.

Turner, A. G. (1982). What subjects of research believe about confidentiality. In J. E. Sieber, (Ed.), *The Ethics of Social Research: Surveys and Experiments* (pp. 151–165). New York: Springer-Verlag.

Turner, G. C., & Coleman, J. C. (1962). Examiner influence on thematic apperception test responses. *Journal of Projective Techniques*, 26, 478–486.

Vikan-Kline, L. (1962). The effect of experimenter's perceived status on the mediation of experimenter bias. Unpublished master's thesis. University of North Dakota, Grand Forks.

Vrolijk, A. (1966). Body posture and hm-hm: A variation. *Nederlands Tijdschrift Voor de Psychologie en Haar Grensgebieden*, 21(7), 438–443.

Williams, J. A. (1964). Interviewer-respondent interaction: A study of bias in the information interview. *Sociometry*, 27, 338–352.

Wilson, E. B. (1952). *An introduction to scientific research.* New York: McGraw-Hill.

Wynne, B. (1979). Between orthodoxy and oblivion: The normalization of deviance in science. In R. Wallis (Ed.), *On the margins of science: The social construction of rejected knowledge* (pp. 9–49). Keele: University of Keele.

Chapter 3 / Informed Consent: Psychological and Empirical Issues

BARBARA H. STANLEY

Department of Psychology, CUNY, John Jay College
Department of Psychiatry, Columbia University
and

JEANNINE R. GUIDO

Department of Neuroscience
New York State Psychiatric Institute

Informed consent of research participants has become an integral part of the research process. In almost all instances the informed consent of potential participants is ethically required and legally mandated (e.g., Committee for the Protection of Human Participants in Research, 1982; Protection of Human Subjects, 1992). While the concern with consent to research has a long history, in modern times the Nuremberg Code (1949) brought informed consent into the forefront of ethical practice in the research setting. This code stresses that voluntary consent to research is essential, that subjects must have the capacity to consent, that they be provided with sufficient information and comprehend that information, and that they are able to exercise their free choice without duress or deceit. Thus, the basic elements of informed consent can be derived from this code: voluntary consent; adequate disclosure; and competency. All three elements of informed consent are important to those engaged in psychological research.

Parts of this chapter were originally included in: Stanley, B. (1987). Informed consent in treatment and research. In I. Weiner & A. Hess (Eds.), *Handbook of forensic psychology*. New York: John Wiley. Reprinted by permission of John Wiley & Sons, Inc.

Elements of Informed Consent

VOLUNTARINESS

Psychologists frequently must confront the issue of voluntariness as a consequence of the many settings in which psychological research is done—mental hospitals, schools, prisons, and work organizations. The real and perceived voluntariness of the individuals to be studied in these settings may be compromised and vary greatly and, hence, must be considered by psychologists conducting research in these settings. For example, a prisoner who participates in a research project that has been strongly endorsed by prison officials may have a very different sense of voluntariness than the shopper in the local mall who is approached by an interviewer to participate in survey research. While the importance of the setting has been stressed in considering the voluntariness of the subjects, other factors must also be explored. The research subject must be free from coercive influences and undue pressure in reaching the decision of whether or not to participate in the research (Culver & Gert, 1982; Meisel, Roth, & Lidz, 1977). This refers to both explicit and implicit efforts to convince or to coerce individuals to participate. Adhering to the doctrine of informed consent means resisting efforts to pressure individuals into participation. This topic will not be explored further in this chapter since it is examined in detail by Grisso (in this volume).

COMPETENCY

The second major dimension of informed consent concerns the competency of the research participants. Competency refers to the functional capacity to give a valid consent to research participation (Stanley & Stanley, 1982). For psychologists conducting research, the question of competency arises most often in research with special populations, such as children, the mentally retarded, the elderly, and the mentally ill. Members of these groups are more likely to have a compromised competency to consent to research. However, this does not mean that membership in one of these groups in and of itself indicates incompetence. Nor does it mean that all incompetent individuals belong to one of these special groups. Because there is no easy way of classifying subjects as competent or incompetent, the burden is on the researcher to determine subject competence if it is questionable.

However, the determination of competency, even on an individual basis, is not straightforward. Competency has been defined in various ways and its assessment is driven by its definition. For a psychological researcher, awareness of competency standards is vital to being able to determine which potential participants are incapable of a valid consent.

The following functional tests of competency have been identified: (1) ability to express a preference regarding participation in research or a treatment; (2) comprehension of the important information relevant to participation in the proposed research project (e.g., risks, benefits); (3) application of rational reasoning in reaching the decision of whether or not to participate in the proposed research; (4) appreciation of the nature of the research and what it means to participate or not to participate; and (5) the reaching of a decision about participation in the research that is consistent with that of a "reasonable" person. Each of these functional tests evaluate somewhat different aspects of the individual. Therefore, using one test rather than another may result in different opinions with regard to the competency of the potential subject. Consequently, it is important to have clearly in mind the test to be used as well as a rationale in determining whether potential subjects are competent. Competency in special populations is discussed at length by Melton and Stanley (in this volume).

DISCLOSURE

The third element of the informed-consent triad is adequate disclosure of relevant consent information (Culver & Gert, 1982; Meisel et al., 1977; Stanley & Stanley, 1981). Adequate information refers to the information an individual would need to make the decision as to whether to participate in research. There is some disagreement as to what is considered "adequate." The federal regulations pertaining to research (Protection of Human Subjects, 1992) specify the following types of information as important: (1) the purposes, procedures, and duration of the research; (2) the risks and discomforts of the research procedure; (3) the benefits of the research (both to the subject directly and to society generally); (4) alternatives to participation; (5) the extent of confidentiality; (6) the voluntary nature of participation; (7) the extent of compensation and treatment for injuries if any should occur in the course of research participation (relevant mostly to biomedical research); and (8) the identification of and the way to contact a key person involved in the research (most relevant in longitudinal studies).

With this overview as a backdrop, the importance of empirical research on informed consent can be discussed, particularly from a psychological perspective. Also, the body of empirical studies that have been conducted on consent will be reviewed.

Empirical Research on Informed Consent

Over the past 25 years, interest in informed consent has grown, as evidenced by the large number of published articles in this time span. Woodward (1979) reported that the number of articles about human experimentation and informed consent increased sixfold in the period following 1960 as contrasted with a 20-year period prior to 1960. Kaufmann (1983), in a review of articles on informed consent, found that medical journals published far more articles on informed consent than did either social-science or law journals. Furthermore, she found that social science lagged behind the other disciplines in both the point at which it began to study informed consent and the number of articles on the topic. Consequently, much of the empirical research on informed consent does not appear to be directly relevant to psychological research. First, the studies tend to examine consent to standard treatment rather than consent to research. Second, the research is usually oriented toward biomedical concerns in either the treatment or research case.

Despite the lack of direct focus on psychological research in this literature, the findings can be readily applied in helping us understand informed consent in psychological research. With respect to informed consent, psychological research differs very little from biomedical research except that the set of risks is different—usually less physically harmful but more likely to wrong (e.g., deceive) an individual. With respect to the comparison of standard treatment and research as well, the informed-consent process should not look that different; the procedures, benefits, risks, and so forth should be clearly identified in both instances. The primary distinction between the two processes is that in research the consent procedure is usually more formal and routine than in the treatment setting because the research-consent process is much more regulated and monitored. Therefore, although much of the empirical research on informed consent is based on standard treatment and is biomedical in nature, it has direct applicability to psychological research. Before any empirical research on informed consent, the literature was philosophical and legal in nature. In addition, there was a series of articles describing the "effects" of informed consent. Interestingly, these articles contained no actual data except case reports. For example, informed consent was reported to "terrify" the individual, cause undue anxiety, and destroy the rapport between the professional and the patient (or, by extension, research subject) (Coleman, 1974; Park, Slaughter, Cori, & Kniffin, 1966). Furthermore, these opinion pieces also found that truly informed consent was a myth (Leeb, Bowers, & Lynch, 1976) or an illusion (Goin, Burgoyne, & Goin, 1976; Hirsch, 1977; Laforet, 1976). While this may be the case, it was a bit premature to draw such conclusions in the absence of empirical substantiation.

The empirical research on informed consent sheds much light on the meaningfulness of the process, what can be reasonably expected from such a procedure in research, who may have trouble giving a valid consent, and how the dimensions of the consent process can be altered to maximize comprehension of the information and genuine participation by the subjects. The empirical research on informed consent falls into several categories: disclosure and comprehension of consent information; reactions to consent procedures; methods of decision making in the consent process; public opinion on the need for and role of informed consent; and reactions to deception research and debriefing and alternatives to deception.

DISCLOSURE AND COMPREHENSION

The largest body of empirical research on the consent process falls into the category of comprehension of consent information. Medical patients or medical research subjects are the most frequently investigated. More than 20 studies have assessed understanding of consent information (e.g., Bergler, Pennington, Metcalfe, & Freis, 1980; Cassileth, Zupkis, Sutton-Smith, & March, 1980; Hassar & Weintraub, 1976; Kennedy & Lillenhaugen, 1979; Marini, Sheard, & Bridges, 1976; Penman et al., 1980; Robinson & Merav, 1976; Schultz, Pardee, & Ensinck, 1975; Singer, 1978). The prototype of these studies is as follows. Subjects are given a consent form for either a research protocol or standard treatment and the form is usually read to them by an investigator. The subjects are then asked questions regarding their knowledge of the consent information. The point at which they are asked such questions varies from immediately afterward to several months later.

Although it is difficult to make comparisons across studies as a result of different methods, it can generally be concluded that comprehension of consent information, irrespective of assessment time, is poor. Overall comprehension ranges from approximately 35% to 80% of the total information conveyed. Subjects tend to be best informed about their diagnosis (if a patient) and the proposed procedure (e.g., that they will be given a series of psychological tests) and least knowledgeable about alternatives available and risks of the proposed procedures. In addition, some studies of research subjects demonstrate that many were not aware or did not acknowledge that they were, in fact, participating in a research study (Mc-Cullum & Schwartz, 1969; Park et al., 1966; Riecken & Ravich, 1982).

While results of these studies are, at first glance, discouraging about the prospects of obtaining a fully informed consent, most of the studies have limitations that make it difficult to consider them conclusive (Meisel & Roth, 1981). First, in several studies exactly what information was conveyed to the subjects is unknown (Cassileth et al., 1980; Goin et al., 1976; Muss et al., 1979; Priluck, Robertson, & Buettner, 1979). Further, some studies gave subjects the consent form to read and then tested knowledge of this form. It is not known whether everyone read the form (Olin & Olin, 1975). In this same vein, the amount of instruction given to subjects varied from study to study. In some, instruction was minimal with no particular effort made to convey the consent information (Benson, Gordon, Mitchell, & Place, 1977). In other studies, investigators went through a good deal of instruction with subjects (Faden & Beauchamp, 1980). There are a number of specific factors that have been investigated as affecting comprehension, including complexity of information, amount of information, clarity of information, modality of disclosure, attitudes toward consent, and subject characteristics.

Varying levels of complexity of language used in consent forms makes it difficult to draw generalizable conclusions from many studies. Grundner (1980) and Morrow (1980) suggest that most consent forms are written in highly technical language. Baker and Taub (1983) investigated the level of difficulty of information sheets and consent forms over a several year period at a Veterans' Administration (VA) medical center. They report that, not only did readability scores increase in difficulty over time, but also the amount of information contained in them increased substantially. Riecken and Ravich (1982) found that consent forms used in 40 research projects at four VA hospitals were written in language requiring a higher level of education than that of most subjects included in the studies. In contrast, one study reports that individuals with education levels commensurate with the consent form reading level were able to answer only four of 10 factual questions correctly (Mariner & McArdle, 1985). Therefore, even having the readability of consent information commensurate with the education level may not be sufficient to ensure adequate comprehension.

What amount of consent information is adequate has been explored in several studies. Cassileth et al. (1980) examined attitudes and perceptions of cancer victims toward informed consent. When asked to evaluate the amount of information given about consent, 76% of these individuals felt they had received "just the right amount" of information and had significantly higher recall scores than individuals who felt that the information given to them was either "too little" or "too much." Epstein and Lasagna (1969) conducted a study that systematically varied amount of consent material presented to subjects. They gave one of three different consent forms of varying length to normal volunteers. Not surprisingly, they found that comprehension was inversely related to the length of the consent form. Their data suggest that consent information should be brief and to the point to maximize comprehension.

The effect of clarity of information on comprehension was reported in another investigation of cancer patients (Muss et al., 1979). It was found that knowledge about chemotherapy side effects was significantly higher when subjects perceived that information regarding side effects was "very clearly" explained than when they perceived the information as "not at all" to "fairly clearly" explained. They also report that knowledge about chemotherapy side effects was significantly higher when explanations were given by health-care personnel (e.g., a nurse) other than or in addition to the physician. They hypothesize that individuals are more likely to feel equal and more at ease with staff members other than physicians and, as a result, ask more questions. It may also be that repeated exposure to the consent material as presented by several staff members helps in clarifying information, thereby improving comprehension.

Modality of disclosure (how information is conveyed to the individual) has been thought to affect comprehension (Barbour & Blumenkrantz, 1978). Some investigators suggest that the manner in which consent information is presented may need to be varied according to the subject's educational level (Freeman, Pichard, & Smith, 1981) and/or age (Taub, 1986) so that comprehension is enhanced. Other investigators (Faden, 1977; Faden & Beauchamp, 1980), in attempting to determine whether comprehension systematically varies according to the type of presentation (i.e., written information, videotape, discussion groups), have shown that modality seems to have no effect on the level of comprehension.

The individual's attitude toward informed consent has been shown to be related to comprehension. Those with no strong opinion about the need for informed consent had significantly lower recall of consent information than those who felt that consent forms were important (Cassileth et al., 1980). Thus, the significance of the consent process to the individual has an important impact on attention and therefore comprehension.

In assessing and comparing studies of comprehension of consent information, one difficulty lies in the varying methods used. Some investigators use multiple-choice or true-false tests as a means of assessment while others use open-ended questions with coded responses. Relevant literature on learning and psychological testing has shown that tests of recognition, such as multiple-choice tests, are easier than tests of recall using open-ended questions. Therefore, comparing results of studies that use open-ended questions with those using objective questions is problematic.

A further difficulty in comparing these studies lies in the fact that immediate understanding and recall are often treated interchangeably. However, results show, not surprisingly, that retention of information declines over time. The utility of assessing retention of all consent information must be questioned. Certainly it is important that research subjects remember that they have the freedom to withdraw from an experiment, but it may not be necessary to keep all the consent information in mind several weeks or months after the initial decision. Further, the fact that individuals forget information does not mean that the information was not used at the time of the decision and then forgotten as part of a normal process.

It must be noted that, in the studies reviewed here, investigators have assumed that knowledge of the consent information as measured by some form of objective test is equated with comprehension of that information. However, the ability of individuals to repeat what they have been told is not what is usually meant by comprehension. A novel approach such as that taken by Mellinger, Huffine, and Balter (1982) seems useful in evaluating comprehension of consent information. They developed an assessment of comprehension that includes an objective test requiring subjects to make judgments about a series of statements in addition to a standard evaluation of comprehension. Illogical judgments indicate a lack of comprehension.

Finally, the sample characteristics of the patients must be taken into account when we examine comprehension. Many of the studies have examined understanding of consent information by individuals with serious medical illnesses. Others have looked at the less seriously ill, and some have researched volunteers without medical illness. Both hospitalized and nonhospitalized patients have been studied. Comparability of these subject groups cannot be assumed. The ill individuals may be under more emotional stress than the healthy volunteer, which may interfere with comprehension of consent information. It was shown by Silva (1985) that 72 of 75 spouses of individuals requiring general surgery displayed adequate comprehension of information for informed consent. Further differences may be found between the hospitalized and nonhospitalized patient. Some research suggests that hospitalization itself makes an individual feel more vulnerable, and this may in turn influence comprehension of consent information. Cassileth et al. (1980) found that ambulatory patients demonstrated greater comprehension of consent information for cancer treatment than those who were bedridden. Further, such factors as education level, intelligence (Cassileth et al., 1980; Freeman et al., 1981; Taub, Kline, & Baker, 1981), and age (Taub, 1980) have shown some relationship with comprehension of consent information, although these are not consistent findings. Overall, the comprehension level of consent information is low. However, instructional aids seem to increase comprehension.

REACTIONS TO CONSENT PROCEDURES
Studies have been conducted on how individuals feel about being informed (Aldifi, 1971; Denney, Williamson, & Penn, 1975; Golden & Johnston, 1970; Lankton, Batchelder, & Ominslay, 1977), as well as professionals' attitudes regarding informed consent (Kaufmann, 1983; Lidz et al., 1983; Levine, 1987; Myers et al., 1987; Taylor & Kelner, 1987). This area of investigation was particularly popular several years ago when the merits of informed-consent doctrine were being hotly debated. While consent is now legally required for most research projects and many standard treatments, current attitudes continue to reflect disapproval of the doctrine and discomfort with following it.

Professionals have argued that informed consent undermines professional rapport and trust (Ingelfinger, 1980). Taylor and Kelner (1987), in their study on physicians' perspectives of informed consent in clinical trials, report that 95% of those investigators surveyed regard informed consent as an intrusion into the professional relationship. Investigators attribute such problems as decreasingly effective communication and less personalized relationships to the informed-consent process. Investigators in this study also viewed informed consent as having a negative affect on patient care. A further concern for investigators in placebo controlled clinical trials is that informed consent can either bias or alter results (Dahan et al., 1987; Levine, 1987; Loftus & Fries, 1979; Myers et al., 1987).

In their study on the informed-consent process, Lidz et al. (1983) listed several barriers to obtaining informed consent. They report that some decisions take place over a long period of time and typically formal disclosure and consent are done after the decision has already been made to have treatment. They also report that there are often many decisions to be made and that the medical decision-making process frequently involves so many individuals that the patient does not know who is responsible. Finally, they observed that most professionals do view informed consent as an integral part of good patient care.

Another criticism of informed consent addresses the consequences of risk disclosure for the subject. Some professionals have expressed concern that individuals who are told of potential risks of a procedure will become unduly alarmed and may reject essential medical treatment (Burnham, 1966; King, 1976). This argument has no validity in the research setting. In their study of decision making about nonsurgical contraceptives, Faden and Beauchamp (1980) report that there was no evidence that disclosed information produced negative consequences such as "irrational" rejection of recommended procedures, psychological harm, or jeopardizing long-term outcome. While these findings are positive, the authors note that disclosed information could have different consequences when more serious issues are being considered.

With regard to subjects' and patients' attitudes toward informed consent, one investigation found that most individuals believed decisions should be primarily or completely left to their physicians (Lidz et al., 1983). While patients expressed a desire for information, this information was rarely wanted in order to direct treatment and was more frequently desired to facilitate patient's compliance with treatment decisions that had already been made by the physician. Some studies have shown that a number of patients (up to 45%) do not really want to know treatment risks (Alfidi, 1975; Lankton et al., 1977). In contrast, Faden, Lewis, Becker, Faden, and Freeman (1981) reported that individuals treated for seizure disorder were more likely to believe that the primary treatment decision should rest with the individual and they preferred far more detailed disclosure than routinely offered by physicians. In this same study, patients and physicians held widely differing beliefs about the consequences of detailed disclosure where patients felt that disclosure would make them more likely to adhere more correctly to their treatment, as well as making them feel more confident in their drug and in their physician. Other studies have also shown that patients appear to prefer full detailed disclosure, including risk disclosure (Alfidi, 1971; Denney et al., 1975; Faden, 1977; Leydhecker, Gramer, & Krieglstein, 1980; Rosenberg, 1973; Saubrey et al., 1984). The decision-making process may also differ according to whether the individual is participating in therapeutic or nontherapeutic research, the individual's setting, and, if applicable, the severity of the problem. Lidz et al. (1983)

reported that acutely ill patients more readily gave up responsibility for their treatment, whereas chronically ill patients tended to be more active in decision making. They also report that inpatients were in general much less likely to question their physicians or participate in making treatment decisions than were outpatients.

Another area of focus has been the level of patient anxiety as a result of disclosure. While there are anecdotal reports that disclosure makes individuals anxious or fearful, empirical studies find no differences in anxiety levels, either self-reported or by physician observers, between informed and uninformed individuals (Denney et al., 1975; Houts & Leaman, 1980; Lankton et al., 1977). While two studies without uninformed controls (Alfidi, 1971; Houts & Leaman, 1980) found that consent information disturbed about 40% of the individuals, only 1% decided not to go ahead with the recommended procedure, and 97% regarded the information as useful. Interestingly, one study (Denney et al., 1975) found that anxiety levels postoperatively were lower in informed rather than uninformed patients. Andrew (1970) found that for some individuals communication given before surgery can result in shorter postoperative hospitalization time and can even diminish the need for stronger pain medication after surgery. These findings suggest that knowledge of expected results seems to make the actual results more emotionally tolerable and less frightening. Other evidence has shown that information disclosure generally enhances calmness and control and can improve health outcome (Faden & Faden, 1978; McClellan, 1982; Oken, 1961; Rockwell & Rockwell-Pepitone, 1979).

In a study of family-planning clinic patients, different methods of disclosing information to the individuals had no impact on patients' level of anxiety (Faden, 1977). About 25% of respondents reported feeling more anxious than usual after the disclosure of information. However, the same percentage of people who were faced with making the decision about contraception also reported more anxiety than usual even though they had not received the detailed information. Characteristics and the behavior of the investigator also have an impact on the mood of the subjects or patients. One study examined chronically ill patients and found that physicians who sounded angry and anxious but whose speech was sympathetic resulted in patients who were satisfied and contented. This suggests that a complicated set of factors is involved in patients' reactions in a medical setting (Hall, Roter, & Rand, 1980).

Overall, this area of investigation would seem to be most fruitful if efforts were placed not in looking at whether consent information makes people upset or anxious, but instead toward identifying subtle cues in the environment or the investigator that produce untoward feelings in subjects or patients.

DECISION MAKING

A small number of studies have investigated factors influencing subject decision making in the consent process. Some studies have shown that people feel they have no choice and must participate (McCullum & Schwartz, 1969). Other studies do not find this, and their primary focus has been to determine whether disclosure of risks discourages subjects from giving consent (Alfidi, 1971; Lankton et al., 1977).

In a study of risk disclosure for anesthesia, individuals did not refuse the procedure after detailed information about the risks (Lankton et al., 1977). A study of 130 individuals who were to undergo cardiac angiography found that when individuals were informed in very explicit language of the serious complications possible from this diagnostic procedure, only 2% refused to undergo the procedure because of the risk information provided them (Alfidi, 1971). Perhaps the best-known study in this area was conducted on kidney donors (Fellner & Marshall, 1970). This study was designed to determine whether kidney donors utilized risk information in their decision to donate a kidney. It was found that decisions were made long before any detailed risk disclosure was made and further that disclosure had little impact on the donors. However, other research (Stanley, Stanley, Lautin, Kane, & Schwartz, 1981; Stanley, Stanley, Schwartz, Lautin, & Kane, 1980) has shown that participation in hypothetical research projects varies according to the risk of the project.

It has been hypothesized that many nonrational variables may affect the decision maker even when circumstances are optimal (i.e., all information is disclosed and individuals demonstrate a high level of comprehension) (Tancredi, 1982). Tversky and Kahneman (1974) have demonstrated that intuitive processes on the part of the decision maker may sometimes thwart an objective evaluation of the probability of events. A few studies have attempted to relate comprehension of consent information to decision making (Epstein & Lasagna, 1969; Stuart, 1978). Findings seem to indicate that higher levels of comprehension are associated with a higher rate of agreement to the proposed procedure by the research participant or patient. However, interpretation of these findings is problematic because the risk-benefit ratio of the procedures must be known to determine whether the individuals' affirmative decisions were sensible.

As an outgrowth of the studies demonstrating that risk disclosure does not seem to influence decision making with regard to medical procedures, some investigators have begun to identify factors that influence decisions. In a study of participation in psychology experiments (Geller & Faden, 1979), the relative influence of standard consent information and personal testimony of one individual was examined. While recall of consent information was affected by testimony that contradicted it, the decision to participate was not affected. In another study, subjects reported that disclosed information was not the primary determinant in decisions regarding contraception. Instead, personal feelings were reported to have a greater influence on the decision (Faden & Beauchamp, 1980).

As an extension of this work, the decision-making techniques developed by investigators who conduct basic research on decision-making and information processing can be applied (Janis & Mann, 1977; Jungerman, 1980). For example, it seems worthwhile to try to adapt the technique of "policy capturing" from the social sciences (Zedeck & Blood, 1974) in research on informed consent. In addition to asking subjects what influenced them, researchers could place subjects in various hypothetical situations and ask them to make a decision about participation. In this way, researchers would not have to depend so heavily on subjects' ability to report influences—an ability that is not completely reliable. This approach can yield a fuller picture of the decision-making process.

PUBLIC OPINION

Investigations of public opinion on informed consent and experimentation have taken several directions. Mellinger, Huffine, and Balter (1979, 1982) have focused on developing procedures for obtaining informed public judgments about ethical issues in nonmedical research. They developed an assessment of comprehension that included an objective test requiring subjects to make judgments about a series of statements in addition to a standard evaluation of comprehension, where illogical judgments indicate a lack of comprehension. While the main finding was that most persons had some comprehension difficulty, their results also demonstrated the feasibility of obtaining informed rather than naive judgments about complex issues from the public. These researchers also gathered data on public opinion about the informed-consent process. They observed that a large majority of those interviewed insisted that informed consent should be required in research with few exceptions.

Holmes, Margetts, and Gibbs (1979) conducted a survey of attitudes of physicians and laypersons about who should be involved in decision making about ethical issues. They found that both groups agreed that the individual facing the dilemma should be highly important in making such decisions. Lesser importance was given to other individuals including governmental leaders, religious leaders, hospital policy boards, and family members by the two groups. Significant differences between physicians and laypersons existed with regard to participation of medical experts on the decision-making process where physicians assigned higher importance to the role of medical experts.

Several studies have looked at public opinion on subject participation in research. Martin, Arnold, Zimmerman, and Richard (1968) assessed both willingness to volunteer one's self and others as subjects for such research. In this study, subjects were asked who of a number of subject classes (e.g., prisoners, chronically ill or dying) should volunteer in several hypothetical biomedical studies that varied in risk (e.g., malaria, common cold). Results indicated a general unwillingness to volunteer subjects who would require proxy consent (e.g., children, institutionalized mentally retarded). It was also found that, the lower the perceived experimental risk, the higher the number of people willing to volunteer for the study. Brackbill and Golden (1979), in a similar study, found comparable results.

REACTIONS AND ALTERNATIVES TO DECEPTION AND DEBRIEFING
Much of the research on ethics and informed consent in psychology has focused on the use of deception in experimentation. Participants in deception experiments, usually college students, are misled as to the true nature of the experiment so certain variables can be manipulated that are otherwise difficult to investigate. While deceptive methodology conflicts with the principle of informed consent, which states that participants should be informed of "significant factors that may be expected to influence willingness to participate" (American Psychological Association [APA], 1992, Std. 6.11(b)), it has been recognized that such experimentation may be useful and necessary. The APA standards indicate that use of deception in psychological experiments may be acceptable under the following conditions: the research problem is considered to be important; the deception is necessary to realize the research objectives; after being informed of the true nature of the research, the subject considers the procedures reasonable and they maintain confidence in the researchers; subject withdrawal is permitted at any time including withdrawal of his or her data on learning of the deception; and the investigator is fully responsible for debriefing subjects.

Deception experiments have elicited both concern for the public's potentially negative opinion of psychologists and their trustworthiness (Ring, 1967), as well as criticism regarding potential harm to participants (Kelman, 1967). Wilson and Donnerstein (1976) presented descriptions of actual nonreactive field experiments to a generally middle-class population who rated each description on such things as ethicality, invasion of privacy, lowering of trust in psychologists, feelings of harassment, and so on. In general, most subjects did not react negatively to the methods. However, a substantial minority for most of the experiments (e.g., 18–47% of respondents perceived the experiment as unethical) and a majority in some cases (e.g., 24–72% of respondents) indicated they would feel harassed by the experiment's methodology. Sullivan and Deiker (1973) compared college students' and psychologists' perception of ethical issues regarding controversial but hypothetical experiments. They found that college students were more tolerant of use of deception than were the psychologists and that, in general, the psychologists expressed ethically stringent views.

For actual subjects who have participated in deception experiments, research indicates that the experience was viewed as positive and enjoyable (Schwartz & Gottlieb, 1981; Smith & Richardson, 1983). After they had participated in a series of deception experiments, Holmes (1967) reported that college students generally perceived experiments as more scientific and valuable. Cook et al. (1970) reported, however, that those college students with a previous history of participating in deceptive experiments believed the experimenter less and reported negative feelings regarding research in general.

With regard to any undesirable aftereffects or potential harm that may occur as a result of participation in deception experiments, the investigator has a duty to identify and remove these consequences, including long-term effects. Thus debriefing, in which all participants must be given a "prompt opportunity . . . to obtain information about the nature, results, and conclusion of the research" (APA, 1992, Std. 6.18), is an integral and necessary part of deception experiments. The use of debriefing has been examined by several investigators. Studies have found that debriefing can be an effective way to eliminate any deleterious effect caused by the research as well as provide educational benefits (Gerdes, 1979; Holmes, 1972; Schwartz & Gottlieb, 1981; Smith & Richardson, 1983). Walster, Berscheid, Abrahams, and Aronson (1967), in contrast, found that debriefing was not effective in eliminating self-perceptions created as a result of the experimental condition before debriefing. Ross, Lepper, and Hubbard (1975) also demonstrated a perseverance effect after a simple debriefing; however, this was not the case when subjects received a more detailed discussion of the possibility that false self-perceptions may continue even after debriefing. While the literature indicates the effectiveness of debriefing when done in a thorough and appropriate manner, it is the responsibility of the experimenter to continually regulate the quality of the debriefing procedures being used (Holmes, 1976a, 1976b).

Because of the obvious ethical considerations associated with the use of deception in psychological research, some investigators have suggested alternative methods. For example, role playing in which a subject is instructed to imagine himself or herself in a particular situation and respond accordingly has been explored as a substitute for deception (Berscheid, Baron, Dermer, & Libman, 1973; Holmes & Bennett, 1974; Horowitz & Rothschild, 1970; Willis & Willis, 1970). In their research, Holmes and Bennett (1974) have suggested that informed consent can be obtained in deception experiments without revealing the deception itself by following a three-step procedure: subjects receive a general introduction to experiments while explicitly being informed that it is sometimes necessary to deceive subjects to get unbiased responses; subjects are informed of the nature of the experiment but not the specific deception; and subjects are informed that they may withdraw at any time.

A Research Agenda on Informed Consent: A Psychological Approach

This chapter has reviewed the empirical studies on informed consent. While there are a substantial number of studies in some areas (e.g., the study of comprehension of consent information), the level of psychological understanding and sophistication brought to bear on this work is limited. Generally, research on informed consent has taken a rather simplistic view of the process and ignores the subtleties and underlying mechanisms inherent in consent procedures. This section will describe some of the possible applications of psychological principles and techniques in refining our understanding of informed consent to research. Areas that can be fruitfully studied using psychological techniques include the following.

First, a well-developed "basic" literature exists on the analysis of risks and benefits and subsequent decision making (Thompson, in this volume). Factors such as the manner of presentation, the emphasis on positive versus negative in a presentation of consent material, and the way in which probabilities of risks are presented (e.g., "There is a 20% chance of the therapy helping" vs. "There is an 80% failure rate") can significantly affect the outcome of a decision. The informed-consent literature would be greatly enhanced by including these factors in trying to understand what influences participation in research.

Second, much is known in the psychological literature about the way in which people process information. The informed-consent literature usually tends to assume that all people process information in the same way and people accurately appraise the degree of risk and act according to the level of risk. An appreciation of the information-processing literature would dispel these misperceptions. There is individual variation in the way information is processed, and the amount of risk is not always perceived accurately. As Thompson (in this volume) points out, people tend to be risk averse in the face of prospective gains and risk taking in the face of prospective losses. This could very well help to explain why people with terminal illnesses or serious conditions with no known treatment willingly consent to high-risk research: the common notion of "What have I got to lose?" takes on real psychological meaning.

Third, most consent studies ignore the context in which the consent is being elicited or assume that it is equivalent across all settings. By *context* we mean the actual setting in which consent is obtained as well as the characteristics and behavior of the researcher who is seeking the consent. Both factors can have a major effect on the actual decision as well as the subject's understanding of the proposed project. As Sieber (in this volume) points out, subtle as well as not-so-subtle aspects of the researcher's behavior can influence the actual results of a study. By extension, this behavior also affects the consent process, including the individual's willingness to become a part of the study. With regard to the setting of the study, the "formality" of the setting and the potential subject's role in that setting can influence and distort the consent process. Psychologists' understanding of demand characteristics can be readily applied. An informal setting (e.g., neighborhood street) in which the individuals are only loosely tied together may result in a different sense of obligation to participate in a research project, if asked, than a setting in which both the researcher and potential subject have some "official" status (e.g., faculty professor and student).

Fourth, the balance of power between the researcher and the potential participant is usually ignored in informed-consent studies. This power balance, which has been studied extensively in social psychology, may be as important or more important than risk assessment in determining whether someone decides to participate in a research project. Consider the example of the college professor and the student. If the professor were conducting a survey of college students, we would anticipate a much higher participation rate than if a college student were conducting a survey of faculty members. Many factors may contribute to this difference, but the power balance would have to be high on the list of important influences.

Fifth, "comprehension" has been narrowly defined in the study of informed consent, and the tools for its assessment are primitive. Comprehension is identified ordinarily as "knowledge." While knowledge is important to comprehension, it is viewed normally in learning and educational psychology as only one aspect of comprehending. Effectively utilizing and integrating the information are more sophisticated aspects of comprehension. With respect to assessment tools, only a little of what is known in psychometrics about reliability and validity has been used in assessing the adequacy of consent. There is a pressing need for the development of psychologically sound assessment techniques in this area.

Sixth, there is a great need for multivariate studies of informed consent, even in those studies that have a solid grounding in psychological theory and principles. As can be seen in this as well as the other chapters in this volume, informed consent is a complex process influenced by a host of factors. Bivariate studies oversimplify this process and cannot capture the texture and complexity of the process. For example, many social-psychology studies have examined the "volunteer effect" and how it can bias the results of a study. Other studies have explored the role of risk perception and its impact on agreement or refusal to engage in a certain behavior. But how do these factors combine and interact to affect decision making in the research setting? Psychologists are well equipped to begin to address the complexity of the consent process and to capture the nuances and dynamics of this process.

References

Alfidi, R. J. (1971). Informed consent: A study of patient reaction. *Journal of the American Medical Association, 216*, 1325–1329.

Alfidi, R. J. (1975). Controversy, alternatives and decisions in complying with the legal doctrine of informed consent. *Radiology, 114*, 231–234.

American Psychological Association. (1992). Ethical principles of psychologists and code of conduct. *American Psychologist, 47*, 1597–1611.

Andrew, J. (1970). Recovery from surgery, with and without preparatory instruction, for three coping styles. *Journal of Personality and Social Psychology, 15*, 223–226.

Baker, M. T., & Taub, H. A. (1983). Readability of informed consent forms for research in a Veteran's Administration medical center. *Journal of the American Medical Association, 250*, 2646–2648.

Barbour, G. L., & Blumenkrantz, M. J. (1978). Videotape aids informed consent decisions. *Journal of the American Medical Association, 240*, 2741–2742.

Benson, H., Gordon, L., Mitchell, C., & Place, V. (1977). Patient education and intrauterine contraception: A study of two package inserts. *American Journal of Public Health, 67*, 446–449.

Bergler, J., Pennington, C., Metcalfe, M., & Freis, E. (1980). Informed consent: How much does the patient understand? *Clinical Pharmacology and Therapeutics, 27*, 435–439.

Berscheid, E., Baron, R. S., Dermer, M., & Libman, M. (1973). Anticipating informed consent: An empirical approach. *American Psychologist, 28*, 913–925.

Brackbill, Y., & Golden, L. (1979). Public opinion on subject participation in biomedical research: New views on altruism, perception, risk and proxy consent. *Clinical Research, 27*, 14–18.

Burnham, P. J. (1966). Letter on medical experimentation on humans. *Science, 152*, 448–450.

Cassileth, B. R., Zupkis, R. B., Sutton-Smith, K., & March, V. (1980). Informed consent: Why are its goals imperfectly realized? *New England Journal of Medicine, 302*, 896–900.

Coleman, L. (1974). The patient-physician relationship: Terrified consent. *Physician's World, 607*.

Committee for the Protection of Human Participants in Research. (1982). *Ethical principles in the conduct of research with human participants.* Washington DC: American Psychological Association.

Cook, T. D., Bean, J. R., Calder, B. J., Frey, R., Martin, L., Krovetz, M., & Reisman, S. R. (1970). Demand characteristics and three conceptions of the frequently deceived subject. *Journal of Personality and Social Psychology, 14*, 185–194.

Culver, C. M., & Gert, B. (1982). *Philosophy in medicine: Conceptual and ethical issues in medicine and psychiatry.* New York: Oxford Press.

Dahan, R., Caulin, C., Figea, L., Kanis, J. A., Caulin, F., & Segrestaa, J. M. (1987). Does informed consent influence therapeutic outcome? A clinical trial of the hypnotic activity of placebo in patients admitted to hospital. *British Medical Journal, 293*, 363–364.

Denney, M., Williamson, D., & Penn, R. (1975). Informed consent: Emotional responses of patients. *Postgraduate Medicine, 60,* 205–209.

Epstein, L., & Lasagna, L. (1969). Obtaining informed consent: Form or substance. *Archives of Internal Medicine, 123,* 682–685.

Faden, R. (1977). Disclosure and informed consent: Does it matter how we tell it? *Health Education Monograph, 5,* 198–214.

Faden, R., & Beauchamp, T. (1980). Decision-making and informed consent: A study of the impact of disclosed information. *Social Indicators Research, 7,* 13–36.

Faden, R., & Faden, A. I. (1978). Informed consent in medical practice with particular reference to neurology. *Archives of Neurology, 35,* 761.

Faden, R., Lewis, C., Becker, C., Faden, A. I., & Freeman, J. (1981). Disclosure standards and informed consent. *Journal of Health Politics and Policy Law, 6,* 255–284.

Fellner, C., & Marshall, J. (1970). Kidney donors: The myth of informed consent. *American Journal of Psychiatry, 126,* 1245–1251.

Freeman, W. R., Pichard, A. D., & Smith, H. (1981). Effects of informed consent and educational background on patient knowledge, anxiety and subjective responses to cardiac catherization. *Catherization and Cardiovascular Diagnosis, 7,* 119–134.

Geller, D., & Faden, R. (1979). *Decision-making in informed consent: Base rate and individuating information.* Paper presented at the annual meeting of the American Psychological Association, New York.

Gerdes, E. (1979). College students' reactions to social psychological experiments involving deception. *Journal of Social Psychology, 107,* 99–110.

Goin, M., Burgoyne, R., & Goin, J. (1976). Facelift operation: The patient's secret motivations and reactions to "informed consent." *Plastic and Reconstructive Surgery, 58,* 273–279.

Golden, J., & Johnston, G. (1970). Problems of distortion in doctor-patient communication. *Psychiatric Medicine, 1,* 127–148.

Grunder, T. M. (1980). On the readability of surgical consent forms. *New England Journal of Medicine, 302,* 900–902.

Hall, J., Roter, D., & Rand, C. (1980). *Communication of affect between patient and physician.* Paper presented at the annual meeting of the American Psychological Association, Montreal.

Hassar, M., & Weintraub, M. (1976). "Uninformed" consent and the wealthy volunteer: An analysis of patient volunteers in a clinical trial of a new anti-inflammatory drug. *Clinical Pharmacology and Therapeutics, 20,* 379–386.

Hirsch, H. R. (1977). Informed consent: Fact or fiction. *Journal of Legal Medicine, 5,* 25.

Holmes, D. S. (1967). Amount of experience in experiments as a determinant of performance in later experiments. *Journal of Personality and Social Psychology, 7,* 403–407.

Holmes, D. S. (1972). Repression or interference: A further investigation. *Journal of Personality and Social Psychology, 22,* 163–170.

Holmes, D. S. (1976a). Debriefing after psychological experiments: 1. Effectiveness of postdeception dehoaxing. *American Psychologist, 31,* 858–867.

Holmes, D. S. (1976b). Debriefing after psychological experiments: 2. Effectiveness of postexperimental desensitizing. *American Psychologist, 31,* 868–875.

Holmes, D. S., & Bennett, D. H. (1974). Experiments to answer questions raised by the use of deception in psychological research (I, II, III). *Journal of Personality and Social Psychology, 29,* 358–367.

Holmes, C., Margetts, J., & Gibbs, G. (1979). Who should decide? A survey of attitudes about bioethical decision-making. *Ethics in Science and Medicine, 6,* 137–144.

Horowitz, I. A., & Rothschild, B. H. (1970). Conformity as a function of deception and role playing. *Journal of Personality and Social Psychology, 29,* 358–367.

Houts, P., & Leaman, D. (1980). *Patient response to information about possible complications of medical procedures.* Paper presented at the annual meeting of the American Psychological Association, Montreal.

Ingelfinger, F. J. (1980). Arrogance. *New England Journal of Medicine, 303,* 1507–1511.

Janis, I., & Mann, L. (1977). *Decision-making: A psychological analysis of conflict choice and commitment.* New York: Free Press.

Jungerman, H. (1980). Speculations about decision-theoretic aids for personal decision making. *Acta Psychologica, 45,* 7–34.

Kaufmann, C. L. (1983). Informed consent and patient decision making: Two decades of research. *Social Science Medicine, 17,* 1657–1664.

Kelman, H. C. (1967). Human use of human subjects: The problem of deception in social psychological experiments. *Psychological Bulletin, 67,* 1–11.

Kennedy, B. J., & Lillenhaugen, A. (1979). Patient recall of informed consent. *Medical Pediatric Oncology, 7,* 173–178.

King, J. F. (1976). The jaws of informed consent. *Maryland State Medical Journal, 25,* 78–81.

Laforet, E. G. (1976). The fiction of informed consent. *Journal of the American Medical Association, 235,* 1579–1585.

Lankton, J., Batchelder, B., & Ominslay, A. (1977). Emotional responses to detailed risk disclosure for anesthesia. *Anesthesiology, 46,* 294–296.

Leeb, D., Bowers, D. G., & Lynch, J. B. (1976). Observations on the myth of "informed consent." *Plastic and Reconstructive Surgery, 58,* 280–282.

Levine, R. J. (1987). The apparent incompatibility between informed consent and placebo-controlled clinical trials. *Clinical Pharmacology and Therapeutics, 42*, 247–249.

Leydhecker, W., Gramer, E., & Krieglstein, G. K. (1980). Patient information before cataract surgery. *Ophthalmologica, 180*, 241–246.

Lidz, C. W., Meisel, A., Osterweis, M., Holden, J. L., Marx, J. H., & Munetz, M. R. (1983). Barriers to informed consent. *Journal of Internal Medicine, 99*, 539–543.

Loftus, E. G., & Fries, J. F. (1979). Informed consent may be hazardous to health [Editorial]. *Science, 204*, 4388.

McClellan, F. M. (1982). Informed consent to medical therapy and experimentation. *Journal of Legal Medicine, 3*, 81–115.

McCullum, A., & Schwartz, A. (1969). Pediatric research hospitalization: Its meaning to parents. *Pediatric Research, 3*, 199–204.

Mariner, W. K., & McArdle, P. A. (1985). Consent forms, readability and comprehension: The need for new assessment tools. *Law, Medicine and Health Care, 13*, 68–74.

Marini, J. L., Sheard, M. H., & Bridges, C. I. (1976). An evaluation of "informed consent" with volunteer prisoner subjects. *Yale Journal of Biological Medicine, 49*, 427–437.

Martin, D. C., Arnold, J. D., Zimmerman, T. F., & Richard, R. (1968). Human subjects in clinical research: A report of three studies. *New England Journal of Medicine, 279*, 1426–1431.

Meisel, A., & Roth, L. (1981). What we do and do not know about informed consent. *Journal of the American Medical Association, 246*, 2473–2477.

Meisel, A., Roth, L., & Lidz, C. (1977). Towards a model of the legal doctrine of informed consent. *American Journal of Psychiatry, 134*, 285–289.

Mellinger, G. D., Huffine, C. L., & Balter, M. B. (1979). Judgments about ethical issues in biomedical research: Methods and findings of developmental studies. *Ethical Issues Monograph Series 1*. Oakland CA: Institution for Research in Social Behavior.

Mellinger, G. D., Huffine, C. L., & Balter, M. B. (1982). Assessing comprehension in a survey of public reactions to complex issues. *Public Opinion Quarterly, 46*, 97–109.

Morrow, G. (1980). How readable are subject consent forms? *Journal of the American Medical Association, 244*, 56–58.

Muss, H. B., White, D. R., Michielutte, R., Richards, F., II, Cooper, M. R., Williams, S., Stuart, J. J., & Spurr, C. (1979). Written informed consent in patients with breast cancer. *Cancer, 43*, 1549–1556.

Myers, M. G., Cairns, J. A., & Singer, J. (1987). The consent form as a possible cause of side effects. *Clinical Pharmacology and Therapeutics, 42*, 250–253.

Nuremberg Code. (1949). From trials of war criminals before the Nuremberg military tribunals under control council law no. 10, 2, 181–182.

Oken, D. (1961). What to tell cancer patients: A study of medical attitudes. *Journal of the American Medical Association, 175,* 1120–1128.

Olin, G. B., & Olin, H. S. (1975). Informed consent in voluntary mental hospital admissions. *American Journal of Psychiatry, 132,* 938–941.

Park, L., Slaughter, R., Cori, L., & Kniffin, H. G. (1966). The subjective experience of the research patient. *Journal of Nervous and Mental Disease, 143,* 199–206.

Penman, D., Bahna, G., Holland, J., Morrow, G., Morse, I., Schmale, A., Long, C., Derogatis, L., & Mellis, N. (1980). *Patients' perceptions of giving informed consent for investigational chemotherapy.* Paper presented at the annual meeting of the American Psychological Association, Montreal.

Priluck, I. A., Robertson, D. M., & Buettner, H. (1979). What patients recall of the preoperative discussion after retinal detachment surgery. *American Journal of Ophthalmology, 87,* 620–623.

Protection of Human Subjects, 45 C.F.R. §§46.101–46.124 (1992).

Riecken, H. W., & Ravich, R. (1982). Informed consent to biomedical research in Veteran's Administration hospitals. *Journal of the American Medical Association, 248,* 344–348.

Ring, K. (1967). Experimental social psychology: Some sober questions about some frivolous values. *Journal of Experimental Social Psychology, 3,* 113–123.

Robinson, G., & Merav, A. (1976). Informed consent: Recall by patients tested postoperatively. *Annals of Thoracic Surgery, 22,* 209.

Rockwell, D. A., & Rockwell-Pepitone, F. (1979). The emotional impact of surgery and the value of informed consent. *Medical Clinics of North America, 63,* 1341–1351.

Rosenberg, S. H. (1973). Informed consent: A reappraisal of patients' reactions. *California Medicine, 119,* 64–68.

Ross, L., Lepper, M. R., & Hubbard, M. (1975). Perseverance in self-perception: Biased attributional processes in the debriefing paradigm. *Journal of Personality and Social Psychology, 32,* 880–892.

Saubrey, N., Jensen, J., Rasmussen, P. E., Gjorup, T., Guldajer, H., & Riis, P. (1984). Danish patients' attitudes to scientific-ethical questions. *Acta Medica Scandanavica, 215,* 99–104.

Schultz, A. L., Pardee, G. P., & Ensinck, J. W. (1975). Are research subjects really informed? *Western Journal of Medicine, 123,* 76–80.

Schwartz, S., & Gottlieb, A. (1981). Participants' postexperimental reactions and the ethics of bystander research. *Journal of Experimental Social Psychology, 17,* 396–407.

Silva, M. C. (1985). Comprehension of information for informed consent by spouses of surgical patients. *Research in Nursing and Health, 8,* 117–124.

Singer, E. (1978). The effects of informed consent procedures on respondents' reactions to surveys. *Journal of Consumer Research, 5,* 49–57.

Smith, S. S., & Richardson, D. (1983). Amelioration of deception and harm in psychological research: The important role of debriefing. *Journal of Personality and Social Psychology, 44,* 1075–1082.

Stanley, B., & Stanley, M. (1981). Psychiatric patients and research: Protecting their autonomy. *Comprehensive Psychiatry, 22,* 420–427.

Stanley, B., & Stanley, M. (1982). Testing competency in psychiatric patients: What is it, how is it assessed? *Institutional Review Board, 4*(8), 1–6.

Stanley, B., Stanley, M., Lautin, A., Kane, J., & Schwartz, N. (1981). Preliminary findings on psychiatric patients as research participants: A population at risk? *American Journal of Psychiatry, 138*(5), 669–671.

Stanley, B., Stanley, M., Schwartz, N., Lautin, A., & Kane, J. (1980). The ability of the mentally ill to evaluate research risks. *IRCS Medical Science, 8,* 657–658.

Stuart, R. B. (1978). Protection of the right to informed consent to participate in research. *Behaviour Research and Therapy, 9,* 3–82.

Sullivan, D. S., & Deiker, T. E. (1973). Subject-experimenter perceptions of ethical issues in human research. *American Psychologist, 28,* 587–591.

Tancredi, L. (1982). Competency for informed consent: Conceptual limits of empirical data. *International Journal of Law and Psychiatry, 5,* 51–63.

Taub, H. A. (1980). Informed consent, memory and age. *Gerontology, 20,* 686–690.

Taub, H. A. (1986). Comprehension of informed consent for research: Issues and directions for future study. *IRB: A Review of Human Subjects Research, 8,* 7–10.

Taub, H. A., Kline, G., & Baker, M. (1981). The elderly and informed consent: Effects of vocabulary level and corrected feedback. *Experimental Aging Research, 7,* 137–146.

Taylor, K. M., & Kelner, M. (1987). Informed consent: The physicians' perspective. *Social Science and Medicine, 24,* 135–143.

Tversky, A., & Kahneman, D. (1974). Judgment under uncertainty: Heuristic and biases. *Science, 185,* 1124–1136.

Walster, E., Berscheid, E., Abrahams, D., & Aronson, V. (1967). Effectiveness of debriefing following deception experiments. *Journal of Personality & Social Psychology, 6,* 126–131.

Willis, R. H., & Willis, Y. A. (1970). Role playing versus deception: An experimental comparison. *Journal of Personality and Social Psychology, 16,* 472–477.

Wilson, D. W., & Donnerstein, E. (1976). Legal and ethical aspects of nonreactive social psychological research: An excursion into the public mind. *American Psychologist, 31,* 765–773.

Woodward, W. E. (1979). Informed consent of volunteers: A direct measurement of comprehension and retention of information. *Clinical Research, 27,* 248–252.

Zedeck, S., & Blood, M. R. (1974). Foundations of behavioral science in organizations. Monterey CA: Brooks/Cole.

Chapter 4 / Fifty Years of Empirical Research on Privacy and Confidentiality in Research Settings

ROBERT F. BORUCH
University of Pennsylvania
MICHAEL DENNIS
Research Triangle Institute
and
JOE S. CECIL
Federal Judicial Center

How do people feel about privacy and confidentiality in the context of social research?[1] What opinions about privacy do respondents to surveys and nonrespondents register? What do they *know* regardless of their opinions or feelings? What do they do? And how do survey interviewers and researchers view the matter?

These questions are important to many behavioral and social scientists, educational researchers, and statisticians. They are not easy to address. This chapter reviews relevant empirical studies undertaken mainly between 1942 and 1992.

Background research on the topic has been supported by the National Science Foundation, Division of Ethics and Values in Science and Technology, the National Institute of Justice, and the U.S. Department of Education. An earlier version of this chapter was presented at the Symposium on Empirical Research on Ethics, jointly sponsored by the University of Nebraska's Applied Ethics Program and Law/Psychology Program, and the American Psychological Association. We are indebted to Michael Saks, Gary Melton, and Joan Sieber for advice on improvements.

TABLE 1

Sensitivity of Different Types of Information in a National Sample

Would Object to Availability of Information About Own	Percentage of Respondents
Sex life	87
Income	78
Medical history	51
Political views	42
Telephone number	34
Address	33
Religious views	28
(Wife's) maiden name	18
Education	17
Occupation	12
Racial origin	10
Nationality	8

Note: Total weighted sample = 1,596.

Source: Reports of the Younger Committee on Privacy, in *Databanks in a Free Society,* pp. 257–258 and 271.2. From Bulmer (1979).

Statistical Evidence and Testimonials about the Role of Privacy

Taking one opinion survey at face value, there has at times been little cause for concern that people are worried about privacy in the context of social surveys. Judging from a probability sample survey by Smith (1983) at the Institute for Social Research, a majority of U.S. households questioned endorsed the idea of voluntary responses to survey inquiries that help inform policy. Most of these respondents even endorsed the idea of data sharing among scientists so long as a nominal anonymity of individual respondents was guaranteed.

The sample on which these conclusions were based was small and therefore suspect. Thus, larger studies, run preferably by disinterested organizations, are worth examination. People are concerned about eliciting information on certain topics in surveys, of course, and about later redisclosure of identifiable records. Some empirical work gauging these concerns has been done; table 1, taken from Bulmer's (1979) description of a survey in the United Kingdom, for instance, suggests that individuals would be most discomfited by redisclosure of data on sex life and income. Education, occupation, and even nationality, however, rank low among order of sensitive topics, judging from national probability samples in the United States and the United Kingdom (Bulmer, 1979).

University-based laboratory studies of the sensitivity of survey questions, often based on small samples of college students, have also been undertaken. The earliest relevant work, undertaken during the 1930s, was designed to determine how requiring identification of survey respondents affected their cooperation. Some of these studies focused on sensitive topics—sexual relations, level of social and personal adjustment, or physical health (especially gastrointestinal problems). They found that, despite promises of confidentiality, anonymous respondents yielded more candid information than did identified ones (see, e.g., Benson, 1941; Ellis, 1947; Fischer, 1946; Olsen, 1936). That is, a simple mechanism for operationalizing an assurance enhances cooperation beyond simple verbal assurance.

Further, early studies involving *innocuous* survey topics suggest that the absence of concrete assurance of confidentiality has no discernible effect on cooperation rate, as one might expect. This was especially true if the inquirer was regarded as trustworthy, as for example, professors seem to have been considered then (and sometimes are now). In particular, Gerberich and Mason (1948), Hamel and Reif (1952), Corey (1937), and Ash and Abramson (1952) found that the effects of an anonymity assurance were negligible when questions that were put to the individual were innocuous.

Work that stems from the personality-test controversies of the 1960s also helps us to understand opinions on privacy and research. Laboratory research at the time suggested that, under diverse conditions, the degree to which a personality inventory "invades privacy" could be roughly gauged by well-known measures of the "social desirability" of response (Walsh, Layton, & Klieger, 1966). The offensiveness of an item depends partly on the respondents' beliefs about how the information will be used and their views about the authority of the user (Simmons, 1968). For example, whether the data are used for research or for supervision of individuals affects the individuals' willingness to cooperate notably (see Barna, 1974, and references therein). Hartnett and Seligsohn's (1967) comparison of levels of anonymity and sensitivity of inquiry suggested that assurances of confidentiality made in an academic setting have little influence on students' reports of their (by and large) innocuous demographic characteristics. But for more sensitive topics, such as emotional stability, various levels of assurance have some influence on even this trusting group.

TABLE 2

Reasons Given for Refusal to Participants in the Washington DC Metropolitan Area Site of the National Household Survey of Drug Abuse

Reason for Refusal	Percent	Number
Person doesn't want to answer that kind of question	11.1	13
Person not interested	42.7	50
Person doesn't use drugs and no one here uses drugs	0	0
Another person wouldn't allow sampled person to participate	11.1	13
Survey is invasion of person's privacy	10.3	13
Person too busy	11.1	13
Survey is waste of resources	.9	1
Person never participates in surveys	4.3	5
Other reasons	8.5	10

Source: From Caspar (1992), based on reports of the reasons for refusal given by non-respondents.

Specialized studies of people who refuse to respond to questions in a large survey are frequently instructive. For instance, the National Institute of Drug Abuse has undertaken a methodological study of its National Household Survey of Drug Abuse (NHSDA) partly to understand how approaches to the survey affect cooperation rates and the role privacy may have. Caspar's (1992) analysis of data from such a study in Washington DC included that in table 2. Individuals who refused to participate in the survey offered reasons for refusal that were recorded by interviewers. As in many other studies, the paramount reason for refusal was disinterest: more than 40% of these nonrespondents said they were not engaged by the survey or the topic. About 10% referred specifically to privacy concerns to justify their refusal.

More recent work has focused on whether the mode of the interview affects respondents' willingness to disclose information. The differences between telephone and personal interviews, for example, have been studied by Groves and Magilavy (1986), Rogers (1976), and Hochstim (1967). Groves and Magilavy (1986), for example, asked respondents how uneasy they felt about answering surveys on several topics. The most difficult topic, as one might expect for American respondents, was income. He also asked about respondents' discomfort with telephone versus in-person interviews. Fifteen percent of the respondents said they felt uneasy being interviewed about the topic in person, while nearly 28% were uncomfortable when interviewed by phone. Their statements, however, are not entirely consistent with their apparent behavior, as will be discussed later.

"Privacy" as a public-policy issue rises and falls in its importance, which varies considerably as well with respect to other issues. Surveys of the late 1960s and early 1970s in the United States and the United Kingdom, during peak political interest in privacy, suggest that privacy for the general public was considerably less important than prices of consumer goods, employment, pensions, and health; it was rated as more important than education (Bulmer, 1979). Further, when people are asked why they declined to participate in surveys, they most frequently declared their disinterest in the survey's topic and lack of time. Asked why they choose to participate, respondents say that the mannerliness of interviewers and feelings of a civic responsibility are important (Shaw et al., 1979).

Public attitudes about the importance of privacy and confidentiality are also reflected in the actions and statements of public officials. Congressional hearings, for instance, led to the special protection of social research, notably to testimonial privilege statutes.

In the U.S. Senate Committee on Labor and Public Welfare (1969, 1970) hearings on drug research legislation, for instance, Senator Howard Hughes reported that an experimental drug-withdrawal program in Des Moines IA was "blown clear out of the water" when the local police infiltrated the program, circumventing staff efforts to ensure the privacy of (volunteer) methadone recipients. Dr. Jonathan Cole testified that a "confidential reporting system for addicts in the city of Chicago . . . after two years was turned over to the police so that the file suddenly stopped being confidential." The reporting system, at least as far as drug research was concerned, was aborted.

In related testimony to the committee, Dr. Helen Nowlis reviewed the disruption of a California survey that failed to obtain reliable statistics on the use of marijuana and hallucinogenic drugs in part because many respondents, recognizing the absence of any legal methods for preserving the secrecy of their response, refused to cooperate. The testimony offered by Bernard Glueck, director of the Institute for Living in Hartford CT, emphasized that at least some major research and treatment institutions had deliberately avoided seeking federal funds for research on sensitive topics (e.g., rehabilitation of drug addicts). He reasoned that the organizations must anticipate the disruption of research, their operations, and the research participants' lives in the event of individuals' records being forcibly disclosed to a law-enforcement agency.

That people will object to a researcher's disclosure of private, sensitive information, whether disclosure is real *or* imagined, is also clear. Cases of disclosure in anthropology have helped illuminate this. For example, publication by "West" on "Plainville" of the late 1930s led easily to deductive disclosure of the town's identity and apparently to a great deal of information about individuals in that town becoming available. Gallaher's follow-up research on Plainville teaches us that discretion as well as privacy issues are important and that individuals will cooperate despite earlier breaches of confidentiality assurance (see Johnson's [1982] summary).

This and kindred work has led some anthropological and clinically oriented scholars to stress the reciprocity between respondent and researcher. According to them, respondents must somehow benefit from the research as compensation for the burdens engendered by cooperating in research. This view does not differ, in the abstract, from statistical researchers' interest in the use of monetary payments to respondents and the stress on interviewer competence. The perspective is also material to researchers' custom of offering feedback to the respondents on the general results of a survey or experiment or feedback on how the work is informative to the respondent about himself or herself. The provision of individual feedback is limited, however, by procedures that guarantee anonymity, so that one objective—reciprocity—is prevented by another—preserving privacy (Hormuth & Boruch, 1986).

Research on privacy and confidentiality has also suggested to Glazer (1982), among others, that the individual who responds to a survey question does not always have complete control of his or her *responses*. That is, the respondent's disclosure of private facts presents a risk, one that has received little attention. The risk, or perception of risk, results partly because of the trust built by the researcher and partly because inquiry is often nondirective. Glazer apparently holds that nondirective techniques are less risky (in this context) than are direct questions. We are aware of no formal research on the topic.

THE RESPONDENT'S KNOWLEDGEABILITY AND PRIVACY CONCERNS

An old Navy aphorism tells us, "Ten percent never get the word." Considering what the general population knows about censuses, surveys, and confidentiality, this may underestimate our collective ignorance. National probability sample surveys in the United Kingdom, for instance, show that in the 1970s about a third of those surveyed believed that census data were available to other government agencies in Britain and that a primary function of the census was to obtain individual's addresses (Bulmer, 1979). Neither belief is true.

Randomized field experiments in the United States also reveal a notable ignorance among respondents. Research overseen by the National Academy of Sciences, for example, suggested that more than a third of the respondents in an ordinary U.S. Bureau of the Census survey could not recall the "institution conducting the survey" or "privacy assurance" when they were asked about these immediately after being interviewed (Shaw et al., 1979). Specific assurances about the institution and about privacy had, in fact, been provided before each interview in the study. About half the respondents said they did not know whether census records were open to other government agencies; these records are in fact not available to others.

Similarly, sample surveys sponsored by the Internal Revenue Service (IRS) suggest that most adults questioned are not informed about rules that govern data sharing among federal agencies, including the IRS. Moreover, it is unclear how well people are able to distinguish statistical and administrative uses of individual records. For instance, nearly 40% of respondents were opposed to the IRS providing farm addresses to the Bureau of the Census to facilitate crop surveys. (See Panel on Confidentiality and Data Access, 1993, for a summary of the IRS surveys.)

Case studies of disrupted research also help illuminate local factual errors concerning privacy. For example, opponents arguing against studies of campus protest conducted by the American Council on Education (ACE) during the late 1960s (Boruch, 1971; Westin et al., 1972) alleged there was no assurance of confidentiality, when in fact there was. They averred that ACE was a government organization, though it is not, and that data allowed near-perfect prediction of who would engage in future protests—an absurd claim to anyone who understands statistics.

Similarly, in a Project Scope study of career development of high school students, critics of the study erroneously maintained that sex-related questions were being asked. The errors were magnified by press coverage and political concerns. "Whereas some . . . believed that Scope computers were connected to the CIA, others seemed convinced that they were connected to the Kremlin" (Tillery, 1967, p. 14). Related errors also emerged in the so-called Rip Van Winkle studies of children's aggression. Such errors did not have much effect on the study itself, apparently because the investigators were thoughtful and accessible to the communities concerned (Eron & Walder, 1961).

It is often easy for the sophisticated individual to exploit ignorance. Before every U.S. decennial census, for instance, some members of interest groups and politicians have claimed falsely that certain questions are being asked, for example, queries about the number of individuals sharing a bathroom. Interest groups usually build local support around a claim or a theme, such as that of Big Brother, that is *at times* fatuous.

INTERVIEWERS AND RESEARCHERS

Survey interviewers' attitudes are important in themselves and can affect the quality of information elicited from survey respondents (Groves & Magilavy, 1986).

Many interviewers recognize that they impose a burden on respondents, for example. Time restrictions and questionnaire technology are often taken for granted, but they do indeed help reduce demands on the respondent. Sharp and Frankel (1983), for example, found that respondents favored brief questionnaires, which also increased their willingness to participate in later surveys. The reduction in the potential for privacy-related harm is, to judge from recent work, also important to interviewers.

Stefan Hormuth, for example, compared interviews based on random-digit dialing (RDD) to interviews drawn from names selected from the telephone directory (Hormuth & Boruch, 1986). An effect he detected was that interviewers felt more comfortable when they knew there was no obvious way to determine identity of the respondent. The use of a telephone-book listing permits easy identification of the individual. Random-digit dialing does not, at least without a reverse directory.

Nelson and Hedrick (1983) studied researchers of drug abuse who had received legal assurances of the confidentiality of their respondents' records. They found that about a quarter of the researchers said that statutory protection mattered to them in the sense of allaying the anxieties of research staff members. They apparently felt that potential conflicts between scientific needs for information and judicial or administrative interests in appropriating the same information were eliminated for the researcher and for the research staff.

In the Hormuth work there does not appear to have been any appreciable difference in quality of data produced by interviewers working with RDD samples versus surveys based on a telephone directory. Some respondents in the Nelson-Hedrick sample, however, maintained that their research could not have been done well without the statutory provision of a testimonial privilege for the researcher and the staff.

It is reasonable to suppose that reducing interviewer and researcher discomfort also reduces the resources needed to cope with discomfort. A lower resource expenditure with no change in output, of course, means improved efficiency. No formal research on this kind of efficiency has apparently been carried out.

The Way People Behave

The thoughtful administrator and researcher know that individuals' opinions may imply little about behavior. How, in fact, do individuals behave when asked to respond to a survey when privacy may be an issue? What accounts for their behavior? Do individuals' opinions about privacy differ from their privacy-related behavior?

COOPERATION RATES IN SURVEYS

Most people cooperate in *well-designed* surveys, in the crude sense that they produce a response. As a matter of fact, cooperation rates in routine observational surveys in the United States are high both in absolute terms and relative to those in other countries: 70–85% is a lower bound for the best of these. For example, the Current Population Survey usually achieves at least a 90% response rate. The internal standards for quality assurance at the National Center for Education Statistics use a minimum response rate of 85% as a target.

Opinion surveys cited earlier, for example, suggest that sexual practices head the list of topics that are regarded as sensitive in surveys in the United States and elsewhere. Questions about sexual behavior and attitudes have nonetheless become important to address on account of AIDS. Syntheses of survey results have then been developed for a National Academy of Sciences Panel on Evaluating AIDS Prevention Programs and reported by Coyle, Boruch, and Turner (1991).

Two standards for cooperation were used in the Coyle et al. (1991) report: agreement to answer questions and validity of the answer. Despite the sensitivity of the topic, AIDS and sexual behavior, the published reports of 15 large-scale surveys had cooperation rates in the 50–80% range. The higher response rates are doubtless a function of high quality in design of ques-

TABLE 3

Reasons for Nonparticipation in Most Recent Survey

	Mail	Telephone	Personal Visit
Total mentions/surveys not participated in	218	154	47
Lack of interest, or inconvenience	165	80	27
Topic uninteresting or inappropriate	43	20	4
General lack of interest, didn't want to bother	62	23	11
Oversight	31	. . .	. . .
Too busy	21	23	9
Inconvenient time	. . .	12	. . .
Other	8	2	3
Objection to approach or content	36	65	16
Topic objectionable	14	11	7
Questions poor	6	1	0
Method objectionable	1	23	1
Distrust			
In research	2	3	2
Of interviewer	. . .	26	. . .
Of sponsor	5	. . .	1
Dislike of interviewer	. . .	. . .	2
Purpose objectionable	8	1	3
Miscellaneous, including no answer and don't know	17	9	3

Note: Derived from Shaw et al. (1979). From Turner, 1982.

tions, interview protocols, and procedures, selection of interviewers, and so on. But they are also explicable in terms of the respondent's interest in the survey's topic. Uninteresting topics, to judge from data in tables 2 and 3, account for a sizable fraction of refusals to participate in a survey. The range in response rates is substantial partly because the surveys differed in design and execution (see Turner, 1991, for deeper analysis).

Calculating the participation rate in a survey on a sensitive topic is an instructive but crude indicator for understanding how people behave. Any response-rate estimate, whether high or low, may be misleading in that individuals' willingness to agree to complete an interview or questionnaire implies little about the truthfulness of their responses to the questions. To the extent that responses are truthful despite privacy being a concern, it seems fair to conclude that the individual, on balance, considers the report to the (arguably trustworthy) researcher more important than privacy.

Methodological researchers have developed a substantial body of analytic and empirical research on the quality of information provided by individuals. This is not the proper place to review it generally; nor can it be reviewed briefly and well when the focus is on privacy. To illustrate the approach and some findings, consider the following.

Methodological studies of the quality of response in the NHSDA have focused partly on prevalence of reporting of use as an indicator of quality (Turner, Leffler, & Gfroerer, 1992a). Mode of survey administration, notably comparing prevalence reported on self-administered questionnaires versus prevalence reported to interviewers was a special focus of one such study. Controlled tests of each mode in the NHSDA yielded evidence that self-report questionnaires, sent by the respondent to the survey firm, resulted in higher prevalence estimates for cocaine and marijuana use. Estimates were roughly 1.5–2.5 times greater when respondents employed the self-report inventory relative to estimates made on the basis of responses to personal interviewer. This finding is consistent with similar comparisons in other research (Turner et al., 1992b). It can be taken as evidence for a peculiar but large effect of questionnaires versus interviewers despite similar privacy guarantees in each and an indicator of how "degree of anonymity" may be interpreted by respondents.

Individuals also vary in cooperativeness in their permitting the transfer of their research records from one organization to another and consenting to reinterview. For example, the National Center for Health Statistics (1987) asked individuals who had been involved in surveys run by the U.S. Bureau of the Census in the late 1970s to comment on transferring and linking their old research records with new interview records and completing a separate health examination. More than 90% of those in the original sample were traced, and more than 90% of those traced provided comment. Similarly, the Survey of Economic Opportunity, run originally by the U.S. Office of Economic Opportunity, was transferred for longitudinal follow-up surveys to the Institute for Social Research. Again, consent for the action was sought and by and large obtained from the targeted respondents. Boruch and Cecil (1979) give examples of similarly positive results in consent-based verification of research records by the U.S. General Accounting Office, school-based surveys of children, and others.

By way of contrast, recall that West Germany's 1982 census was delayed on account of a partly sham privacy controversy. Sweden's cooperation rate in government surveys was also lower in 1985 partly, it is believed, as a consequence of alleged data sharing between a survey research organization and a tax organization. Concerns about public perception now prevent the U.S. Bureau of the Census from conducting further linkage studies with the IRS, studies that could illuminate the statistical structure of errors in records generated by both organizations.

The privacy-related factors that enhance public cooperation in surveys have become clearer partly from large-scale randomized trials. Two national controlled experiments on the level of confidentiality assurance, one undertaken by the Bureau of the Census and the Institute for Social Research and monitored by the National Academy of Sciences (Shaw et al., 1979), and one designed by Eleanor Singer (1978) and the National Opinion Research Center, are pertinent. Shaw et al. (1979) provided evidence of how level of assurance counts. The effect of assurance is weak. A sample size of 2,500, for instance, is large enough to pick up a trend, but it is too small to produce reliable estimates of the magnitude of the effect for any pairwise comparison of increasing confidentiality assurance levels. The Census Bureau's work on five levels of assurance suggests refusal rates ranging from 2 to 3% (for the lowest assurance), for the kinds of questions asked in the Current Population Survey, that is, relatively innocuous ones. This order of magnitude of the fraction is small, but the number in the population that is affected is large and so the effect has been deemed important to those who must construct census policy.

To judge from respondents' reports, the variables that matter most to them include the innocuousness of the questions that are posed and good interviewers' conduct. Repeated follow-ups have remarkable effects in mail surveys.

These results are not entirely consistent with those of Singer (1978): different levels of confidentiality assurance produced no discernible differences in overall cooperation rate. The level of assurance appeared to influence cooperation in answering sensitive rather than innocuous items.

What do we know about noncooperation on account of privacy concerns? To judge from surveys of noncooperators, around 3–5% are likely to be too busy or to be unreceptive to any inquiry regardless of subject, or at least to say they are too busy. Even for fertility surveys, privacy concerns account for less than 4% of nonrespondents.

Trends in nonresponse rate are important, however. Steeh (1981) examined the nonresponse rates during 1952–1979 for two well-known continuing studies at the Survey Research Center: the National Election Studies and the Surveys of Consumer Attitudes. In both surveys, she found that the nonresponse rate rose notably, from 5–8% in 1952 to 15–22% in the late 1970s. This trend was particularly strong in urban areas. The nonresponse rate in these areas in the 1979 National Election Studies was just under 30%. Since the noninterview rate remained relatively constant during this period, most of these nonrespondents represent outright refusals or terminated interviews.

EPISODIC DISRUPTION

Serious disruption of surveys may be based on sham issues. For example, in a case described in Sieber (1982), a Harlem-based community organization attempted to organize resistance to a health survey run by Columbia University. The issue the organization raised, "trickery in the survey," was eventually perceived as phony by respondents, partly as a consequence of the conscientiousness of the researchers and partly as a consequence of the incompetence of the antagonistic organization. There were few negative effects on the survey in this instance.

Oyen's examination of the controversy over Project Metropolitan in Oslo in 1964 is one of the best of its kind and illustrates some remarkable parallels with similar episodes in the United States (Oyen 1965, 1966, 1976). In a cooperative longitudinal study involving Norway, Denmark, and Sweden, a large sample of children was to be tracked from age 11 onward to discover how their views of social class developed and changed, influenced their vocational choice and occupational mobility, and were linked to their achievement.

Despite the approval of the Oslo school board and assurances that the data would be used only for research purposes, protests against the study were aired by a major Oslo newspaper, *Afterposten*, and others, over the radio, and in the Norwegian parliament. About 10% of the children's parents put their complaints into writing. The project was directed by sociologists, who drew fire partly because "sociologist" was evidently easily confused at the time with "socialist." Further, "while several critics made claims about the evils of sociology, some felt that the proposed research reminded them too much of psychology and thus fired their charges at the psychologists."

Here, as in other incidents, media coverage magnified errors. References were made to Kinsey's studies of sexual behavior, for instance, even though Project Metropolitan involved no questions about sex. Provocative references were made to "human experimentation," when, in fact, the goal was merely to survey students. The more direct and legitimate concerns that privacy was being invaded, that the research itself harmed the target population, and that the research data would be misused by corrupt politicians or sociologists were, in Oyen's judgment, part of a general public interest in the legitimacy of sociological research. The study was aborted in Norway, but continued in Denmark and Sweden with more than 20 thousand participants (Janson, 1975; Magnusson, Duner, & Zetterblom, 1975).

Project Metropolitan became controversial again in Sweden in 1986. The project was attacked on grounds that respondents were not told data were being accumulated on them and that they did not understand that their survey data were being linked periodically with administrative records. Here, as in the earlier controversy and as in U.S. debates over privacy in social research, errors and hyperbole in journalistic reporting were not uncommon. Reuters' Stockholm-based reporter, for instance, announced that the respondents were guinea pigs when in fact no experiments were being carried out (*Chicago Tribune*, 11 February 1986). Mistakes or poor judgment by researchers complicated matters still further: informed consent for record linkage appears not to have been sought despite the apparent legal requirement to do so. Some respondents interviewed by the press said they were unaware that data were accumulated even though they were periodically provided information in response to queries over this 20-year term of study. Organized opposition to the project was mounted amid public debates on the propriety of the work (Dalenius, 1986a, 1986b).

Serious disruptions of surveys, despite such episodes, have been infrequent in the United States, Sweden, and other democratic countries. One of the plausible reasons for their relative infrequency is the social researchers' and government's wariness about topics that may have lead to controversy. Controversial matters such as mental illness, AIDS, tax payments by affluent individuals or organizations, and so on are *not* often the subject of high-quality field research in the behavioral and social sciences.

A second plausible reason for the infrequent disruption of field research in recent years may lie with the oversight activity of institutional review boards (IRBS), which can prevent gratuitously controversial studies by helping ensure that the research is competently carried out relative to professional standards. A final reason lies perhaps in government rules (considered later) bearing on access to identifiable administrative records and the special protection for research records generated by the law and the re-

TABLE 4
Simple Variation on Randomized Response

Sample A

    $\frac{1}{6}$: Did you cheat on last year's tax returns?

    $\frac{5}{6}$: Did you have toast for breakfast last week?

Sample B

    Did you have toast for breakfast last week?

$P_A(Y)$ = Proportion of "Yes" responses observed in sample A

P_C = Unknown portion of people who affirm cheating

P_T = Fraction of those having toast in sample A, estimated using sample B

$$P_A(Y) = \frac{1}{6} P_C + \frac{5}{6} P_T$$
$$P_C = [P_A(Y) - \frac{5}{6} P_T] 6$$

searchers' special procedure for ensuring confidentiality. The technical procedures are considered next.

STATISTICAL METHODS TO ENSURE PRIVACY: FIELD TESTS

Warner's (1965) randomized response technique was a major breakthrough in ensuring the privacy of individuals in direct, personal interviews. Ignored for a time, analytic work on and empirical tests of the approach were undertaken during 1976–1986 by statisticians such as Dalenius in the United States and Sweden, Bourke in Ireland, Goodstadt in Canada, and experts in the United States such as social psychologists Dawes and Smith (1985) and Locander, Sudman, and Bradburn (1976).

In a simple variation on the approach, illustrated in table 4, the interviewer simultaneously presents a sensitive inquiry to each individual in a large sample, for example, "Did you cheat on your income taxes last year?" and an innocuous one, for example, "Did you have toast for breakfast last week?" (The true relation of the former and the latter must be zero, i.e., toast eating and tax cheating should be unrelated.) Each individual, on being presented with the questions, is then instructed to roll a die and to respond to the first question if a one or a two shows on the die and to the second question if a three, four, five, or six appears. The respondent is also told to refrain from giving the interviewer any indication of which question was answered.

When the process is carried out on two large samples of individuals and the odds on asking each question are changed from one sample to the next, one can estimate the proportion of individuals in the population who have cheated on their income tax and the proportion of toast eaters. In particular, from the laws of probability, the odds on answering one or the other question in each sample, and the observed proportion of affirmative responses, one can develop two simultaneous independent equations in two unknowns that are easily solved.

The technique permits social scientists to estimate the incidence of sensitive properties of individuals. More important here, the technique results in no disclosure, to the interviewer or anyone else, of any specific information about a particular respondent. There is no deterministic link between the state of the individual and his or her response. The major disadvantages of the approach are that large samples are generally needed for precise estimation and of course the process of eliciting information is more complicated.

At best, the approach reduces embarrassment or distress associated with questions. The extent to which it does so is measurable in principle. In practice, the results of more than two dozen field studies suggest that the method *sometimes* works in the sense of increasing quality of the data (table 5). It *always* works in the sense of assuring the respondent of privacy: neither the interviewer nor the researcher knows the respondent's true state.

For example, study of drug use among Canadian high school students (Goodstadt, Cook, & Gruson, 1978) involved a randomized field test of alternative ways to elicit information about students' drug abuse. One way consisted of the randomized response method. The sensitive question concerned drugs, and the inoffensive one concerned legal forms of recreation. Students were remarkably more willing to answer questions under the randomized response scheme. Mean reported drug use was significantly higher with this method than with direct questions.

Similarly encouraging results were obtained in studies sponsored by the U.S. Army. In one large experiment, for instance, servicemen were asked about their use of illicit drugs, racial attitudes and race-related behavior, and military attitudes. Comparing a regime of anonymous response plus statistical protection against a program of anonymous response, Reaser, Hartsock, and Hoehn (1975) found that the respondents were more than twice as likely to admit undesirable behavior when the randomized response device was used.

In Canada (Krotki & Fox, 1974), Taiwan (Chi, Chow, & Rider, 1972; Liu, Chow, & Mosley, 1975), and the United States, comparisons have also been made to understand how responses to direct questions about fertility control coupled with a promise of confidentiality differ from responses to

TABLE 5

Field Results of Randomized Response Methods

	Sample Size for RR	Percentage Response to RR	Percentage Responses to Standard	Crude Reduction in Response Bias
Abernathy, Greenberg, Horvitz	3,113	97	NR	YES
I-cheng, Chow, Rider	1,021	89	89	YES
Liu, Chen, Chow	353	85	NR	YES
Krotki and Fox	352	97	73	INC
Shirnizu and Bonham	9,797	99	NR	YES
Goodstadt and Gruson	431	95	87	YES
Brown and Harding	1,100	NR	NR	INC
Brown (mail)	2,114	18–50	32–65	INC
Reaser, Hartsock, Hoehn (mail)	2,400	23	26	YES
Bartth and Sandler	64	100	NR	YES
Berman, McCombs, Boruch	156	100	100	INC
Dawes	270	100	NR	NR
Zdep and Rhodes	995	98	75–85	YES
Locander, Sudman, Bradburn	233	60–78	48–90	INC
Folsom	423	100	. . .	. . .
Erickson	76	97	NR	INC
Fidler and Kleinknecht	132	100	100*	YES
Illinois Inst. of Technology	1,200	100	NR	INC
Kim and Flueck (1)	54	NR	NR	NR
Kim and Flueck (2)	50	NR	NR	NR
Fox and Tracy	530	NR	NR	YES
Aitken and Bonneville	1,825	NR	NR	YES

Note: The gross number of respondents involved in a survey using the methods is reported in the first column. Cooperation, registered by crude response rate, is indexed in the second column for the randomized response sample. When an estimate of response rates for direct questions or some other standard is available and reported, that is listed in column three. *NR* implies that the information was not included in the report. The fourth column contains a judgment, based on the published report, as to whether the use of randomized response led to reduced bias in reporting by respondents. *INC* indicates that results are inconlusive. *YES* indicates a clear reduction in bias, relative to a standard. Ellipses indicate that the study was not designed to provide the information. See text for citations for topics covered in each study. References are given in Boruch and Cecil except for the last three studies.

questions that use such statistical devices for ensuring confidentiality. The results favor randomized response more often than not, and at least one postinterview survey of attitudes suggests that many respondents are inclined to trust the method and to believe that their friends would too.

A study of responses to questions about child abuse yielded results that further support the idea that at least some people are more candid in reporting when the mechanism for preserving confidentiality, such as randomized response, is clear. Zdep and Rhodes (1977) found respondents about five times more likely to admit corporal punishment of their children under the randomized-response method than under a sealed-envelope approach. Refusal rate was considerably lower with the statistical technique, which alone could account for the difference.

The methods are novel, and some experts are skeptical about their effectiveness. Bergman, Hanve, and Rapp (1978), for instance, argue that "it appears doubtful if a randomized response technique . . . has any advantages in their situation," namely, their study of cooperation rates in Swedish surveys of living conditions. In fact, using the randomized-response device appeared, at times, to undermine response rate at worst and complicate research at best. Tests on college students' responses to questions about drug use, seeking psychiatric assistance, and other questions, for example, led to mixed results at the University of Nebraska (Berman, McCombs, & Boruch, 1977). The problem seems to be tied to the novelty of the statistical methods, the extent to which interviewers use them properly, and the extent to which college students are proud of behaviors that others would regard as distressing.

In a larger and more sophisticated field experiment, Locander et al. (1976) compared the randomized-response method with three other methods: face-to-face interviews, telephone interviews, and self-administered questionnaires. The randomized-response method provided more accurate estimates for sensitive questions about drunk driving and bankruptcy, slightly better estimates for low-threat questions on voter registration, and poorer estimates for questions with socially desirable associations such as primary voting or having a library card. *Better* is defined as estimates of the incidence of a sensitive trait that is higher than the estimate provided by alternatives. A "poorer" estimate is defined as one that inflates the incidence of a socially desirable trait or behavior.

Judging from the results of all the field tests listed in table 4, the conditions under which randomized approaches perform well cannot always be anticipated. The methods must be tested in pilot studies before being adopted in main surveys.

The randomized-response idea invites development, which is partly the source of its scientific merit. Development has been frequent. There are variations for multicategory and ranked responses to questions. The approach has been coupled to Guttman scaling of attitudes by social psychologists (Dawes & Smith, 1985). It has been adapted to settings in which continuous or ranked responses to questions (e.g., How *much* did you steal?) are wanted (e.g., by Bourke, 1982, among others). It is mathematically possible to permit one to estimate relations between variables measured using randomized response and variables measured with more direct techniques. Statistical tests of hypotheses based on such data are possible. A monograph giving a thoughtful, practice-oriented, treatment has been produced by Fox and Tracy (1986).

Related technical devices have also been invented to ensure confidentiality of identifiable records in data processing, in release of statistical tables, and in release of public-use data tapes. We are unaware of published empirical research on these devices though there is abundant analytic work (e.g., Dalenius, 1986a, 1986b).

Government Rules

Four kinds of government rules reflect how public representatives and civil servants have handled privacy in research contexts. The first involves statutes, regulations, and policies that restrict access to individuals or to information on individuals that is maintained by administrative government agencies. The second pertains to a smaller class of statutes and so forth that provide special legal protection to *research* records on identifiable individuals who furnish information for research purposes. The third and fourth types bear on sharing data in the interest of legitimate statistical research.

RESTRICTED ACCESS TO PEOPLE AND TO INFORMATION
Researchers may at times be prohibited by government from eliciting information from individuals under the government's jurisdiction. As an extreme example, consider an ordinance issued in 1940 by the Nazi government in occupied Krakow (Republic of Poland, 1941):

(1) The carrying out of statistical inquiries . . . is the exclusive privilege of the Governor General's Bureau of Statistics

(2) Collection of statistics by any other body is subject to . . . express permission

(3) Whoever, either deliberately or through negligence, shall, without having received permission . . . conduct a survey . . . shall be punished by fine and imprisonment for not more than one year.

The United States has not been visited with similarly severe problems. But the freedom of inquiry that social scientists in the United States now enjoy has had an uneven history. Edward Shils, for example, writing in a 1938 issue of the *Annals of the American Academy of Political and Social Science*, reported on faculty members who were fired for conducting surveys about sexual mores of college students and producing books on the topic (Shils, 1938). The same issue of the *Annals* reported that during the 1930s considerable pressure was brought to bear on sociologists carrying out (then) controversial research on the prohibition of sale of alcoholic beverages and on economists doing work on public utilities.

Governments in many societies have restricted researchers' and others' access to records collected by government for administrative purposes, that is, for making decisions about individuals. The restrictions are important insofar as they preserve individual privacy and influence the extent to which legitimate research can be based on the records. Some empirical research on researchers' access to individuals has been undertaken at the macropolitical level by legal scholars such as Flaherty (1980) and sociologists such as Mochman and Muller (1979). For instance, Flaherty (1986) reviewed the implementation of national privacy legislation to understand how government surveillance of individuals is controlled by agencies such as data-inspection boards.

Flaherty, among other experts, does not always distinguish between administrative record systems and statistical research systems, despite the precedent set by the U.S. Privacy Protection Study Commission, among others. Partly as a consequence, what appears to be legitimate research, such as French efforts to construct a screening system for high-risk infants, is lumped with surveillance systems that are designed to track individuals for police purposes (Flaherty, 1986). Census surveys in various countries are often similarly regarded as surveillance devices. One of the reasons Flaherty chooses not to distinguish administrative and research systems is that, until recently, national laws frequently did not do so. The distinction is made in neither the French nor the Swedish privacy acts, for instance.

Researchers have periodically undertaken studies on the extent to which administrative records maintained by governments are accessible for statistical research purposes. A sociologist, for instance, may be interested in examining records on child abuse held by a state protection agency in the interest of understanding cross-generation influences on child-rearing. Understanding which agencies permit access to such administrative records for research purposes and which do not is critical in the particular instance. This understanding is important, more generally, in developing a portrait of how privacy-based access rules vary across government entities.

The Bureau of Justice Statistics of the U.S. Department of Justice, for instance, has sponsored legal studies and field research to illuminate access rules in the criminal-justice arena. The bureau's reports, summarized tersely in Reiss and Boruch (1991), cover the public's and researchers' access to such records. For instance, a survey of 160 agencies suggested that, for about two thirds of these units, the laws under which they operate contain explicit provisions that enable the researcher to use data on identifiable individuals for legitimate research purposes (U.S. Department of Justice Bureau of Justice Statistics, 1982a, 1982b, 1988).

The bureau has also supported surveys of the *practices* of these agencies, that is, how they behaved when asked to supply records for legitimate statistical research within the constraints of law. For agencies that operate under statutes that provide for researcher access, the results suggest that a legitimate researcher's failure to obtain access would be unusual and infrequent. In the state agencies whose governing laws have no explicit provision for research, however, about half the agencies said they refused all requests by researchers.

Such empirical work suggests that public concerns about privacy have not led to the creation of laws that uniformly restrict researchers' access to administrative records in criminal justice. More to the point, privacy concerns in this arena take a second place at times to public interests in reliable research on germane topics.

Records on individual juveniles who come into contact with the courts are usually maintained by the relevant state court system. Such records are not a matter of public information; disclosure is specified by state laws. Until recently, little research had been done on the statutes and no in-depth research appears to have been conducted on whether these laws provide access to records for research purposes.

A compendium of laws bearing on release of such records has, however, been summarized by the National School Safety Center (1991). Though designed to inform administrators in schools, courts, law-enforcement agencies, and so on about who is legally mandated to access individual records in each state, the compendium is a useful source on access for research or statistical purposes. We learn, for instance, that the laws of Colorado, Florida, Idaho, Iowa, Maryland, Mississippi, Missouri, South Dakota, Virginia, and West Virginia contain a provision for research on deliquency. West Virginia's law is illustrative. It prohibits disclosure of an identifiable record to anyone but the child, court and government service agencies responsible for the child, and "a person doing research provided [that] identifying information is left out" (National School Safety Center, 1991, p. 60). No empirical study appears to have been done on which research studies have capitalized on access to the records or how the provisions came into being.

What is known about fields other than criminal justice in which administrative records might be useful in research but may be governed by rules that impede the researcher's access to the information? Robbin and Jozefacki (1983) were exceptional in conducting well-designed surveys on individual state regulations of social scientists' access to state health and welfare records. Their results imply that researchers are *not* often recognized explicitly in the laws governing access to such records. Of 18 pertinent laws of the state of Illinois, for example, only two provide explicit legal authority for access to the records by social researchers: they concern child abuse and neglect and vital statistics records on births and deaths. The state of Nebraska has 13 statutes on administrative records that are relevant in principle to research on child and family services, justice, and other areas. Only one statute, pertaining to records on child abuse, provides access authority to researchers.

The matter is similarly complicated in the federal arena. One of the few exceptions includes federal law and regulation on the use of drug-treatment records. Under the Food, Drug, and Cosmetic Act and the regulations embodied in Title 21 of the Code of Federal Regulations, such records can be used for audits and program evaluations or research projects, provided that privacy of individuals on whom records are maintained is protected.

PRIVILEGE STATUTES, SUBPOENAS, AND THE COURTS

"Testimonial privilege" statutes are designed to protect the researcher who elicits sensitive information from individuals and the individuals themselves. The existence of such laws indicates how one public interest, learning something about people in general, is balanced against another, learn-

TABLE 6

Statutes Providing Grants of Qualified Immunity for Research Information and Their Provisions

Statute	1	2	3	4	5	6	7
Public Health Services Act Sections 303(a) and 308(d) Pub. L. No. 91-513, 42 U.S.C.A. § 242a(a)	Y	N	N	Y	Y	Y	Y
Crime Control Act of 1973. Pub. L. No. 93-83, 42 U.S.C.A. § 3771	Y	Y	Y	Y	Y	N	Y
Juvenile Justice and Delinquency Prevention Act of 1977. Pub. L. No. 95-115	Y	Y	Y	Y	Y	N	Y
Controlled Substances Act, Section 502(c) Publ. L. No. 91-513, 21 U.S.C.A. § 872c	Y	N	N	Y	Y	Y	N
Drug Abuse Office & Treatment Act Pub. L. No. 92-255, Amended, § 408 Pub. L. No. 93-282, 21 U.S.C. § 1175a	Y	Y	Y	YC	N	YC	Y
Alcohol Abuse Act Pub. L. No. 93-282, 45 U.S.C.A. § 4582a	Y	Y	Y	YC	N	YC	Y
Privacy of Research Records Act	Y	Y	Y	Y	Y	Y	Y
Hawkins-Stafford Act, Pub. L. No. 100-297	Y	Y	Y	Y	Y	N	Y

Notes: Columns are as follows: 1, protects identification if research data; 2, protects identifiable information; 3, automatic rather than authorized; 4, immunity from administrative inquiry; 5, immunity from legislative inquiry; 6, immunity from legislative inquiry; 7, provisions for secondary analysis, in regulations or law. Abbreviations are as follows: Y, yes, covered explicitly; N, not, covered explicitly; YC, court order required for disclosure.

ing about a particular individual. These laws have been the object of considerable analytic research on how and how well they protect respondent privacy. Less often, they have been the subject of empirical research designed to learn how and how well the statutes work.

Table 6 augments study of the topic by Boruch and Cecil (1979) and summarizes the federal statutes that protect researchers and respondents and provides data on the extent to which each law meets certain legal standards. Section 524(a) of the Omnibus Crime Control and Safe Streets Act, for example, provides a constrained guarantee that research records generated on identifiable respondents will not be appropriated for nonresearch purposes. In other words, the information "shall be immune from legal process." There are related provisions in the Controlled Substances Act (1988) and the Public Health Service Act (1988). The "nonresearch purposes" prohibited by the laws include the criminal prosecution of a respondent on the basis of the information an individual may provide to a researcher. Figure 1 illustrates a confidentiality certificate issued under the Public Health Service Act. It was used to protect privacy of respondents who were willing to cooperate in research on drug involvement in traffic accidents.

The Hawkins-Stafford Act is among the most recent laws that include special provisions on privacy. The law covers research data obtained from students, teachers, and so forth by the National Center for Education Statistics (NCES). Modeled after privacy law that governs the statistical research of the U.S. Bureau of the Census, the Hawkins-Stafford Act is remarkable in offering assurances that heretofore have not been made in education statistics.

The relevant section of the law holds that, except as provided, no person may:

(i) use an individually identifiable information furnished under . . . the section for any purpose other than statistical purposes for which it was provided.

(ii) make any statistical publication whereby the data furnished by any particular person . . . can be identified.

(iii) permit anyone other than the individuals authorized by the Commissioner to examine the individual reports.

Further, Section B of the law requires that "copies of . . . reports . . . shall be immune from legal process, and shall not without the consent of the individual concerned, be admitted as evidence or used for any purpose in any action, suit, or other judicial or administrative proceeding." This protection extends to contractors to the NCES (Section D).

The statute ensures that courts cannot compel government employees or contractors to disclose information that individuals provide for educational research. It covers sanctions against researchers who disclose individually identifiable information collected under the act.

FIGURE 1

CONFIDENTIALITY CERTIFICATE
No. DA-93-45

issued to

EMPLOYEES OF THE RESEARCH TRIANGLE INSTITUTE
AND OTHER PARTICIPANTS

conducting research known as

"TRAINING AND EMPLOYMENT PROGRAM (TEP)"

In accordance with the provisions of section 301(d) of the Public Health Service Act (42 U.S.C. 241(d)), this Certificate is issued in response to the request of the Principal Investigator, Michael L. Dennis, Ph.D., Center for Social Research and Policy Analysis, Research Triangle Institute, P.O. Box 12194, Research Triangle Park, North Carolina 27709, to protect the privacy of research subjects by withholding their identities from all persons not connected with the research. Dr. Dennis is primarily responsible for the conduct of this research.

Under the authority vested in the Secretary of Health and Human Services by that section, all persons who:

1. are employed by the Research Triangle Institute and its contractors and cooperating agencies; and

2. have, in the course of that employment, access to the information which would identify individuals who are the subjects of a research project entitled "Training and Employment Program (TEP);"

are hereby authorized to protect the privacy of the individuals who are the subjects of that research by withholding their names and other identifying characteristics from all persons not connected with the conduct of that research.

The overall objective of this study is to compare the effectiveness of two levels of increased vocational services in a randomly controlled trial with 960 subjects in three methadone treatment programs in Buffalo, NY; Pittsburgh, PA; and San Jose, CA. The specific aims of

FIGURE 1 continued

the application are to: (1) determine the effectiveness of enhancing standard methadone treatment with vocational services in terms of educational attainment, employment, earnings, ability to pay for treatment, drug use, needle use, criminal behavior, psychological functioning, and social functioning; (2) determine the relative effectiveness of two levels of enhanced vocational services in terms of the preceding outcomes; (3) estimate the cost-effectiveness and benefit-cost ratio of standard methadone treatment and treatment with enhanced vocational services in terms of the preceding outcomes and as a payback mechanism for treatment; and (4) determine the relative cost-effectiveness and benefit-cost ratio of two levels of enhanced vocational services in terms of employment.

As provided in section 301(d) of the Public Health Service Act (42 U.S.C. 241(d)):

"Persons so authorized to protect the privacy of such individuals may not be compelled in any Federal, State, or local civil, criminal, administrative, legislative, or other proceedings to identify such individuals."

This authorization is applicable to all information obtained pursuant to the research project entitled, "Training and Employment Program (TEP), NIDA grant no. 1 RO1 DA-07964-01," which could identify the individuals who are the respondents in the research conducted under that research project.

This Certificate does not represent an endorsement of the research project by the Department of Health and Human Services.

The Certificate is effective upon date of the commencement of the research project and will expire at the end of March 1996. The protection afforded by this Confidentiality Certificate is permanent with respect to subjects who participate in the research during any time the Certificate is in effect.

(dated 12/9/85)   (signed)
                        Richard A. Millstein
                        Acting Director
                        National Institute on Drug Abuse

At least three aspects of the protection provided in the Hawkins-Stafford Act are remarkable: extension of protection to organizational data when organizational and individual data are comingled in a data set; the loophole in protection arising from the exemption for the specific survey that the American Counsel on Education was interested in, resulting in a retreat to the inadequate protection of the Privacy Act for records in this particular survey; and the greater willingness of NCES (as compared with the Bureau of the Census) to experiment with off-site licensing agreements as a means of permitting access to restricted identifiable data (see Newton & Pullin, 1991).

No empirical research has apparently been undertaken on the effect, effectiveness, or ramifications of this act, despite its importance in educational statistical research that costs well over $50 million annually in the United States. The little that is understood about this act and others is based on the analytic work summarized in table 6.

How do individual states protect the researcher engaged in legitimate research on sensitive topics and respondents? Charles Knerr's (1982) survey showed that about 28 of the 50 states enacted laws that protect respondents in research on substance abuse. Nebraska is not included on his list; Illinois is. There is spotty coverage of an assortment of other research topics. One New York statute is remarkable, for instance, in that it protects psychiatric research records.

Subpoenas of a researcher's records on identifiable research respondents are an indirect indicator of official attitudes toward the privacy of the respondents and social research. "Official" here means the courts, certain administrative agencies that can issue a subpoena (e.g., a district attorney's office), state legislatures, and Congress.

Until the 1970s, little was understood about subpoenas, the legal appropriation and use of research records on identifiable individuals. Analyses of laws and their sequelae have been undertaken by Boruch and Cecil (1979) and Gray and Melton (1985), among others. At least one field survey has illuminated how legal privilege is awarded and used. Consider the special case of privilege under §502(c) of the Controlled Substances Act. Nelson and Hedrick (1983) found that *no* federal agency refused the confidentiality grant authorizing researchers to withhold identifiers on their respondents. Eighty-seven researchers had received the grant during 1971–1976. Seven of the researchers who were surveyed by Nelson and Hedrick were approached by government agencies during their projects to disclose respondent information. They could and did refuse to disclose it on legal grounds. About 25% of the researchers said they could not have done the work without the privilege.

The benefit of a confidentiality grant does not lie solely in ensuring the cooperation of potential research participants. More than half the researchers who provided information to Nelson and Hedrick said their respondents would have cooperated without the limited statutory guarantee of respondents' privacy. On the other hand, about a third of the researchers viewed the legal grant as critical in gaining cooperation from institutions that control access to the individuals on whom the institution maintains records. Federal, state, and local government agencies, for example, exercise control over records on students, prisoners, and others, and the agencies must attend to law on privacy or confidentiality. Few of Nelson and Hedrick's researchers acknowledged, incidentally, that the privilege was helpful in gaining approval from IRBS.

Charles Knerr (1982) also surveyed researchers who were subpoenaed to determine how the privacy of the researchers' respondents may have been threatened by legal appropriation of records. He identified 13 major episodes of subpoenas issued since the mid-1960s. Seven of these resulted in a court's quashing the subpoena or negotiating a termination of the request for records. In the remaining cases, records were produced or the researchers were imprisoned, or both.

Three attempts to legally appropriate research records on identifiable individuals have received considerable attention from researchers and legal scholars. The case studies of these episodes are summarized briefly in what follows.

Case: The Graduated Work Incentive Experiments. The New Jersey Negative Income Tax Experiment (Kershaw & Small, 1972) generated individual records containing identification of respondents in the research and limited information about them. The research-related material had been elicited under a promise of confidentiality. Initially, disclosure by subpoena was compelled for records on fewer than 35 research respondents (of over 1,000) in Mercer County NJ. The disclosure was followed by a subpoena of complete records.

Disclosures at the first site, made of 14 records during a grand-jury investigation of alleged fraud and during congressional hearings on the experiment, apparently had little effect on the conduct of the experiment. There were no cases of subsequent respondent loss directly traceable to the investigation. The subsequent release of the identities of 18 families participating in the experiment by a welfare officer in Passaic County, however, did "upset a number of respondents," who then refused to continue to participate in the project.

Case: The Woodlawn Project. A second pertinent case involved a government-supported community-action program. The Woodlawn Project attempted to use youth gang structure as a base for a community-service organization, and gang members were offered the opportunity to participate in a related manpower-training program. No explicit promise of confidentiality was made initially to gang members from whom information was elicited. No formal demands for a confidentiality assurance were made by gang members at the beginning of the project.

The first threat of disclosure was induced by a congressional subcommittee's subpoena of all records pertaining to the project. The "administrative and fiscal documents" were shown to an investigatory agent and copied. A second subpoena demanded records of attendance at training sessions and the researchers' related observational records. According to Dr. Irving Spergel, director of the study, "The records taken were statistical observation forms containing data on attendance and comments about general program activity," *not* records of identified individuals. Though individually identified records were not at issue, this first subpoena was followed by increased difficulty in eliciting further information from respondents.

The second subpoena made it impossible to continue the research. Both trainees and their employers expressed concern over public access to research data on identified individuals. Consequently, the principal investigator laid plans for terminating his research on the program. The training program itself, including the evaluation, was ended before completion, however, by the federal agency that had supported it.

This case, like others, is complicated by factors other than privacy or confidentiality, concerns that also helped produce disruption of research. Those factors included errors made by journalists and congressional representatives in reporting details about the conduct of the project and the program's status as a political football (Spergel, 1969; Walsh, 1969).

Knerr (1982) points out that the relatively low incidence of subpoena is not a good indicator of the pressure that is brought to bear on researchers. The Nelson-Hedrick survey revealed, for instance, that Newman's methadone maintenance program in New York "frequently" handled up to five requests a month for information on research participants from officials in government welfare departments, the Federal Bureau of Investigation, fire departments, and so on. While few of these involved formal legal action, Newman (1977) in one instance had to spend time in jail in defense of his records. Other, more recent cases are more important partly because they deal with requests that are not as easy to handle.

COMPELLED DISCLOSURE OF RESEARCH EVIDENCE IN CIVIL LITIGATION

In particular, there have been a number of civil-justice cases in which the courts sought to compel the production of confidential research information. Unlike the examples of subpoena in criminal cases cited by Knerr and others, these cases attempted to use research information as evidence in a tort suit alleging injury due to a faulty product.

For instance, in 1971, Dr. Arthur Herbst of the University of Chicago demonstrated a relationship between the development of a certain cancer in young women and the earlier ingestion of the drug diethylstilbestrol (DES) by their mothers during their pregnancies. To study the treatment of the disease Herbst developed a data registry collecting the medical records of women who had the cancer and information concerning their mothers' possible use of DES. All information was gathered under a promise of confidentiality.

Access to the data was sought by a DES manufacturer that was sued by women who alleged they were injured when their mothers ingested DES while pregnant, causing the plaintiffs to contract cancer some years later. Herbst's data registry contained the only evidence of a possible causal link between DES and the cancer. The manufacturer contended that it would be confronted by the published findings of Herbst and others concerning the relation between DES and cancer. Further, the manufacturer maintained that it must have access to the data to examine the findings critically and to cross-examine the plaintiffs' expert witnesses adequately. Herbst was not a witness in the case. He had refused to become personally involved in DES litigation, partly to avoid the likelihood of such intrusions into the data registry.

The lower court did not require the registry information to be released, citing the affidavits of physicians and medical researchers that stated they would no longer cooperate in the reporting of cases to the registry if confidentiality could not be ensured (*Andrews v. Eli Lilly & Co.*, 1983). Rather than jeopardize the flow of research information, the lower court permitted the research records to remain confidential.

The court of appeals, however, reversed this decision. It ordered some disclosure of research information (*Deitchman v. Squibb & Sons, 1984*). The appeals court emphasized the importance of the data in permitting the manufacturer to cross-examine the plaintiffs' experts on the data underlying their opinions. This court did not ignore the threat such a disclosure would pose to maintaining the research data. Indeed, it instructed the lower court to investigate ways to permit access to the information *and* to guard against a loss of confidentiality. Only disclosure of nonidentifying information was ordered, as well as information on the statistical methodology.

In a similar case in 1986 Irving Selikoff of Mount Sinai School of Medicine received a subpoena for 18,000 medical records, including raw data and identifiable responses to questionnaires, relating to two articles published in medical journals six years earlier. The articles asserted that smoking, combined with exposure to asbestos, heightens the risk of lung cancer. Tobacco manufacturers, who were defendants in a law suit charging that their products caused lung cancer, sought access to the data to verify the findings and cross-examine plaintiffs' experts. After much procedural wrangling, the federal courts permitted access to computer tapes on nonidentified respondents and supporting documentation from the published studies (*In re American Tobacco Co., 1989*). In these and similar cases (see *Farnsworth v. Procter & Gamble Co.*, 1985; *Lampshire v. Procter & Gamble*, 1982) courts struggle to fashion standards for disclosure that permit access to information critical to the resolution of litigation while avoiding burdens that would impede productive research activity.

The most difficult circumstance arises when the courts must decide whether access to such information should extend to sensitive information offered under a promise of confidentiality. In both *Deitchman* and *Farnsworth* the courts attempted to honor the spirit of such promises by stripping the research data of information that would make the records easily identifiable and entering an order prohibiting efforts to deduce the identity of the research participants.

Amendments to Rule 45 of the Federal Rules of Civil Procedure provide general standards for considering whether and under what conditions disclosure of such information should be compelled. First, the requesting party must demonstrate a "substantial need for the [research data] that cannot be otherwise met without undue hardship." While interpretation of these terms remains unclear, at a minimum they would seem to require a demonstration that requested information addresses an essential issue in the litigation and a conscientious but unsuccessful effort to find such information elsewhere. The research community can urge a more demanding standard, such as requiring some showing that the published account on which testimony is based is likely flawed in such a way as to undercut the validity of the findings. Second, the requesting party must ensure that the person responding to the subpoena will be "reasonably compensated." In addition to compensation for time and effort responding to the subpoena, some previous cases have included a degree of compensation for the cost of the original research and the extent of disruption of professional activities that will result from responding to the subpoena.

Finally, the amendment grants courts broad discretion to structure the terms and conditions under which the information may be disclosed. One possibility may be to disclose the research information to a neutral third party from the relevant research community who will undertake an independent verification of the research findings at the expense of the requesting party. Such an arrangement was recommended in *Deitchman*. Disclosure to other scientists should be more acceptable to researchers who must respond to a subpoena, since any shortcomings of the research can be assessed in relation to the standards of the profession and the strength of the findings. Some indication of the willingness of the research community to undertake such assignments will present courts with an attractive option to denial of access and turning over the research data to a *hostile* requesting party.

DATA SHARING AND SCIENCE

Good science, at times, requires the disclosure of statistical microrecords generated in research as a way of ensuring that the data are well exploited by scholars apart from the original data collector. The functions of such data sharing in the scientific community include independent verification of earlier analyses, testing new hypotheses, and reducing the costs or burdens engendered by new data collection. Since the 1980s, considerable attention has been directed to the topic, partly because of its importance and partly because of the privacy issues it may engender. Much of the pertinent research has been reported by Fienberg, Martin, and Straf (1985). A more recent summary (Cordray et al., 1991) is the basis for what follows.

Various empirical studies have focused on federal agencies that sponsor research and encourage scientists to make available the data produced during the research. These agencies include the National Institute of Justice, National Science Foundation, and National Heart, Lung, and Blood Institute. Each agency requires scientists to share their data with other scientists and analysts; each operates under guidelines that prohibit disclosure of data on identifiable individuals. They vary considerably, however, in when and how disclosure occurs.

Some scholars have attended to professional practice, for example, the natural incidence of data sharing. For instance, review of a small sample study of articles appearing in nearly 20 scientific journals suggests that a large fraction of publications rely to a greater or lesser extent on existing data (Cordray et al., 1991). The potential influences on the practice of capitalizing on shared data are easy to identify from case studies and field work, but their relations and relative level of influence are not well understood. These influences include standards of professional ethics and laws, policies of research sponsors and employers, and journal editorial policies. Respondents in research are at times also important, to judge from the empirical studies cited earlier. Each source of influence has been the target of research. For instance, studies of codes of ethical conduct developed by professional societies reveal that few of them direct explicit attention to data sharing and the balance between standards of privacy and those of data sharing. Exceptions include the codes of the American Sociological Association, American Evaluation Association, and the American Statistical Association. Almost all professional societies that have developed a code direct some attention to privacy. Similarly, a study of journal editorial practice and policy reveals that "the majority of journal editors have been slow to embrace . . . recommendations" made by the National Academy of Sciences that foster access (Cordray et al., 1991). The *American Journal of Public Health* is exceptional in having a policy that requires supplying primary statistical data to the editor and other scientists.

EMPIRICAL RESEARCH ON DEDUCTIVE DISCLOSURE

A narrative description of what an individual said to a researcher may, with a little collateral information, be sufficient to identify the individual if no clear identifier, such as a name, is attached to the description. It was partly in the interest of forestalling such deductive disclosure that Kinsey's study of sexual behavior involved coding responses to open-ended questions (Turner et al., 1992a). That is, a simple yes-no record of whether anonymous individuals referred, for example, to childhood fantasies is far less vulnerable to deductive disclosure than a prose description that reveals idiosyncratic characteristics of the individual. Coding responses and otherwise expunging information that may lead to deductive disclosure is a common approach to ensuring privacy of subjects of anthropological and ethnographic research (see Boruch & Cecil, 1979, for other illustrations).

Anonymous records of individuals' responses to questionnaires might also be used to deduce a respondent's identity. Collateral public information must of course be available to the inquirer and must be contained in the anonymous file.

Mathematical work has been done to understand the probability of deductive disclosure based on anonymous statistical records. Much of the work is done by statistical agencies, such as the U.S. Bureau of the Census and NCES, that are governed by laws requiring they protect the privacy of respondents. Data tapes and statistical data sets that are being considered for release to the public are routinely screened to ensure that deductive disclosure is not a significant problem. Data sets that are vulnerable in this respect are not released or are adjusted in various ways to make the possibility of deductive disclosure remote.

There appear to be few published reports of *empirical* work on the topic, however. We are aware of no journal articles that have been published on the deductive-disclosure probabilities for a given data set or an array of data sets. Some unpublished reports exist. Kerr and Boruch for example, examined the Survey of Doctoral Recipients files under the auspices of the National Science Foundation (Panel on Confidentiality and Data Access, 1993). This work suggests that nearly 100% of certain records are identifiable given the anonymous record and public data on the Ph.D. recipient, for example, males receiving a Ph.D. in nursing. More than 20% of some less vulnerable files are identifiable.

Similarly, we have been unable to locate any research on public perception of deductive disclosure, at least none leading to a published article or report. Nor have we encountered any empirical research on legal *or* illegal attempts to exploit public-use data tapes to build an information file on identifiable individuals.

Research That Needs to Be Done

What should social scientists better understand about the topic of privacy in research contexts? The research prospects can be divided into three categories dealing with individuals as respondents, institutions, and countries or governments.

INDIVIDUALS

Disjunctions between an individual's attitudes and behavior are common. For instance, even though many people rate sexual activity as a highly sensitive topic for a survey inquiry and say they would object to questions about it, the cooperation rates achieved in well-designed worldwide surveys of fertility control practices, surveys of attitudes, knowledge, and beliefs about AIDS among other topics are remarkably high.

Part of this disjunction doubtless lies in the way survey questions are sometimes asked. To the extent questions about fertility control are tactful, cooperation is more likely. Part of the disjunction lies in the generally low correlations between expressed attitudes and actual behavior found in many social surveys. This general phenomenon is not well understood and deserves attention in the privacy arena and elsewhere.

Little is known about how the respondent decides to cooperate in a sensitive survey that uses novel statistical methods to ensure privacy. For example, randomized response works well some of the time to induce greater cooperation. But it is not clear *why* it works or why it fails at times. Are the probabilities that are manipulated crucial to the respondent? Are perceived probabilities or the mechanism for randomization important? One possible approach to informing ourselves about these and related matters is to consider recent research on cognitive processes in survey research (e.g., Jabine et al., 1984). Similar work may help us to understand the decision processes and baseline information that influence cooperation rate.

We often do not know why and when special groups in the population will be sensitive to privacy concerns. Much of what is known about individual cooperation rates in surveys is based on national probability sample surveys and multisite randomized field experiments for testing social programs. These are sufficient to permit general statements. But they are usually not sufficient to characterize privacy concerns of especially vulnerable groups that are asked to engage in research. For instance, new immigrants cooperate with requests for information in some respects and do not cooperate in others in the United States and elsewhere. Many illegal aliens in the United States pay their taxes, for instance. But this does not mean they cooperate in legitimate social research. The wealthiest citizens in any country are particularly difficult to survey. Plausible reasons for noncooperation in any of these cases include scarce time and disinterest. But privacy concerns and distrust of social research may be important too. We know less than we should about their relative importance.

Spillover or ripple effects of controversy are poorly understood. Dalenius (1986b) points out that the cooperation rate in Sweden's monthly employment surveys dropped during the well-publicized Project Metropolitan controversy. Similar observations have been made about surveys undertaken during public debate over privacy issues in other surveys (Boruch & Cecil, 1979). The ripple effect of press coverage seems important. But it is hard to estimate and difficult to disentangle from cyclic variations in response rate, variations in the quality of surveys, and so on. The problem invites creative attention from the methodologist, statistician, and theorist.

None of the empirical research done so far on privacy in social research helps us to understand how and why privacy attitudes change. Changes in culture, custom, information, and age may influence individual privacy concerns, but we know little about such effects. Fine contributions to our understanding have been made by historians such as Duffy (1968), Flaherty (1972, 1980, 1984, 1986), and Cohen (1982). But their example seems not to have been followed often by historians or social scientists. As a consequence, we know little about how ideas about privacy or confidentiality have been altered, abandoned, or invented alongside changes in ethnic and racial culture, communications technology, and other arenas.

Although there has been considerable analytic work on deductive disclosure, published reports based on empirical studies are few. Virtually nothing is known about public perceptions of the risks of deductive disclosure. Little evidence is readily available about the empirical probabilities of deductive disclosure for a given data set or sets of data sets. No research has been published on illegal attempts to build augmented identifiable files from anonymous records despite claims in some quarters that the matter is important.

INSTITUTIONS

Institutions such as welfare agencies and criminal justice systems vary considerably in their willingness to permit the collection of information about the institution or about individuals for whom the institution is responsible. There are various reasons an institution may or may not cooperate in research in either sense. However, we lack hard information about actual practices and the reasons for them. Statutes, regulations, and bureaucratic customs are a target of research opportunity.

Compendia of state and federal statutes, for example, bearing on researchers' access to administrative records and on the confidentiality of researchers' records are useful products of research. The few compendia that have been produced are often available only in reproduced report form (e.g., Robbin & Jozefacki, 1983). The frequent need to update our understanding of law, judicial decisions, and the institution's actualization of either is difficult. For instance, no one has updated the Robbin-Jozefacki study on state laws, the Nelson-Hedrick survey of researchers on their opinions of testimonial privilege statutes, or the Knerr work on subpoena of research records.

Similarly, little evidence has been generated on why special provisions exist, as few as they are, to permit researcher access to administrative records in the juvenile court systems and elsewhere. No studies have apparently been carried out to learn about what research has been undertaken on the basis of this access, the value of the research to various stakeholders, and whether special privacy problems emerged in the research.

The compendia of laws or rules or judicial decisions also need to be augmented with commentaries. For instance, the statutes relevant to mental-health research in Virginia include the state's Freedom of Information Act, which exempts medical and mental-health records from disclosure, and the Privacy Protection Act, which permits the state to "disseminate records . . . only . . . to accomplish a proper purpose." The proper purpose in a recent endeavor was determined by the state's Joint Legislative Audit and Review Panel, a unit whose statutory authority includes access to records of every agency financed by the state. Brief legal commentary on these was essential in determining the legal feasibility of evaluating certain features of substance-abuse treatment programs, an effort undertaken partly by external researchers under contract to the state (Pethtel, 1985). Because compendia and commentaries are few, far less is known than should be about how they affect social research, how to build model statutes, regulations, or guidelines, and about how they protect privacy without impeding good research.

The complex arena of sharing data collected for research purposes also deserves research attention. Institutional rules, professional practice, laws, and so forth vary considerably across jurisdiction, academic discipline, and government agency in whether and how they encourage data sharing and how privacy issues are handled. Competent reviews have been undertaken at times (e.g., Cordray et al., 1991). A systematic and coherent work agenda seems justified because of the topic's complexity and the relatively brisk movement toward data sharing over the last decade.

COUNTRIES AND THEIR GOVERNMENTS

Do Sweden, Germany, or Poland differ much from North and South American countries in the extent to which each is concerned about privacy? Are the citizens of these countries any less or more concerned than Norwegian,

Danish, Indian, Kenyan, or Colombian citizens? Questions such as these are partly answerable by virtue of the studies cited earlier, but large gaps remain in our understanding. We know how privacy is handled in research contexts, access law, or privacy practice for countries of the Middle East, the Far East, and Africa.

The People's Republic of China is an especially interesting case on account of the country's statistics law (People's Republic of China, 1983). Article 14 of the law, for example, includes the statement that "individual . . . data belonging to any private person or his family [that is collected in the census] should not be divulged without the consent of the said person." But little is known of the extent to which the statute is implemented, recognized, understood, or trusted by Chinese citizens. Law in the United States is no less interesting on this account. The Hawkins-Stafford Act provided remarkable privacy protection to individuals who agreed to cooperate in educational research sponsored by the NCES. But little is understood from empirical study of whether and why the law influences public perception, willingness to cooperate in surveys, and so on. Nor is much understood formally about how innovative NCES inventions, such as licensing agreements, enhance the public's access to data without appreciably reducing individual privacy.

Work that helps us understand the reasons people agree to provide information in a survey or field experiment and how the accuracy of the information they provide is influenced by law and other social custom also seems sensible. This includes empirical investigations of randomized response to understand its efficacy with populations whose members are suspicious of social research or of probabilistic mechanisms that ensure privacy, the government sponsors of such research, and how conclusions based on data elicited in this way differ from those collected in other ways. The People's Republic of China, for instance, is justifiably concerned about tax cheating and racial sentiments. Whether good data on these or more volatile topics can be collected without threat to the Chinese respondent seems worthy of exploration, as it has been in the United States.

Concluding Remarks

More than 50 years ago, George Bernard Shaw is said to have declared that "an American has no sense of privacy. He does not know what it means. There is no such thing in the country." Shaw was wrong by contemporary standards and empirical data from privacy research. There *is* such a sense among Americans, as well as among Germans (the state of Hesse passed the first modern privacy law on individuals), Swedes (the Swedish privacy statute antedates the U.S. Privacy Act of 1974), and others. He was also wrong by the standards of the 1930s, to judge by faculty members fired for asking the wrong survey questions (Shils, 1938) and the early history of vital statistics and the census in the United States.

Where Shaw was correct should be of no small interest to the social scientist. We lack much understanding of privacy and of confidentiality assurance. We know only a little about vulnerable and powerful groups in Western societies, and less about other societies. There is a need to know more for three reasons: better research in the social and behavioral science and education, more effective accommodation of the individual's right to privacy in research contexts, and a better understanding of how privacy interests, custom, and law can be balanced against society's need to understand itself.

Notes

1. The distinction between privacy as a "state of the individual" and confidentiality as a "state of data" is important (Dalenius, 1986a, 1986b). But it is not drawn sharply here because, rightly or wrongly, empirical research does not depend heavily on the separation of the two.

References

Andrews v. Eli Lilly & Co., 97 F.R.D. 494 (N.D. Ill. 1983), vacated *sub nom*. Deitchman v. E. R. Squibb & Sons, Inc., 740 F.2d 556 (7th Cir. 1984).

Ash, P., & Abramson, E. (1952). Effect of anonymity in attitude and opinion research. *Journal of Abnormal and Social Psychology, 47,* 722–723.

Barna, J. D. (1974). Invasion of privacy as a function of test set and anonymity. *Perceptual and Motor Skills, 38,* 1028–1030.

Benson, L. E. (1941). Studies in secret ballot technique. *Public Opinion Quarterly, 5,* 79–82.

Bergman, L. R., Hanve, R., & Rapp, J. (1978). Why do some people refuse to participate in interview surveys? *Sartryck vs. Statistisk Tidskrift, 5,* 342–356.

Berman, J., McCombs, H., & Boruch, R. F. (1977). Notes on the contamination method. *Sociological Methods and Research, 6,* 45–62.

Boruch, R. F. (1971). Educational research and the confidentiality of data: A case study. *Sociology of Education, 44*, 59–85.

Boruch, R. F., & Cecil, J. S. (1979). *Assuring the confidentiality of social research data.* Philadelphia: University of Pennsylvania Press.

Bourke, P. D. (1982). Randomized response multivariate designs for categorical data. *Communication Statistics: Theory Methodology, 11*, 2889–2901.

Bulmer, M. (Ed.). (1979). *Censuses, surveys, and privacy.* London: MacMillan.

Caspar, R. (1992). Follow-up of nonrespondents in 1990. In C. F. Turner, J. T. Lessler, & J. C. Gfroerer (Eds.), *Survey measurement of drug use: Methodological studies* (pp. 155–176). Washington DC: U.S. Government Printing Office.

Chi, I. C., Chow, L. P., & Rider, R. V. (1972). The randomized response technique as used in the Taiwan Outcome of Pregnancy Study. *Studies in Population Planning, 3*, 265–269.

Cohen, P. C. (1982). *A calculating people: The spread of numeracy in early America.* Chicago: University of Chicago Press.

Controlled Substances Act, 21 U.S.C. §§801 to 904 (1988).

Cordray, D. S., et al. (1991). Sharing research data: With whom, when, how much? In *Data management in biomedical research: Report of a workshop* (pp. 39–85). Washington DC: U.S. Department of Health and Human Services.

Corey, S. M. (1937). Signed versus unsigned attitude questionnaires. *Journal of Educational Psychology, 28*, 144–148.

Coyle, S. L., Boruch, R. F., & Turner, C. F. (Eds.). (1991). *Evaluating AIDS Prevention Programs* (2nd ed.). Washington DC: National Academy of Sciences Press.

Dalenius, T. (1986a). *Protecting the right to privacy in censuses and surveys.* Providence RI: Brown University, Mathematics Department.

Dalenius, T. (1986b). *The 1986 invasion of privacy debate in Sweden.* Providence RI: Brown University, Mathematics Department.

Dawes, R. M., & Smith, T. L. (1985). Attitude and opinion measurement. In G. Lindzey & E. Aronson (Eds.), *The handbook of social psychology* (Vol. 1, pp. 509–566). New York: Random House.

Deitchman v. E. R. Squibb & Sons, Inc., 740 F.2d 556 (7th Cir. 1984).

Duffy, J. (1968). *A history of public health in New York City.* New York: Russell Sage.

Ellis, A. (1947). Questionnaire versus interview methods in the study of love relationships. *American Sociological Review, 12*, 541–553.

Eron, L. D., & Walder, L. O. (1961). Test burning II. *American Psychologist, 16*, 237.

Farnsworth v. Procter & Gamble Co., 758 F.2d 1545 (11th Cir. 1985).

Fienberg, S. E., Martin, M. E., & Straf, M. L. (Eds.). (1985). *Sharing research data.* Washington DC: National Academy of Sciences Press.

Fischer, R. P. (1946). Signed versus unsigned personal questionnaires. *Journal of Applied Psychology, 30,* 220–225.

Flaherty, D. H. (1972). *Privacy in colonial New England.* Charlottesville: University Press of Virginia.

Flaherty, D. H. (1980). *Privacy and government data banks: An international perspective.* London: Mansell.

Flaherty, D. H. (1984). *Privacy and data protection: An international bibliography.* New York: Knowledge Industry.

Flaherty, D. H. (1986). Governmental surveillance and bureaucratic accountability: Data protection agencies in western societies. *Science, Technology and Human Values, 11,* 7–18.

Fox, J. A., & Tracy, P. E. (1986). *Randomized response* (Quantitative Applications in the Social Sciences Series, No. 58). Beverly Hills CA: Sage.

Gerberich, J. B., & Mason, J. M. (1948). Signed versus unsigned questionnaires. *Journal of Educational Research, 42,* 22–26.

Glazer, M. (1982). The threat of the stranger: Vulnerability, reciprocity, and fieldwork. In J. E. Sieber (Ed.), *The ethics of social research: Fieldwork regulation and publication* (pp. 49–70). New York: Springer.

Goodstadt, M. S., Cook, G., & Gruson, V. (1978). The validity of reported drug use: The randomized response technique. *International Journal of Addictions, 13,* 359–367.

Gray, J. N., & Melton, G. B. (1985). The law and ethics of psychosocial research on AIDS. *University of Nebraska Law Review, 64,* 637–688.

Groves, R. M., & Magilavy, L. J. (1986). Measuring and explaining interviewer effects in centralized telephone surveys. *Public Opinion Quarterly, 50,* 251–266.

Hamel, L., & Reif, H. G. (1952). Should attitude questionnaires be signed? *Personnel Psychology, 5,* 87–91.

Hartnett, R. T., & Seligsohn, H. C. (1967). The effects of varying degrees of anonymity on responses to different types of psychological questionnaires. *Journal of Educational Measurements, 4*(2), 95–103.

Hawkins-Stafford Act (Public Law 100–297).

Hochstim, J. R. (1967). A critical comparison of three strategies of collecting data from households. *Journal of the American Statistical Association, 62,* 976–989.

Hormuth, S. E., & Boruch, R. F. (1986). Schutz der privatsphare wider wissenschaftliche Neugierde: Personen- und informationsbezogene Verfahren zur Losung des Interessenkonfliskts. In A. Spitznagel & L. Schmidt-Atzert (Eds.), *Sprechen und Schweigen: Zue Psychologie der Sebsten Thullung* (pp. 169–182). Bern: Huber.

In re American Tobacco Co., 880 F.2d 1520 (2d Cir. 1989).

Jabine, T. B., Straf, M., Tanur, J., & Torangeau, R. (Eds.). (1984). *Cognitive aspects of survey methodology.* Washington DC: National Academy Press.

Janson, C. G. (1975). *Project Metropolitan: A longitudinal study of a Stockholm cohort.* (Research Report No. 1). Stockholm: Stockholm University (S-10405), Department of Sociology.

Johnson, C. J. (1982). Risks in the publication of fieldwork. In J. E. Sieber (Ed.), *The ethics of social research: Fieldwork, regulation, and publication* (pp. 71–92). New York: Springer.

Kershaw, D. N., & Small, J. C. (1972). Data confidentiality and privacy: Lessons from the New Jersey Negative Income Tax Experiment. *Public Policy, 20,* 258–280.

Knerr, C. R. (1982). What to do before and after the subpoena arrives. In J. E. Sieber (Ed.), *The ethics of social research: Surveys and experiments* (pp. 191–206). New York: Springer.

Krotki, K., & Fox, B. (1974). The randomized response technique, the interview, and the self-administered questionnaire: An empirical comparison of fertility reports. In *Proceedings of the American Statistical Association: Social Statistics Section* (pp. 367–371). Washington DC: American Statistical Association.

Lampshire v. Procter & Gamble, 94 F.R.D. 58 (N.D. Ga. 1982).

Liu, P. T., Chow, L. P., & Mosley, W. H. (1975). Use of the randomized response technique with a new randomizing device. *Journal of the American Statistical Association, 70,* 324–332.

Locander, W., Sudman, S., & Bradburn, N. (1976). An investigation of interview method, threat, and response distortion. *Journal of the American Statistical Association, 71,* 269–275.

Magnusson, D., Duner, A., & Zetterblom, G. (1975). *Adjustment: A longitudinal study.* Stockholm: Almqusit & Wiksell.

Mochman, E., & Muller, P. J. (Eds.). (1979). *Data protection and social science Research.* Frankfurt: Campus.

National Center for Health Statistics (1987). *Plan and operation of the NHANES I epidemiologic follow up: Study 1982–1984* (DHHS Publication No. 87–1324). Washington DC: U.S. Government Printing Office.

National School Safety Center (1991). *The need to know: Juvenile record sharing.* Malibu CA: National School Safety Center.

Nelson, R. L. & Hedrick, T. E. (1983). The statutory protection of confidential research data: Synthesis and evaluation. In R. F. Boruch & J. S. Cecil (Eds.), *Solutions to ethical and legal problems in social research* (pp. 213–236). New York: Academic.

Newman, R. G. (1977). *Methadone treatment in narcotics addiction.* New York: Academic.

Newton, K. B., & Pullin, D. C. (1991). *The implications of Section 252 of the Excellence in Mathematics, Science, and Engineering Act of 1990 on the policies and practices of the National Center for Education Statistics*. Paper commissioned by the National Research Council, Committee on National Statistics, Washington DC.

Olsen, W. C. (1936). The waiver of signature in personal data reports. *Journal of Applied Psychology, 20,* 442–450.

Oyen, O. (1965). Encounter with the image of sociology. *Sociologiske Meddeleser, 10,* 47–60.

Oyen, O. (1966). *Social class, conservatism, and submission to longitudinal research: The reaction to Project Metropolitan in Norway*. Paper presented at the Sixth World Congress of Sociology, Evian, France.

Oyen, O. (1976). *Social research and the protection of privacy: A review of the Norwegian development*. Unpublished manuscript. University of Bergen, Department of Sociology, Bergen, Norway.

Panel on Confidentiality and Data Access (1993). *Private lives and public policies: Confidentiality of and access to information in a free society*. Washington DC: National Academy of Sciences Press.

People's Republic of China (1983). *Statistics law*. (Adopted by the Third Session of the Standing Committee of the Sixty National People's Congress on December 8, 1983). Bejing: State Statistical Bureau.

Pethtel, R. D. (1985). *Compliance with Privacy Act: Memorandum to community service board executives*. Available from Richmond, Commonwealth of Virginia, Joint Legislative Audit and Review Commission.

Public Health Service Act, 42 U.S.C. §§201–300aaa-3 (1988).

Reaser, J. M., Hartsock, S., & Hoehn, A. J. (1975). *A test of the forced alternative random response questionnaire technique* (HUMRO Technical Report 75–9). Arlington VA: Human Resources Research Organization.

Reiss, A. J., & Boruch, R. F. (1991). The program review team approach and multisite experiments: The Spouse Assault Replication Project. In R. Turpin & J. Sinacore (Eds.), *New directions for program evaluation: Multisite evaluations* (pp. 33–44). San Francisco: Jossey-Bass.

Republic of Poland, Ministry of Foreign Affairs (1941). *German occupation of Poland: Extract of note addressed to the allied and neutral powers*. New York: Greystone.

Robbin, A., & Jozefacki, L. (1983). *Compendium of state legislation on privacy and access*. Madison: University of Wisconsin Press.

Rogers, T. F. (1976). Interviews by telephone and in person: Quality of response and field performance. *Public Opinion Quarterly, 40,* 51–65.

Sharp, L. M., & Frankel, J. (1983). Respondent burden: A test of some common assumptions. *Public Opinion Quarterly, 47,* 36–53.

Shaw, W., Aydellotte, W. O., Boruch, R. F., Cannell, C. F., Felleg, I. P., Fellman, D., Merriam, I. C., Meyer, P. E., Reynoso, C., Spradley, J. P., Taylor, H. F., & Williams, P. N. (Eds.). (1979). *Privacy and confidentiality as factors in survey response* (Report of the Panel, Committee on National Statistics). Washington DC: National Research Council.

Shils, E. A. (1938). Limitations on the freedom of research and teaching in the social sciences. *Annals of the American Academy of Political and Social Science, 200,* 144–164.

Sieber, J. E. (Ed.). (1982). *The ethics of social research.* (Vols. 1–2). New York: Springer.

Simmons, D. S. (1968). Invasion of privacy and judged benefit of personality test inquiry. *Journal of General Psychology, 79,* 177–178.

Singer, E. (1978). *Informed consent procedures in surveys: Some reasons for minimal effects on response.* Paper presented at the Conference on Solutions to Ethical and Legal Problems in Social Research, Washington DC.

Smith, T. W. (1983). The hidden 25 percent: An analysis of nonresponse on the 1980 General Social Survey. *Public Opinion Quarterly, 47,* 386–404.

Spergel, I. A. (1969). Community action research as a political process. In I. A. Spergel (Ed.), *Community organization: Studies in social constraint* (pp. 231–263). Beverly Hills CA: Sage.

Steeh, C. G. (1981). Trends in nonresponse rates: 1952–1979. *Public Opinion Quarterly, 45,* 40–57.

Tillery, D. (1967). Seeking a balance between the right of privacy and the advancement of social research. *Journal of Educational Measurement, 4,* 11–16.

Turner, A. G. (1982). What subjects of survey research believe about confidentiality. In J. E. Sieber (Ed.), *The ethics of social research: Surveys and experiments* (pp. 151–166). New York: Springer.

Turner, C. F., Leffler, J., & Gfroerer, J. (1992a). Effects of mode of administration and wording on reporting of drug use. In C. F. Turner, J. Leffler, & J. Gfroerer (Eds.), *Survey measurement of drug use: Methodological studies* (pp. 221–244). Washington DC: U.S. Government Printing Office.

Turner, C. F., Leffler, J. T., & Gfroerer, J. C. (1992b). *Survey measurement of drug use: Methodological studies.* Washington DC: U.S. Government Printing Office.

U.S. Department of Justice, Bureau of Justice Statistics (1982a). *Criminal justice information policy: Research access to criminal justice data.* Washington DC: U.S. Government Printing Office.

U.S. Department of Justice, Bureau of Justice Statistics (1982b). *Research access to criminal justice data.* Washington DC: U.S. Government Printing Office.

U.S. Department of Justice, Bureau of Justice Statistics (1988). *Public access to criminal history record information.* (NCJ Publication No. 111458). Washington DC: U.S. Government Printing Office.

U.S. Senate Committee on Labor and Public Welfare (1969). *Hearings on the Compre-hensive Narcotic Addiction and Drug Abuse Care and Control Act of 1969* (91–1). Wash-ington DC: U.S. Government Printing Office.

U.S. Senate Committee on Labor and Public Welfare (1970). *Hearings on the Compre-hensive Narcotic Addiction and Drug Abuse Care and Control Act of 1969* (91–2, Part 2). Washington DC: U.S. Government Printing Office.

Walsh, J. (1969). Antipoverty R & D: Chicago debacle suggests pitfalls facing OEO. *Science, 165,* 1243–1245.

Walsh, J. A., Layton, W. L., & Klieger, D. M. (1966). Relationships between social desirability scale values, probability of endorsement, and invasion of privacy ratings of objective personality items. *Psychological Reports, 18,* 671–675.

Warner, S. L. (1965). Randomized response: A survey technique for eliminating eva-sive answer bias. *Journal of the American Statistical Association, 60,* 63–69.

Westin, A. F. & Baker, M. (Eds.). (1972). *Databanks in a free society.* New York: Quad-rangle.

Zdep, S. M., & Rhodes, I. N. (1977). Making the randomized response technique work. *Public Opinion Quarterly, 41,* 531–537.

Part 2 / Special Populations and Contexts

Psychological research on special populations or in special contexts tends to be accompanied by atypical ethical and procedural problems because of the vulnerabilities of those who are studied. Research populations that are vulnerable and noteworthy for the atypical ethical problems they raise include people with mental illness or mental retardation, children, older persons, abused or neglected persons, persons with HIV infection, criminals, the homeless, delinquent youngsters, and troubled families. Such populations raise problems because they are vulnerable, lacking in resources or autonomy, unable to speak for themselves, or subject to potential stigma or public embarrassment.

Issues of research-participant vulnerability interact with those such as consent, risk/benefit, research validity, and what is done with the data. These issues also interact with the prevailing theories and attitudes of the times, the institutional setting of the research, and the way in which the research findings are disseminated and translated into policy and practice. Such issues are key to developing a true partnership in which people who are studied are participants in that endeavor and not subjects of it. For a more detailed examination of such elements of risk and vulnerability and how one can recognize these potentials, the reader is referred to *Planning Ethically Responsible Research,* especially part 3 on risk and benefit and part 4 on vulnerable populations (Sieber, 1992).

In chapter 5, Gary Melton and Barbara Stanley examine ethical issues surrounding research on populations of uncertain competence to consent (adults with mental disabilities and children), populations that often are dependent. They show that competence to consent is not a stable trait of the individual but interacts with contextual factors such as the complexity of the communication, the restrictiveness of the institutional setting in which it occurs, and the perceived power of those in authority in relation to the consent giver. They review research showing that persons of uncertain competence are often more capable of rational consent than has been supposed, particularly if interacting factors are adjusted to maximize autonomy and competency of decision making.

In chapter 6, Thomas Grisso examines the way in which various institutional and organizational settings may influence the degree of coercion, threat, and candor of research participants. Drawing extensively on social, ethical, and organizational theory and research, he demonstrates that persons in such settings are likely to enter into research with preconceptions and assumed constraints that differ significantly from those of persons in contexts in which it is reasonable to consider oneself as autonomous. He provides suggestions for research methods that increase participant autonomy and a research agenda for gaining a clearer understanding of issues of coercion and autonomy in institutional and organizational settings.

Chapter 5 / Research Involving Special Populations

GARY B. MELTON
Institute for Families in Society
University of South Carolina
and
BARBARA H. STANLEY
John Jay College of Criminal Justice
City University of New York
and Department of Psychiatry
Columbia University School of Medicine

It is somewhat arbitrary to separate the topics of special populations and special settings (see Grisso, in this volume). Research involving prisoners obviously must take into account the special features of prisons. Similarly, issues regarding research involving children are often colored by the characteristics of the places (e.g., schools) in which children typically are a captive audience and relatively easily solicited for participation in research. Analogous issues arise in the settings from which mentally disordered and mentally retarded persons are drawn. In each of these settings, the potential participants are usually in situations in which they have little power, and those who are in authority often have minimal expectation that their charges will be able to make decisions on their own. These factors may combine to create an environment in which the potential participants perceive little freedom of choice.

Although separation of *competence* and *voluntariness* in decision making is conceptually coherent in general, it is not necessarily so among groups of people of uncertain competence. As Grisso and Vierling (1978) discussed in their application of developmental theory to issues related to consent to treatment, cognitively immature persons may fail to understand that they have a right to make their own decisions. Theory and research on moral and social development suggest that young children (and presumably, by analogy, moderately and severely retarded adults) are apt to perceive significant adults as powerful and authoritative and unlikely to understand the concept of entitlement to make a decision to consent or refuse consent (see, e.g., Melton, 1980).

More generally, it is most helpful to conceptualize competence as an *interactive* construct rather than a stable trait of the individual. For example, an individual's understanding of information disclosed during a consent process is likely to vary with the complexity of the syntax and vocabulary used, the effort invested in communicating (rather than merely handing the potential participant a form or unexpressively reciting a rote warning), and the extent that the setting is stressful and thus deflects attention and interferes with concentration. Similarly, as already discussed, voluntariness involves the interaction among the degrees of freedom in the environment with the expectations of the individual.

There is little research directly assessing such interactions between settings and the personal skills and expectations of special populations. Most of the research that has been conducted on special populations' competence to consent has focused on treatment decisions. As with analogous research involving general-population and medical-patient samples (see Stanley & Guido, in this volume), most of the studies on special populations' decision making about treatment have been limited by obvious methodological flaws. Notably, most studies have not differentiated disclosure, comprehension, and retention. Rather, most studies have simply assessed the quality of patients' memory for information material to the decision at hand, without ensuring that information was disclosed in a comprehensible fashion or that the information disclosed was understood at the time that it was presented.

Nonetheless, the research on treatment decision making, particularly by minors, has become increasingly sophisticated in both its legal framework and its methodological rigor. Moreover, research on consent to treatment is obviously directly relevant for therapeutic research, and much of the research involving persons of uncertain competence fits into that category. More generally, the elements of consent to treatment and consent to research are similar.[1] Therefore, it is useful to consider the substantial literature on consent to treatment among persons of uncertain competence, along with the few studies directly focused on consent to research among special populations.

The choice of the rather awkward phrase *persons of uncertain competence* is intentional. The commonality among the various groups whom the law and/or professional practice treat as "different" in research ethics is that the law historically has regarded them as incompetent to make their own decisions. However, as we shall see, research generally does not support such de jure concepts of incompetence when they are applied en masse to special populations. "Special populations" may be less "special" than commonly believed, at least with respect to competence in decision making about treatment and research. The phrase *uncertain competence* thus captures both the historic presumptions and the empirical reality. Special populations are treated as incompetent, but a substantial proportion can reason as well about treatment and research decisions as the average normal (unlabeled) adult at least part of the time.

Minors

ETHICAL FRAMEWORK

Ethical issues in regard to minors' involvement in research have received considerable attention, largely because such issues are extraordinarily difficult to resolve.[2] The National Commission for the Protection of Human Subjects of Biomedical and Behavioral Research (1977) commissioned special studies of the issues related to research involving children, and special regulations ("Additional Protections," 1983 & 1993) ultimately were promulgated. The commission debated at length whether *any* nontherapeutic research involving children could be justified, and a minority report on the issue was issued (for a summary of the discussions and the ultimate recommendations, see McCartney, 1978).

The difficulty of the issue arises because the assumptions that underlie the usual distribution of decision-making authority in matters involving children cannot be easily sustained in decision making about research. The questions, themselves thorny, that typically arise in problems of child and family policy about the proper distribution of decision-making authority among child, family, and state are compounded in research by the question of the propriety of using individuals for social benefit, particularly when they themselves have not consented to such sacrifice.

In general, the law presumes minors to be incompetent to make decisions on their own behalf, whatever their actual level of competence may be. At the same time, parents generally are presumed to act in their children's best interests and, therefore, are given authority to make decisions on their children's behalf.[3] In most research, though, the study is unlikely to benefit the participants directly. Therefore, the presumption that parents are acting to promote their children's welfare is questionable on its face.

Whether this problem is intractable was the subject of a protracted debate within the National Commission for the Protection of Human Subjects and between ethicists McCormick (e.g., 1974) and Ramsay (e.g., 1976). Following the logic above, Ramsay took the position that research involving children should be barred. A substituted judgment would be improper if it were not really on behalf of the incompetent minor. To the contrary, McCormick argued that, if children were competent, they would consent to research, because such an altruistic response is the morally proper course of action. Therefore, parents should be permitted to give permission for their children to participate in research.

With somewhat similar logic, Baumrind (1978) argued that children's participation in research should be encouraged as a morally socializing event. In such a view, parents should require their children to participate in research as part of their education in the norm that one should give unto others. Bartholome (1976) took a similar position that functionally is midway between McCormick and Ramsay. Like Ramsay, Bartholome argued that research involving children could be justified only if a benefit accrued to the participants. However, he also viewed improved moral character as a personal benefit; thus, child research that was not otherwise beneficial to the participants themselves could be justified if it fostered altruistic motives.

LEGAL FRAMEWORK

Ordinary Allocation of Decision-Making Authority. Stimulated by the debate in the National Commission for the Protection of Human Subjects, federal regulators ("Additional Protections," 1983/1993) have acted under the assumption that decisions about research can be differentiated from other decisions involving children. Therefore, the fact that parents are said to give *permission* for, rather than consent to, their children's participation in research emphasizes that the decision is not a substituted judgment. Moreover, for most research, the regulations grant power of *assent* to older children and adolescents themselves. Although minors are not considered legally competent to consent to research, older children and adolescents— more or less, those minors old enough to express a preference—have a veto power, such that they are free to abstain from participation in research even if they are de facto incompetent to consent and their parents have given permission for their participation. Child assent is required unless "the capability of some or all of the children [participating] is so limited that they cannot reasonably be consulted" or the research may offer a therapeutic benefit "that is important to the health or well-being of the children and is available only in the context of research" ("Additional Protections," 1983/1993, 46.408(a)).

Involvement of Adults Other than Parents. The drafters of the regulations also recognized circumstances in which children's parents or guardians may have conflicts of interest. The regulations provide for an exemption from parental permission when it "is not a reasonable requirement to protect the subjects (for example, neglected or abused children)" ("Additional Protections," 1983/1993, 46.408(c)). In such an instance, IRBs have the discretion to determine "an appropriate mechanism" for protection of participants, with the choice of procedure dependent on "the nature and purpose of the activities described in the protocol, the risk and anticipated benefit to the research subjects, and their age, maturity, status, and condition" ("Additional Protections," 1983/1993, 46.408(c)).

The regulations also presume that state wards and their guardians do not have the same interests. Apparently remembering instances in which institutionalized persons served as a convenient population of "guinea pigs" for risky medical research[4] and mindful of evidence that guardians often have little relationship with their wards in foster care (Bush & Gordon, 1978), the authors of the regulations established a general, although rebuttable, presumption against wards' participation in research. State wards are permitted to participate in research only when the study is directly related to their status as wards, or the wards are selected by chance as potential participants from a different population of which they also are a part (e.g., schoolchildren). Thus, wards might legitimately be recruited for a study of the experience of children involved in child-protection proceedings or an evaluation of treatment in a group home where they reside, or they might participate in a study of cognitive development for which their classmates are also invited to be participants. Foster children cannot be used as a sample of convenience, though, when others might also serve as well as participants in a given study.

Even when participation by wards can be justified, the regulations require special protection for wards. Permission is required not only from a ward's guardian but also from an advocate "not associated in any way . . .

with the research, the investigator(s), or the guardian organization" ("Additional Protections," 1983/1993, 46.409(b)). The regulations give no guidance about how such advocates are to be selected, and they give no express guidance to the advocates about how they should decide whether to give permission for a ward's participation. In the absence of guidelines, IRBs might conceptualize the process as one of community consultation (see Melton, Levine, Koocher, Rosenthal, & Thompson, 1988), in which surrogates for a vulnerable population act as intermediaries with the population of interest and speak on their behalf. Protection and advocacy agencies for persons with disabilities, child-advocacy agencies and organizations (especially those outside government), and lists of adult "graduates" of foster care might be appropriate sources of advocates.

Independent Consent by Minors. Although the regulations do not establish a mature-minor rule (see Wadlington, 1983) under which de facto competent minors a fortiori have power of consent, minors' consent is legally sufficient under some circumstances. Minors are treated as adults for purposes of consenting to research if state law permits their "consent to treatments or procedures involved in the research" ("Additional Protections," 1983/1993, 46.402(a)).

At first glance, this provision would appear to permit research without parental permission whenever treatment for a related condition (e.g., pregnancy, venereal disease) can be obtained by minors independently. However, the matter may not be so simple. First, state law is often ambiguous about the existence of a mature-minor rule in regard to treatment. Second, no state has adopted a mature-minor rule for consent to research. Thus, the common-law principle that minors are incompetent to consent to research may still prevail under state law even when minors have independently achieved a right to make decisions about treatment, itself a matter of considerable ambiguity in most state laws (Melton & Ehrenreich, 1992; Wadlington, 1983). For example, a statutory provision permitting minors to consent to psychotherapy may be based more in a paternalistic desire to increase the likelihood that emotionally disturbed adolescents will obtain treatment than a libertarian wish to protect their privacy. In such an instance, it is unlikely that the right of independent access to psychotherapy implies a corollary right to consent independently to research related to child mental disorders. Virginia is one of the few states with a special statute on research.[5] It is noteworthy that Virginia appears to require co-consent by a parent, even when the minor is competent to consent and even though Virginia has a statute that provides for independent consent to treatment by minors.[6] When the right to consent is based on the common law without an express statutory provision, the matter is likely to be even more ambiguous or contradictory.

Because state law that bars participation without parental permission may be more protective than the federal regulations, the former may not be preempted by the latter, unless an interest protected by the U.S. Constitution is implicated. Given the narrow construction that the Supreme Court has applied to the constitutional right to privacy in recent years, researchers would be ill-advised to assume that it applies to research, even in domains where it has been recognized to apply at least to some minors (e.g., abortion decision making). Researchers studying conditions or treatments covered by special minor-consent statutes would be wise to seek express legislative authority for research or, at a minimum, an attorney general's opinion about the sufficiency of minors' consent to research in various circumstances.

EMPIRICAL QUESTIONS RELATED TO ALLOCATION OF AUTHORITY
Most of the arguments in the debate about child-research policy have involved empirical assumptions. For example, the various ethical theories of decision-making authority in child research have focused on beliefs about the effects of children's participation in research on their moral development, factors affecting parental decision making, and children's competence.

Socializing Effects. Conclusions about the socializing effects of research participation are largely speculative at this point. Participation by children in *decision making* about research may increase their moral and legal sophistication (Melton, 1983). It is unlikely, though, that participation at the behest of others would have that effect unless children perceived themselves as making an affirmative effort to help others. In other words, altruistic values would be unlikely to develop further unless children "owned" the benevolent behavior and understood its rationale. Coercion to participate would provide neither modeling of altruistic behavior nor new ways of thinking about social norms. In short, whatever the potential effects of research participation on moral development, psychological theory suggests that positive effects will be enhanced if children's participation in decision making is promoted. Therefore, the Baumrind and Bartholome arguments and analogous moral theories may be valid only if parental permission is accompanied by respect for children's autonomy, at least to the degree that they are able to exercise it competently.

Protection of the individual interests of children and youth is also consistent with psychological research and theory on development of concepts of privacy (see, e.g., Melton, 1983; Wolfe, 1978). Privacy is a salient concept even for children of elementary school age, and its application may be important in development of self-esteem and personal identity. Protection of control over personal information is especially important to adolescents, and stringent safeguards to prevent compulsory revelation of such information and to maintain adolescents' personal control over the range of individuals with access to their data are warranted on psychological as well as ethical grounds.

Considerations about minors' subjective experience of participation in research under varying levels of deference to their wishes and protection of their confidentiality may become especially significant in longitudinal studies (see Weithorn, 1984). The burden on a child when a strange adult spends a couple of hours asking him or her many personal questions, posing many problems to solve, and/or performing minor physical procedures (e.g., blood tests) may be quite different when the exercise is repeated every three months over a period of years. The psychological effects may be multiplied if the research subjects the child to labeling or intervention that would not otherwise have occurred (see, e.g., Cadman et al., 1987).

Surrogate Decision Making. Particularly if socializing effects (and, therefore, even remote personal benefits) of participation cannot reasonably be expected, questions about the adequacy of advocacy for children participating or potentially participating in research must be considered seriously. A limited body of knowledge is available about the reasoning of parents who give permission for their children's participation in research. The data available suggest that parents who do give permission probably are more effective on average than parents who fail to comply and that the foibles of decision making about research among adults apply with at least equal force to parents.

In regard to the former point, Beck, Collins, Overholser, and Terry (1984) found that elementary school students whose parents permitted their participation in school-based research on social comparisons were less likely to be aggressive or withdrawn than children for whom permission forms were not returned. Given the relation between child-behavior problems and family dysfunction (see Hetherington & Martin, 1979), it is reasonable to assume that those parents who are relatively "out of sync" with their children are also relatively unlikely to volunteer their children for research. However, the fact that the difference is relative should not be ignored. Some 40% of children identified by their parents as aggressive or withdrawn (compared with 65% of other children) were permitted to participate. Therefore, researchers and institutional review boards (IRBS) cannot assume that the parents who give permission for their children to participate are the "good" parents.

Even when parents presumably do have good relationships with their children, they may make foolish decisions about their children's participation, sometimes because of their concern for their children. In a study of a pediatric cancer ward, McCullom and Schwartz (1969) found that only about 5% of mothers understood that the purpose of their children's hospitalization was purely research. Even though they had been explicitly informed to the contrary, almost half thought that the hospitalization was for diagnosis, treatment, or both. When asked why they had permitted their children's hospitalization, parents often spontaneously lamented, "I have no choice." They believed they must do anything possible to help their children, even though in that instance they were mistaken in thinking the hospitalization was for their children's own benefit. Because of the confusion about research and treatment, parents may give permission for their children's participation in research because they believe (erroneously) that the children will receive direct benefit, especially when they are in need of treatment.

Of course, parents are not the only decision makers in child research other than the children themselves. Researchers themselves make decisions about the risks that are reasonable for children and youth to assume; so do IRBS and others involved in peer or citizen review or consultation. In some cases (e.g., research involving state wards), third parties other than parents have legal authority to give or refuse permission for minors to participate in research.

Little research is available about the criteria such unrelated adults use in decisions about research involving minors or the quality of such adults' decision making. The data that are available suggest little consensus about the appropriate norms. In a survey of 45 leading child-development researchers, Keith-Spiegel (1983) found a wide range of beliefs about the age at which children themselves are as competent as adults to make a decision about participation in research (range = 2–17 years; mean = 11 years). The researchers also showed little consistency in their response to children's tacit expression of a desire to withdraw from research:

> Signs interpreted to mean that a minor participant did not want to fulfill the obligations of participation once assent was given fell into two categories. Among the behavioral indicators commonly mentioned were passivity, distractiveness, off-task behavior, lack of cooperation, random responses, shyness, fussiness, silence, crying or puckering, going to sleep, hand or foot dancing, constant looks toward the door, excessive nervousness, lack of eye-contact with the experimenter, and signs of boredom such as multiple yawns. Among the verbal expressions on the part of children that indicated a desire to disengage from the research trials were, "I want to go to the bathroom," "I'm tired," "When will I be done?," responding repeatedly to direct and age-appropriate questions with "I don't know," and any expression of a desire to be doing something else. *Several of the respondents noted that they did not necessarily interpret these reactions as indicating a blanket unwillingness to participate in the project. Rather, such behavior or verbal expressions may indicate a temporary lack of cooperation and an attempt could be made to schedule the session at another time.* (Keith-Spiegel, 1983, p. 197, emphasis added)

The degree of unreliability of researchers' decision making about minors' participation in research was most vividly illustrated by the respondents' attitudes toward use of deception in research involving children. About one third argued that deceptive techniques should never be used with children. Some of these researchers were concerned about the consequences of such deception; if professionals working with children cannot be believed, children may have no one left to trust. Another third approved of deception in studies involving children if the research held sufficient promise of benefit. The remaining third conditioned their approval on the nature of the techniques used rather than the level of benefit expected:

> Common limitations criteria included no use of outright lies or tactics that would make the child feel foolish or a failure and no use of any technique that would betray a trust or encourage the child to act in a way that might create guilt or anxiety or the expression of feelings or attitudes that the child might not ordinarily express. False negative feedback was also discouraged. This group generally found deception or concealment as also acceptable if such techniques assisted the

child or the parents in feeling better about their participation than they might have otherwise. (Keith-Spiegel, 1983, p. 202)

The "vast majority" of the respondents in Keith-Spiegel's survey agreed with commentary by the American Psychological Association's Committee for Protection of Human Participants in Research (1982) that children who are deceived in research, unlike adult participants, should not be informed during debriefing that they had been told lies as part of the research procedure. The respondents, like the committee, were concerned that such information would be harmful to many children. As Keith-Spiegel (1983) pointed out, the researchers' approach "implicitly singles out children as being incapable of handling the truth" (p. 202), an ironic belief in view of the majority's approval of deceptive research designs under some circumstances.

COMPETENCY TO CONSENT

Consent to Treatment. Of course, direct study of children's understanding of research and response to research procedures would provide a stronger basis for judging such matters than reliance on experts' personal experiences and opinions. However, virtually no systematic research exists on the matter.

The most substantial tangentially relevant literature pertains to minors' competence in decision making about treatment. Generally, this body of research has supported conclusions derived from developmental theory (e.g., Grisso & Vierling, 1978) that minors are often more competent in decision making than the law has presumed. In the most widely cited study, Weithorn and Campbell (1982) asked 9-, 14-, and 18-year-olds to decide several hypothetical situations involving physical- or mental-health problems. Nine-year-olds did not differ from the (presumptively competent) legal adults in their ability to express a preference or reach a reasonable outcome (i.e., the choice that a panel of experts would have made). Fourteen-year-olds approximated adult decisions according to those standards as well as the other two standards used as criteria (i.e., understanding of the alternatives and their risks and benefits; a reasonable process of decision making—rational weighing of such information). These laboratory findings have been validated by studies of real-life treatment decision making suggesting that, at least for routine medical and mental-health decisions, even children of elementary school age tend to make "good" (i.e., adultlike) choices, that their reasons approximate those used by adults, and that such involvement facilitates treatment (see, e.g., Adelman, Lusk, Alvarez, & Acosta, 1985; Adelman & Taylor, 1986; Bastien & Adelman, 1984; Bonner & Everett, 1986; Bush & Gordon, 1978; Bush, Gordon, & LeBailly, 1977; Holmes & Urie, 1975; Lewis, 1983; Taylor, Adelman, & Kaser-Boyd, 1985).

Consent to Research. Few studies have examined minors' decision making about research per se, some of which are unpublished. None have evaluated specific skills (e.g., risk perception) in decision making about research.[7] Moreover, as Keith-Spiegel (1983) has pointed out, the nature and degree of developmental differences in competence to consent to research probably vary with the complexity of the experimental procedure.

The research available, however, indicates that minors are typically at least as competent in decision making about research as they are in consent to treatment. In hypothetical decision making about research, Keith-Spiegel and Maas (1981) found children of elementary school age to give reasons similar to those of adults for participating or not participating. Haber and Stephens-Bren (1981) found some six-year-olds to be better able than some adults to recall information about a simple memory study; by age 10, all the children demonstrated similar competence as adults, according to a standard of understanding of critical elements of the proposed study.

In one of the few published studies of children's consent to research, Lewis, Lewis, and Ifekwunigue (1978) approached a sample of six- to nine-year-old children already involved in making simple health-care decisions at school about participating in a trial swine-influenza vaccine. The initial assent procedure was conducted in classroom groups prior to seeking written permission from the parents. After briefly describing the nature of the study, the authors solicited questions and answers from the children. Then the risks and benefits as outlined in the protocol were described (usually amounting to a reiteration of the answers to the questions that the children themselves had posed) and children were asked to indicate their assent (writing "Yes" on a form), their veto ("No"), or their desire to discuss the matter with their parents before deciding ("?"). Almost half the children vetoed participation; for the remainder, only 15% of the children's parents gave permission for their children to participate in the trial.

Although Lewis et al. (1978) did not study the competence of individual children, the quality of the questions raised in groups was remarkable, given the youth of the participants and the riskiness and complexity of the study.

The presentation in each classroom lasted approximately five minutes. Question-and-answer sessions took from 15 to 30 minutes. All presentations were made on the same morning. The form of the question-and-answer sessions was remarkably similar. All questions were initiated by the students; the presenters' only question was, "Anything else you'd like to know?" Children verified that the study would involve getting "shots." They asked about the side effects; these were described. They asked how soon the side effects might occur and how likely these were to occur. They also asked why blood samples (to determine antibody responses) would be taken. Younger children (age 6) often asked the presenter to demonstrate how much blood would be taken (two teaspoonfuls) and the size of the needle to be used.

Children asked about the magnitude of the side effects with such questions as, "Will I be sick enough to have to stay home from school?" Children in more than one class asked if "it" (the vaccine) had been tried on anyone else and why *they* in particular had been chosen for this study. They also asked if the presenter had taken the shot (answer: no). With regard to benefits, they asked what would happen if they were exposed to, or got influenza. (Lewis, 1983, p. 81)

The only published study of individual decision making by child participants in research gave IRBs further—although qualified—reason to be generally sanguine about school-age children's involvement. Abramovitch and her colleagues (Abramovitch, Freedman, Thoden, & Nikolich, 1991) studied children's decision making about actual psychological studies in which they were asked to be involved and a set of hypothetical studies. Participants ranged in age from 5 to 12.

The majority of five- and six-year-olds correctly answered open-ended questions about the nature of the studies in which they were asked to participate. By age nine, there was unanimity in doing so. Until age nine, however, most children could not correctly describe the studies' purposes. The majority of five- and six-year-olds (and almost all the children by age nine) knew how they could withdraw from participation, although many children—perhaps accurately, as findings from Keith-Spiegel's (1983) survey of researchers demonstrated—did not believe the researchers would honor their request more than temporarily. Similarly, many did not understand or believe experimenters' promises of confidentiality (a point on which the children's beliefs actually match prevailing law in regard to parents' access to records about their children). Perhaps the most disturbing

finding was that children typically indicated they would assent to participation in ethically questionable studies even though the children were able
to identify the problems in the studies.

Interestingly, the majority of children in Abramovitch et al.'s (1991)
studies tended to approve of policies in agreement with current law about
the distribution of decision-making authority. They generally believed that
participation should not occur if parental permission or child assent was
denied, although older and brighter children often argued that child consent ought to be sufficient.

In short, the existing studies give considerable reason to believe that
school-aged children can participate competently in decision making
about research. Their understanding of information about studies in which
participation is sought and their reasons for participation (or refusal to participate) are similar to those of adults. At the same time, Abramovitch et
al.'s (1991) findings about the difficulty in convincing children that their
choices will be honored (i.e., that they *really* can decline or withdraw from
participation or maintain privacy) also suggest the need for third-party involvement (e.g., parental permission) in such decisions.

THE PROCESS OF DECISION MAKING

Although the process of decision making was not a focus of the Lewis et al.
(1978) study, the use of a group question-and-answer session (analogous to
the community-consultation process that has been attempted with adult
participants in some sensitive research; see Melton et al., 1988) raises interesting questions about the nature of informed assent. Federal regulations
give no guidance on how assent is to be obtained and only implicit guidance about the elements of informed assent. Scholarly commentary on
these points is also virtually absent.

As Katz (1984) has argued, informed consent is meaningful only if it sig-
nifies a true partnership between investigator and participant. The same
principle should apply in informed assent. Because children are not used
to having their views solicited, special efforts may be necessary to convince
them that opinions will be taken seriously and denials of assent honored.
Belter and Grisso (1984) found that even adolescents would not identify
rights violations in a videotaped therapy session until the investigator had
modeled such whistle-blowing and, by so doing, had demonstrated explicit permission for it. In samples of younger participants, children who
have had minimal experience with entitlement because of their socioeconomic situation have been shown to be especially skeptical about their

rights (Melton, 1980) and especially difficult to convince that adults have vested them with decision-making authority (Lewis, 1983). Systematic evaluation of various means of inculcating a perception of personal control in child-research participants would be useful.

Evaluations of diverse media for presenting information would also be useful to potential participants. For example, by showing a videotape of a child going through the entire research procedure, researchers might teach children about a research design in which various physiological measurements (e.g., electroencephalogram readings) are to be taken. Such a modeling exercise might result in vicarious desensitization of procedures that could be frightening to young children, at the same time that it gives each child sufficient knowledge to make an informed judgment whether to assent to participation.

Most broadly, researchers should be creative in applying knowledge about developmental trends in information processing and adult-child relations to the process of informed assent to studies of various degrees of complexity. Such developmentally and ecologically sophisticated research on child-by-situation interactions in the research context is essentially nonexistent. In drawing that conclusion, we are aware, of course, that the potentially available data are vast, because every study involving children is coincidentally a study of children's response to the research situation. Unfortunately, however, researchers rarely have systematically debriefed child participants and recorded their responses.

Mentally Disabled Persons

PERSONS WITH MENTAL RETARDATION

Empirical research on the ethics of research involving persons with mental retardation is even less available than such research on child participants. In fact, we are aware of no research at all on competence to consent among persons with mental retardation.

For now, the best one can do in describing the likely competence to consent of a person with mental retardation is to combine the developmental literature with knowledge about the situational demands of the setting from which the individual has been selected. However, we should caution that such generalizations are apt to be far from exact. A nine-year-old with a mental age of nine is likely to be quite different in social competence from a 25-year-old with a mental age of nine. Also, the population of people labeled mentally retarded is enormously heterogeneous in level of adaptive skills and experience in making complex decisions and dealing with professionals.

PERSONS WITH SEVERE MENTAL DISORDERS

Legal Framework. More attention has been given to competence in decision making among persons with severe mental disorders, probably as a result of the vitriolic debate and corresponding litigation about mental patients' competence to refuse treatment (specifically antipsychotic medication). In general, relevant legal authority (both from case law and scholarly commentary) supports the principle that mental disability by itself (whether it is one of mental retardation or severe mental disorder) does not negate a specific competency, such as competence to consent to research, absent an express judicial finding of incompetence in the particular domain (for a review, see Melton, Petrila, Poythress, & Slobogin, 1987, chap. 9). That principle applies even if an individual is involuntarily committed, unless the grounds for commitment include a finding of the particular form of incompetency. As a general rule, both the ethical principle of respect for persons and the constitutional principle of the least drastic alternative demand that limitations on the liberty and privacy of adults with mental disabilities be no greater than necessary to meet compelling state interests.

Because research participation is typically done for the benefit of others and because persons with mental disabilities, especially when they are institutionalized, are presumed to be vulnerable to the exploitation of others, the drafters of the federal regulations on research proposed special procedures, including third-party review (analogous to the procedures required for research involving children who are state wards), for research with such populations.[8] The proposed federal regulations on research with institutionalized persons with mental disabilities have never been promulgated, at least in part because they were believed to be overly paternalistic. Although we recognize that the question is not an easy one, our preference is for continued recognition of autonomy in decision making about research among people with mental disabilities (Stanley & Stanley, 1981), in the absense of a formal legal declaration of their incompetence or a de facto showing of incompetence when a researcher seeks an individual's consent. Our preference is based on a combination of adherence to the ethical and legal principles noted earlier and of empirical research showing that guardians for adults with mental disabilities often have obvious conflicts of interest (American Bar Association, 1989; Melton et al., 1987, chap. 9.02) and that adults with severe mental disorders often are at least as competent as general medical patients in decision making about treatment and research.

Empirical Research. The capacity of individuals with mental illness to make competent decisions about participation in research has been the subject of much speculation, debate, and controversy. Opinions run the gamut from the assumption that people with serious mental disorders have a nearly complete lack of capacity to the belief that most people with mental illnesses are capable of independent decision making. Despite the diversity of viewpoints and the fervor with which they are endorsed, only a few empirical studies directly address the issue.

In studies examining the comprehension of consent material by psychiatric patients, a mixed picture emerges that depends in part on the diagnostic category being studied. Studies using control groups have generally shown that psychiatric patients do not demonstrate poorer comprehension of consent information than comparable medical patients (Grossman & Summers, 1980; Soskis & Jaffe, 1979). Other findings indicate that psychiatric patients may have more difficultly in understanding certain aspects of the consent material, while medical patients may experience more difficulty in other areas. For example, Soskis (1978) found that medical patients were more aware of the name and dosage of their medication than patients with schizophrenia, but the psychiatric patients were more knowledgeable about the risks and side effects of the drugs they were taking. In other studies using comparison groups (e.g., Stanley, Stanley, Lautin, Kane, & Schwartz, 1981), medical and psychiatric patients (predominantly with diagnoses of either schizophrenic disorder or major affective disorder) did not differ significantly from medical patients in their evaluation of the risks and benefits of proposed research projects.

An argument could be made that psychiatric patients are more vulnerable in the research setting because their lack of understanding of consent material would lead them to agree to risky research, but empirical findings contradict this assertion. Grossman and Summers (1980) and Roth et al. (1982) found that psychiatric patients who understood more of the information disclosed during the consent process were more likely to agree to proposed procedures.

There are many other studies that examine decision-making capacities in the psychiatric population. Such research sheds little light, however, on our understanding of this population's capacities, because the studies have not included comparison groups. The few controlled studies suggest a cautious approach in the development of additional protections for the psychiatric populations as a whole. The question remains whether certain subpopulations, such as people whose thought processes have been grossly disorganized by schizophrenia, should receive special safeguards in research.

Elderly Persons

ELDERLY POPULATIONS

A discussion of the involvement of elderly people in research entails separation of the population into four subgroups: those who are normal and healthy, those with medical illnesses, those with disorders affecting cognitive function, and those with emotional disturbances. Within the latter three subgroups, participants' place of residence—institutional or non-institutional—at the point of recruitment into the research and during the research must be considered. Also, it is not sufficient to consider only the presence or absence of an impairment in these subpopulations; the extent of the impairment must be taken into account.

ETHICAL AND LEGAL FRAMEWORK

Although federal policymakers have given special attention to adults with mental disabilities and to children as research participants, elderly people have not been the subject of special regulations (Stanley, Stanley, & Pomara, 1985). This omission probably reflects the diversity of people covered by the term *elderly*—ranging from institutionalized senile individuals with no capacity for independent decision making to fully functioning older persons living independently with responsible positions in their families and workplaces. The lack of attention is probably also an indicator of more general negligence in regard to concerns of the elderly.

Elderly people share in the legal presumption of competence enjoyed by adults in general (Stanley & Stanley, 1986). Competence of elderly people to make decisions about research will be questioned only when there is a specific reason, such as the presence of senile dementia or institutionalization. Consequently, the law recognizes a negligible role for surrogate decision makers for the elderly, unless there is a specific judicial finding of incompetence to make health-care decisions (Dubler, 1988). The law contrasts with common clinical practice, however, in which family members of elderly individuals are often utilized as surrogate decision makers without a formal legal determination of incompetence of the elderly family member.

In considering each of the four subgroups of elderly separately, the relevant issues of involving them in research differ somewhat. For the healthy normal elderly individual or the older person with a medical illness, the ethical considerations in research participation are the same as for their younger adult counterparts. General ethical guidelines, as incorporated into federal regulations regarding research with all human participants ("Protection," 1981/1992), apply. Although some have argued that older adults should be considered a vulnerable population (Lawton, 1980), this perspective is usually thought to be overly paternalistic and discriminatory (Ostfeld, 1980).

Thus, to be considered vulnerable, elderly individuals must be in a setting that leaves them vulnerable or have a disorder that affects their decision-making capability. For elderly people, two institutional settings that may place them in a vulnerable position are the nursing home and the hospital. In both situations, elderly people are often in dependent positions in which they are completely reliant on others for their care. Therefore, when asking elderly residents in these settings to participate in research, the researcher should be mindful of the dependent position of the population. Institutionalized elderly people may feel obliged to participate in research, or they may feel that their care would be adversely affected by their refusal. This situation is covered by the requirement in the general regulations on research with human participants that "appropriate additional safeguards" be applied when "some or all of the subjects are likely to be vulnerable to coercion or undue influence" ("Protection," 1981/1992, 46.111(b)).

With regard to elderly people with emotional disturbances and those with cognitive disorders, the controversy that arises for adults with mental disabilities is relevant. The proposed research regulations for institutionalized people with mental disabilities would be applicable to the institutionalized portion of this population. As with other adults with mental disorders, however, there is a wide spectrum of severity and symptomatology among elderly people with emotional or cognitive disorders. Therefore, dichotomous categorization of the elderly as those with or without cognitive impairment is not very meaningful. According to legal standards, the presence of a disorder is not sufficient to result in a finding of incompetence to give consent or to require additional protections in the research setting. Instead, a functional capacity evaluation must be performed. This evaluation is designed to address the extent to which the cognitive or emotional disorder interferes with decision-making capacity. Depending on the extent of interference, the protections can range from none to the need for a surrogate decision maker.

EMPIRICAL EVIDENCE

Until recently, little empirical information was available about the decision-making capacities of elderly research participants. The studies now available generally show that the elderly or certain subgroups of elderly individuals demonstrate specific difficulties in the consent process. Taub, Kline, and Baker (1981) found that elderly individuals with lower educational backgrounds and poorer vocabulary did not retain consent information as well as did elderly people with higher educational levels and better vocabulary. Furthermore, elderly individuals did not remember consent information as well as younger normal individuals (Taub, Baker, & Sturr, 1986). The simplification of the information presented did not lead to an increment in retention (Taub, 1980). Comprehension of consent information was found to diminish with age (Taub et al., 1986).

In a study of elderly medical patients, Stanley et al. (1984) found that the elderly tended to evaluate ratios of risks to benefits in the same way as younger medical patients. However, elderly patients comprehended less consent material than did younger medical patients. Not surprisingly, in a study of elderly people with Alzheimer's disease of moderate to severe levels, Stanley et al. (1988) found that comprehension of consent information was substantially lower than that for normal elderly individuals. This study also examined comprehension of consent material for depressed elderly persons and found no difference, however, when such patients were compared with normal elderly individuals.

In an effort to identify strategies useful in enhancing decision-making capacity in the elderly, Tymchuk, Ouslander, and Rader (1986) compared four methods of providing consent information. For the entire sample of elderly individuals (including those with significant short-term memory problems), no method resulted in improvement. However, a simplified-language approach did result in significant improvement when participants with severe memory deficits were removed from the analysis.

Taken together, these results seem to indicate that, although elderly people are a diverse group, they tend to have somewhat more difficulty in the consent process. This difficulty is particularly pronounced for those subgroups that enter the consent process with a cognitive disorder. Furthermore, efforts aimed at improving the decision-making capacities provide mixed results and seem to be effective only in limited situations.

Conclusions

As illustrated by the publication but lack of promulgation of regulations on research participation by institutionalized adults with mental disabilities, the law is ambivalent about the participation of persons of uncertain competence, especially when research is not for participants' own benefit (as is usually the case). At the same time, although research has shown some group differences, the bigger message may be that populations of uncertain competence often are not so "special" in their approach to the research enterprise.

What *is* special is the settings in which such populations often are found, and research does give some basis for questioning dependent populations' perceptions of voluntariness, even when coercion is not being directly applied. In that regard, there is a need for empirical research that would provide the foundation for modifications in the *process* of informed consent or assent so that the goal of a partnership between researcher and participants can be fulfilled, even when participants begin with a substantially lower status than the researcher.

In that regard, Abramovitch et al.'s (1991) work "piggybacking" research ethics studies onto actual studies is a model that ought to be a standard feature of the research process, especially when participants are drawn from dependent or vulnerable populations. There is also a need, however, to go beyond studies tapping comprehension of consent information to theory-driven, ecological research that identifies key factors in the process of interaction between researcher and "special" participants. Competence is not a static trait; it varies with the context, and researchers need the knowledge critical to maximizing participants' active and informed involvement in decision making about research.

Notes

1. Consent to research differs from consent to treatment primarily in the necessity to understand (in the former) the concept of research itself. In that regard, the

social aspects of the decision may be more salient in decision making about research, because it rarely offers the participants direct benefit. Also, by its nature, research often involves a greater degree of uncertainty and therefore may require a somewhat different kind of risk assessment than that employed in a competent treatment decision.

2. For more extensive discussion of the law, ethics, and psychology of children's participation in research, see Stanley and Sieber (1992).

3. Protection of the interests of incompetent minors is not the only theory on which parental authority is based. Such deference to parental judgments may be based in part on promotion of the integrity of the family and a particular social order therein (see, e.g., *Bellotti v. Baird* 1979).

Also, in some instances, parental authority may be supported in the interest of protection of their economic interests under a contract theory. In other words, if parents' financial resources are obligated in some way by a decision, fairness may dictate that parents decide whether and how such funds are to be spent or invested. Obviously, this consideration generally will not apply in research if the project agrees to reimburse participants for their expenses (e.g., transportation, medical bills) involved in the research itself and in remediation of any harm resulting from participation. The most common potential application of the contract theory may be the distraction from other activities in which parents have invested resources for the child. However, even that rather indirect rationale for protection of parental interests is unlikely to apply unless the research demands substantial investment of time, as most behavioral research does not.

4. The most famous example of such exploitation of state wards was the hepatitis virus injection of residents of the infamous Willowbrook facility for mentally retarded persons in New York. The stated rationale (more precisely, the rationalization) for the practice, which did in fact contribute substantially to knowledge about hepatitis, was that Willowbrook residents were likely to contract hepatitis even without such intentional exposure. For a historical account of the study, see Rothman and Rothman (1984).

5. Va. Code Ann. 37.1–235(A)(iii) (Repl. Vol. 1990).

6. Va. Code Ann. 54.1–2969(D)(4) (Repl. Vol. 1991).

7. One study (Lewis, 1981) did assess adolescents' spontaneous mention of risks in response to several hypothetical problems, one of which involved research (consent to a clinical trial of a medication for acne). Although Lewis did not report separate findings by vignette, she indicated that spontaneous mentions of risks and adult professionals' conflicting interests increased across adolescence.

8. The proposed regulations were published at 43 Fed. Reg. 53,590 (1978).

References

Abramovitch, R., Freedman, J. L., Thoden, K., & Nikolich, C. (1991). Children's capacity to consent to participation in psychological research: Empirical findings. *Child Development, 62,* 1100–1109.

Additional Protections for Children Involved as Subjects in Research, 45 CFR §§119.30–119.40 (1993) (originally 1983).

Adelman, H. S., Lusk, R., Alvarez, V., & Acosta, N. K. (1985). Competence of minors to understand, evaluate, and communicate about their psychoeducational problems. *Professional Psychology: Research and Practice, 16,* 426–434.

Adelman, H. S., & Taylor, L. (1986). Children's reluctance regarding treatment: Incompetence, resistance, or an appropriate response? *School Psychology Review, 15,* 91–99.

American Bar Association, Commission on the Mentally Disabled and Commission on Legal Problems of the Elderly (1989). *Guardianship—an agenda for reform: Recommendations of the National Guardianship Symposium and policy of the American Bar Association.* Washington DC: American Bar Association.

Bartholome, W. G. (1976). *The ethics of non-therapeutic clinical research on children.* Paper prepared for the National Commission for the Protection of Human Subjects of Biomedical and Behavioral Research. Washington DC: Department of Health, Education, and Welfare.

Bastien, R. T., & Adelman, H. S. (1984). Noncompulsory versus legally mandated placement, perceived choice, and response to treatment among adolescents. *Journal of Consulting and Clinical Psychology, 52,* 171–179.

Baumrind, D. (1978). Reciprocal rights and responsibilities in parent-child relations. *Journal of Social Issues, 34*(2), 179–196.

Beck, S., Collins, L., Overholser, J., & Terry, K. (1984). A comparison of children who receive and who do not receive permission to participate in research. *Journal of Abnormal Child Psychology, 12,* 573–580.

Bellotti v. Baird, 443 U.S. 662 (1979).

Belter, R. W., & Grisso, T. (1984). Children's recognition of rights violations in counseling. *Professional Psychology: Research and Practice, 15,* 899–910.

Bonner, B. L., & Everett, F. L. (1986). Influence of client preparation and problem severity on attitudes and expectations in child psychotherapy. *Professional Psychology: Research and Practice, 17,* 223–229.

Bush, M., & Gordon, A. C. (1978). Client choice and bureaucratic accountability: Possibilities for responsiveness in a social welfare bureaucracy. *Journal of Social Issues, 34*(4), 22–43.

Bush, M., Gordon, A. C., & LeBailly, R. (1977). Evaluating child welfare services: A contribution from the clients. *Social Service Review, 51,* 491–501.

Cadman, D., Chambers, L. W., Walter, S. D., Ferguson, R., Johnston, N., & McNamee, J. (1987). Evaluation of public health preschool child development screening: The process and outcomes of a community program. *American Journal of Public Health, 77,* 45–51.

Committee for the Protection of Human Participants in Research, American Psychological Association. (1982). *Ethical principles in the conduct of research with human participants.* Washington DC: American Psychological Association.

Dubler, N. N. (1988). Improving the discharge planning process: Distinguishing between coercion and choice. *Gerontologist, 28,* 76–81.

Grisso, T., & Vierling, L. (1978). Minors' consent to treatment: A developmental perspective. *Professional Psychology, 9,* 412–427.

Grossman, L., & Summers, F. (1980). A study of the capacity of schizophrenic patients to give informed consent. *Hospital and Community Psychiatry, 31,* 205–206.

Haber, S., & Stephens-Bren, S. (1981, April). *Do children understand enough to consent to participate in research?* Paper presented at the meeting of the Western Psychological Association, Los Angeles.

Hetherington, E. M., & Martin, B. (1979). Family interaction. In H. C. Quay & J. S. Werry (Eds.), *Psychopathological disorders of childhood* (2nd ed., pp. 247–302). New York: Wiley.

Holmes, D. S., & Urie, R. G. (1975). Effects of preparing children for psychotherapy. *Journal of Consulting and Clinical Psychology, 43,* 311–318.

Katz, J. (1984). *The silent world of doctor and patient.* New York: Free Press.

Keith-Spiegel, P. (1983). Children and consent to research. In G. B. Melton, G. P. Koocher, & M. J. Saks (Eds.), *Children's competence to consent* (pp. 179–211). New York: Plenum.

Keith-Spiegel, P., & Maas, T. (1981, August). *Consent to research: Are there developmental differences?* Paper presented at the annual meeting of the American Psychological Association, Los Angeles.

Lawton, M. (1980). Psychological vulnerability. *IRB: A Review of Human Subjects Research, 2,* 5–6.

Lewis, C. C. (1981). How adolescents approach decisions: Changes over grades seven to twelve and policy implications. *Child Development, 52,* 538–544.

Lewis, C. E. (1983). Decision making related to health: When could/should children act responsibly? In G. B. Melton, G. P. Koocher, & M. J. Saks (Eds.), *Children's competence to consent* (pp. 75–91). New York: Plenum.

Lewis, C. E., Lewis, M. A., & Ifekwunigue, M. (1978). Informed consent by children and participation in an influenza vaccine trial. *American Journal of Public Health, 68,* 1079–1082.

McCartney, J. J. (1978, October). Research on children: National Commission says "yes, if . . . ." *Hastings Center Report*, pp. 26–31.

McCormick, R. A. (1974). Proxy consent in the experimentation situation. *Perspectives in Biology and Medicine, 18*, 2–20.

McCullom, A. T., & Schwartz, A. H. (1969). Pediatric research hospitalization: Its meaning to parents. *Pediatric Research, 3*, 199–204.

Melton, G. B. (1980). Children's concepts of their rights. *Journal of Clinical Child Psychology, 9*, 186–190.

Melton, G. B. (1983). Decision making by children: Psychological risks and benefits. In G. B. Melton, G. P. Koocher, & M. J. Saks (Eds.), *Children's competence to consent* (pp. 21–40). New York: Plenum.

Melton, G. B., & Ehrenreich, N. S. (1992). Ethical and legal issues in mental health services for children. In C. E. Walker & M. S. Roberts (Eds.), *Handbook of clinical child psychology* (2nd ed., pp. 1035–1055). New York: Wiley.

Melton, G. B., Levine, R. J., Koocher, G. P., Rosenthal, R., & Thompson, W. C. (1988). Community consultation in socially sensitive research: Lessons from clinical trials of treatments for AIDS. *American Psychologist, 43*, 573–581.

Melton, G. B., Petrila, J., Poythress, N. G., & Slobogin, C. (1987). *Psychological evaluations for the courts: A handbook for mental health professionals and lawyers.* New York: Guilford.

National Commission for the Protection of Human Subjects of Biomedical and Behavioral Research. (1977). *Research involving children* (Publication No. OS 77–004). Washington DC: Department of Health, Education, and Welfare.

Ostfeld, A. M. (1980). Older research subjects: Not homogeneous, not especially vulnerable. *IRB: A Review of Human Subjects Research, 2*, 7–8.

Protection of Human Subjects, 45 CFR §§46.101–46.124 (1992) (originally promulgated in 1981).

Ramsay, P. (1976, August). The enforcement of morals: Nontherapeutic research on children. *Hastings Center Report*, p. 21.

Roth, L. H., Lidz, C., Meisel, A., Soloff, P., Kaufman, K., Spiker, D., & Foster, F. (1982). Competency to decide about treatment or research. *International Journal of Law and Psychiatry, 5*, 29–50.

Rothman, D. J., & Rothman, S. M. (1984). *The Willowbrook wars.* New York: Harper & Row.

Soskis, D. A. (1978). Schizophrenic and medical inpatients as informed drug consumers. *Archives of General Psychiatry, 35*, 645–647.

Soskis, D. A., & Jaffe, R. L. (1979). Communicating with patients about antipsychotic drugs. *Comprehensive Psychiatry, 20*, 126–131.

Stanley, B., Guido, J., Stanley, M., & Shortell, D. (1984). The elderly patient and informed consent. *Journal of the American Medical Association, 252,* 1302–1306.

Stanley, B., & Sieber, J. E. (Eds.). (1992). *Social research on children and adolescents.* Newbury Park CA: Sage.

Stanley, B., & Stanley, M. (1981). Psychiatric patients in research: Protecting their autonomy. *Comprehensive Psychiatry, 22,* 420–427.

Stanley, B., & Stanley, M. (1986). Competency and informed consent in geriatric psychiatry. In H. Schwartz & R. Rosner (Eds.), *Geriatric psychiatry and the law,* (Vol. 3, pp. 17–28). New York: Plenum.

Stanley, B., Stanley, M., Guido, J., & Garvin, L. (1988). The at risk: The functional competency of the elderly at risk. *Gerontologist, 28,* 53–58.

Stanley, B., Stanley, M., Lautin, A., Kane, J., & Schwartz, N. (1981). Preliminary findings on psychiatric patients as research participants: A population at risk? *American Journal of Psychiatry, 138,* 669–671.

Stanley, B., Stanley, M., & Pomara, N. (1985). Informed consent and geriatric patients. In B. Stanley (Ed.), *Geriatric psychiatry: Ethical and legal issues* (pp. 17–35). Washington DC: American Psychiatric Press.

Taub, H. A. (1980). Informed consent, memory and age. *Gerontologist, 20,* 686–690.

Taub, H. A., Baker, M., Sturr, J. F. (1986). Informed consent for research: Effects of readability, patient age, and education. *Law and Public Policy, 34,* 601–606.

Taub, H. A., Kline, G. E., & Baker, M. T. (1981). The elderly and informed consent: Effects of vocabulary level and corrected feedback. *Experimental Aging Research, 7,* 137–146.

Taylor, L., Adelman, H. S., & Kaser-Boyd, N. (1985). Exploring minors' reluctance and dissatisfaction with psychotherapy. *Professional Psychology: Research and Practice, 16,* 418–425.

Tymchuk, A. J., Ouslander, J. G., & Rader, N. (1986). Informing the elderly: A comparison of four methods. *Journal of the American Geriatric Society, 34,* 818–822.

Wadlington, W. J. (1983). Consent to medical care for minors: The legal framework. In G. B. Melton, G. P. Koocher, & M. J. Saks (Eds.), *Children's competence to consent* (pp. 57–74). New York: Plenum.

Weithorn, L. A. (1984, January). *Informed consent for prevention research involving children: Legal and ethical issues.* Paper presented to the National Institute of Mental Health, Center for Prevention Research, Rockville MD.

Weithorn, L. A., & Campbell, S. B. (1982). The competency of children and adolescents to make informed treatment decisions. *Child Development, 53,* 1589–1598.

Wolfe, M. (1978). Childhood and privacy. In I. Altman & J. F. Wohlwill (Eds.), *Human behavior and environment: Advances in theory and research* (Vol. 3, pp. 175–222). New York: Plenum.

Chapter 6 / Voluntary Consent to Research Participation in the Institutional Context

THOMAS GRISSO

Department of Psychiatry
University of Massachusetts Medical Center

Research by medical and social scientists often involves participants in institutional settings, especially universities, hospitals, and correctional facilities. Special circumstances in these settings require close scrutiny when informed consent for research participation is sought from institutional residents. Characteristics of institutions, their staff, and residents themselves can threaten the satisfaction of the three basic criteria for valid informed consent: adequate disclosure, participant competency, and voluntariness.

For example, institutional staff sometimes have been insensitive, paternalistic, or unclear when disclosing risks of research participation, thereby failing to provide institutional residents with information to which they are entitled (Andrews, 1984; Lidz et al., 1984). Further, it is often difficult to determine whether residents of some institutions are competent to make critical decisions about their participation in research (Appelbaum & Roth, 1982; Grisso, 1986). Finally, guidelines for ethical research procedures, (e.g., American Psychological Association, 1981) have warned that many institutional residents are especially vulnerable to coercion and exploitation. Questions about the voluntariness of their research participation have been raised especially in settings such as prisons where freedom of choice is greatly restricted (Capron, 1973; Keith-Speigel & Koocher, 1985; Swan, 1979).

The author wishes to acknowledge the encouraging and challenging reflections of Paul Appelbaum, James Korn, Julian Rappaport, and William Thompson during preparation of this chapter.

While all three criteria for informed consent are worthy of discussion, this chapter focuses primarily on questions of voluntariness of consent by research participants in institutions. *Voluntariness* can be defined in several ways, which will be explored later in this chapter. Legal interpretations have tended to define consent as involuntary when it is the consequence of overt duress and coercion. In contrast, this chapter deals with more subtle threats to independence and self-determination of research participants.

For example, let us imagine that a university's institutional review board (IRB) receives a research protocol from a professor describing a proposed study in a mental hospital. The review board determines that the proposed disclosure to patients during the consent process will be complete, crystal clear, and simple in wording and content. The proposal describes a careful and reasonable method for screening potential participants for their competency to make the decision to refuse or to participate. Confidentiality will be explained in a forthright manner, as will the participants' complete freedom to refuse to participate (and to discontinue if they start) without any penalty whatsoever. Furthermore, the researcher's past record indicates a highly conscientious and sensitive handling of patients and research participants. The described procedures will be carried out to the letter.

This situation would seem to cover the bases both legally and ethically. Few reviewers would doubt that any consent borne of this procedure would compromise the patient's autonomy. The point of this chapter, however, is that this conclusion may be shortsighted, because neither the review board nor the investigator have considered the special characteristics of the social milieu in which consent will be sought.

The research-consent procedure so neatly described in a proposal will not occur in a vacuum. It will come to life at a particular time and place that has its own history. When the place is an institution, everything characterizing everyday life in that place becomes the backdrop and context within which the proposed consent procedure must be considered.

Life in many institutions has taught residents that they have little autonomous choice in everyday matters that influence their lives. With this as the backdrop for a research-consent procedure, can we view the consent of an institutional resident as "choiceful" and voluntary? Or do the subtle consequences of institutional life for residents "taint" the voluntariness of their consent, even in the absence of overt coercion?

This question has rarely been the subject of research or analysis. This chapter considers the issue by explaining more fully why we should be concerned about the institutional milieu when considering questions of voluntary research consent, proposing a construct—the "normative power residual"—with which to conceptualize an institution's influences that may subtly inhibit residents' autonomous decisions about research participation, describing the variable's relation to voluntariness and potential methods for studying it, and finally recommending a research agenda.

The Institutional Context

In a seminal treatise on the rights of subjects in social research, Kelman (1972) noted that research participants are doubly disadvantaged in terms of their power to control their participation in research. First, they are drawn disproportionately from relatively powerless segments of society. They thus enter the research situation with a "power deficiency," Kelman claimed, that increases their vulnerability at the stage of recruitment for research participation. Second, once they are in the research situation, participants are on the researcher's "turf." The investigator takes charge and defines the situation on his or her own terms. This can contribute further to decreased power and control by participants. The participant's power is especially reduced, Kelman noted, "when the research is carried out in a setting 'owned' by the investigator" (Kelman, 1972, p. 991).

Kelman's treatise focused generally on participants in social research, not specifically on research participation by institutional residents. The "power deficiency" may be especially salient when institutional residents' research participation is sought by an investigator with institutionally sanctioned authority. The following discussion considers this possibility from three perspectives—sociological theory, psychological research on compliance, and clinical observations of the research-consent process—using selected examples rather than an exhaustive review.

SOCIOLOGICAL PERSPECTIVE

Goffman's (1961) sociological concept of the "total institution" offers a relevant theoretical context within which to consider institutional residents' research participation. The concept can be applied equally well to schools, hospitals, and correctional settings. For this reason, Goffman refers to the total institution's inhabitants as "members" (rather than students, patients, or prisoners) and "officials" (rather than professors, doctors, or wardens). The concept of total institution is not absolute; it describes a condition with effects that may vary depending on the institution's approximation of certain critical features of the concept.

The primary features of the total institution include a physical space and organization within which officials control virtually all aspects of life for the members. Officials' rules and decisions are guided ostensibly (but often not in reality) by an institutional plan associated with the formal mission of the institution (e.g., education, treatment, correction, and rehabilitation). Officials also sanction entrance and exit with regard to "membership"; that is, they control who will become or will cease to be a member. All these features serve to establish and maintain clear status superiority for officials over members.

The institution is more or less "total" to the extent that all aspects of members' lives (work, play, sleep) occur in the same space and in the immediate company of each other at about the same time. Finally, members' contacts with the outside world are more or less restricted by officials and their rules.

Given these conditions, Goffman postulates a number of consequences associated with members' adjustments to the institution. One of the most important is "mortification," which refers to the process by which the institution's practices cause matters of personal identity to fall away or weaken and to be replaced by member identity. Thus socialized, the member adapts to the institution's officially controlled rules, customs, and prescribed interactions, many of which are quite different from those of the outside world. The institution's system, therefore, reshapes virtually all the member's assumptions, expectancies, and decisions about daily life and interpersonal encounters.

This theoretical construction of institutional life poses critical challenges to presumptions about members' exercise of choice when they are asked to participate in research. When a member has adapted to a system of few choices, substantial dependence on official-controlled rewards, and functional regimentation, what does it mean to him or her when an official (or a professional from outside the system) walks up and says: "Here's something I'd like you to do—but it's up to you; do you want to do it or not?" What would it take to convince the institutionally socialized member to shed member identity and to resume personal identity as an autonomous individual for this one specific purpose?

PSYCHOLOGICAL PERSPECTIVE

Let us place in this context Thompson's (1983) review of social-psychological research on compliance. Thompson used the results of such research to hypothesize ways in which doctors might subtly influence their hospitalized patients' consent to treatment decisions. These can be applied equally well to the question of voluntariness of research consent in other institutions, even when the investigator who requests participation is not an institutional official.

For example, Asch (1956) demonstrated that a person can be induced to give answers to questions that he or she knows are obviously wrong, as a consequence of others' endorsements of the wrong answer and the individual's reluctance to contradict their judgment. Further, Milgram (1963) demonstrated that the presence of an authority figure can induce research participants to agree to administer supposedly dangerous electric shocks to another person, even when the participant's personal values would contradict such actions under other circumstances.

Imagine now a member of the total institution seeing one fellow member after another nod in consent and enter a research room with a professional. Imagine the professional—clearly more in the status position of official than of member, even if from outside the institution—walking up to the member and asking research participation. Given the pressures experienced by Asch's and Milgram's noninstitutionalized participants, how much greater are the compliance effects for the person who is socialized to member status in the total institution in which the research request is being made?

Thompson commented also on research demonstrating the compliance-producing effects of the "foot-in-the-door technique" (Freedman & Fraser, 1966). That is, a person can often be induced to comply with requests of increasing demand if he or she has first been induced to comply with a relatively small, "easy" request. Might a member's daily acts of compliance in small matters of life in the total institution create this effect a thousandfold? Isen and Levin (1972) have shown how one can increase compliance by first doing a person a small favor, thus creating in the recipient a feeling of obligation to reciprocate. How much more powerful is the cumulative effect of small acts of kindness toward institutional members by officials whose status requires no such beneficence?

CLINICAL PERSPECTIVE

Lidz et al. (1984) have observed some of what sociological theory and psychological research lead us to infer about consent in institutions. Their ethnographic study described treatment and research-consent procedures as practiced in a highly regarded psychiatric hospital. Generally, they found that most patients passively accepted the treatment and research decisions already selected by staff before consent was sought.

After watching consent situations and interviewing staff and patients over a period of years, Lidz et al. (1984) reported that "informed consent in the pristine form envisioned by law and by ethicists was only rarely, if ever, to be found in the Hospital" (p. 315). For example, when informing patients of proposed treatment or research procedures, doctors tended to offer information not as though patients were expected to decide whether to accept the treatment but as though the doctors were being kind enough to tell patients what needed to be done. The authors explained that this approach often interacted with patients' self-doubts to produce a lack of assertiveness in consent decision making.

One interpretation would construe the behaviors of both the doctors and the patients in these situations as a consequence of socialization to Goffman's "official" and "member" roles. The officials control rules and procedures in a way that will minimize resistance to the institution's espoused objectives and other, more mundane concerns of the staff. Further, members in Goffman's institution are socialized to a role that diminishes their sense of a capacity to decide matters that affect their welfare. This view does not deny the possibility that some members of many types of institutions have actual incapacities to make decisions. Yet many clinical researchers have noted that institutional members' already-tenuous abilities are further diminished by the mortification process described by Goffman (Barton, 1959; Braginsky, Braginsky, & Ring, 1969; Paul, 1969; Sommer & Whitney, 1961; Wing, 1962).

Therefore, the socialization of officials and members to their institutional roles can arguably inhibit both parties from expecting anything other than member compliance with official requests. Herein lies a major reason for concern about threats to choices about participation in institutional residents' consent.

Normative Power Residuals

How should we conceptualize this institutional expectancy that may influence members and officials in the research-consent process? I will use the term *normative power residual* as a label for a construct that may be useful at least for discussion and potentially for research.

DEFINITION OF THE CONSTRUCT

Power is the central element in this construct. In an institutional context, it refers to the degree and balance of influence that members and officials have on each others' behaviors and decisions. The word *normative* refers to what is usual or typical in interactions between officials and members within a given institution or type of institution. The word *residual* suggests that the pattern and history of these interactions in a given institution create for its inhabitants a general expectancy that they bring to future interactions. The normative power residual, therefore, is defined as an institution's shared expectancy about generalized power arrangements and modes of influence in interactions between officials and members of the institution.

The residual quality of the construct places it in the company of other cognitive constructs in social-learning theories. Carson (1969), for example, has spoken of learned "images" of interpersonal behavior, with which a person plans and executes approaches to future interactions. Similarly, an institution's normative power residual is its collective, shared image of the prevailing power arrangements between its officials and its members.

An institution's normative power residual is our "backdrop" for the consent procedure. It is the relevant institutional context, often not described in research protocols, in which a researcher will seek residents' consent to research participation.

All consent procedures are exercises in power and influence (Thompson, 1983). Some element of coercion is involved in any investigator-participant transaction (Keith-Spiegel & Koocher, 1985); one person is seeking the cooperation of another who, prior to the interaction, has no particular interest in the arrangement. Researchers working in institutional settings can often offer residents certain incentives that are in short supply in institutional life, and one must be careful not to exploit institutionalized individuals in this way.

The researcher's power in consent situations, however, comes not merely from the words, formal incentives, and demeanor suggested in the research-consent protocol. It comes also from the normative power residual of the institution in which consent is sought. That is, the potential volunteer brings to the situation certain expectancies about members' interactions with institutional officials. These expectancies may generalize to other persons (such as the researcher) whose status may be perceived to be more nearly that of an institutional official than that of an institutional member.

RESEARCH EXAMPLES

Currently there is little research literature concerning the expectancies of institutional members in research-consent situations. Two studies, however, are illustrative, and others will be offered later. The first demonstrates the effects of such expectancies even among patients who are not institutionalized, and the other demonstrates the presence of subtle expectancies despite a researcher's attempts to counteract them.

The first study (Rosen, 1977) was performed in outpatient mental-health facilities in Georgia. The state's mental-health services system included a central computer file that stored demographic, socioeconomic, and diagnostic statistics on recipients of public mental-health services. Data were coded with Social Security numbers so that individuals in the file could be identified for purposes of subsequent data entries. All recipients of mental-health services had the right to refuse entry of information about themselves in the state file.

Rosen observed that all applicants for services at an outpatient clinic were given a form describing the computer file plan. The form indicated the specific data that would be entered in the state computer, the state's research reasons for the file, and other relevant information. It clearly indicated the voluntary conditions of data entry and the patient's right to refuse it. Rosen found that, during an eight-month period, 100% of 962 applicants for services at the mental-health center complied with the request.

Startled that no one would object to such recording of personal information and concerned that applicants might not be attending closely to the terms of the request, Rosen for a time had the form read aloud to patients at intake in two mental-health clinics. Once again she found a 100% compliance rate. Finally, she added a sentence on the end of the form. It told patients that the type of services the mental-health clinic would provide them would not depend on their choice concerning data entry in the state computer system. The compliance rate in this new condition dropped to 41% in one clinic and 20% in the other.

The sentence Rosen added explains why 60–80% of the applicants in the original condition complied with the research request. They apparently believed that refusal would result in clinic staff decisions to reduce the type or quality of services they would receive. No one would accuse the clinic of overt coercion in this procedure, yet it is difficult to conclude that the majority in the original condition *felt* "free" in the psychological sense to decide to refuse. They were apparently influenced by their inaccurate expectancies about staff powers based on assumptions they brought to the situation.

Rosen's study does not demonstrate the effects of a normative power residual based on institutional socialization, because the study investigated neither the previous treatment histories of these outpatients nor whether the expectancy was shared among the institution's officials and members. The study does show, however, how expectancies about interactions between officials and members that are brought to the consent situation by individuals might influence them to make consent choices contrary to those they would make on the basis of their unencumbered personal preferences.

In Rosen's study, the expectancy was easily overcome by providing information to counter it. The second study suggests that the effects of an institution's normative power residual on consent situations might not always be so easily overcome.

In this study (Grisso, 1981), 15- and 16-year-olds in a juvenile court detention center were asked to participate in a research procedure as part of a study of juveniles' abilities to understand *Miranda* rights, rights to silence and legal counsel, of which juveniles are informed when they are arrested and faced with questioning by law-enforcement officers. The sessions did not occur at the time of police questioning; rather, they took place several days into juveniles' detention after arrest. The research procedure included standardized interviews and measures designed to assess juveniles' understanding of *Miranda* rights and their perceptions of juvenile court procedures and actors.

Consent information was provided verbally in a preexperimental session with each juvenile. The information stressed that participation was voluntary (there was no inducement incentive or punitive consequences of refusal), that it could be discontinued by the volunteer at any time during the research, that the researcher was not part of the court but rather an independent researcher from Saint Louis University, and that nothing in the research sessions would be told to anyone connected with the court or police. Most of this information was repeated at least twice during the information session. The compliance rate was about 90%.

For 192 juveniles, the 45-minute experimental session ended with several questions concerning the participant's recall of the researcher's institutional affiliation and certain thoughts that might have occurred to the juvenile while participating in the research. Despite the careful preexperimental informing process, only 54% of the juveniles remembered that the examiner was a researcher from a university. In response to the question "Do you think that most kids here believe us when we tell them that we work for a university and not the court?" 39% said that other juveniles probably would not believe this. About 22% said that sometime during the session it had occurred to them that the researcher might report their answers to the court, and about one quarter of these more skeptical participants said they had thought about it "often" during the session.

These results do not directly address the question of voluntariness of consent. They do suggest, however, that residents' expectancies based on their socialization to the power and control of institutional officials are not always easily undermined by providing contradictory information. Further, the results demonstrate the generalization of the institution's normative power residual to authority figures without official status who enter the institutional setting.

Voluntariness and the Normative Power Residual

From the perspective of the preceding discussions, we could question the voluntariness of otherwise "adequate" informed-consent procedures when an institution's normative power residual is heavily balanced in favor of members' compliance with officials' requests. In fact, we could avoid much further discussion if we could conclude that the normative power residual of virtually all institutions balances power in favor of its officials and, therefore, that research consent by a member of any institution can never be truly voluntary. For two reasons, however, this conclusion is difficult to reach: variability in definitions of "involuntariness" and the other is variability among institutions.

NOTIONS OF INVOLUNTARINESS

The concept of involuntariness can be interpreted in at least three ways. First, the law generally defines consent as involuntary when it is the product of coercion, unfair persuasions, or inducements (*Relf v. Weinberger*, 1974; also "Protection of Human Subjects," 1992/1981). Thompson (1983) has noted that, while this legal definition invalidates a consent obtained with blatant forms of duress and coercion, it provides little protection from more subtle forms of influence such as that encountered in normative power residuals in institutions. For example, courts have recognized that the mere fact that a mental patient is hospitalized and dependent on hospital personnel does not create automatically a condition for involuntary consent (Wexler, 1975, 1981). Therefore, from a legal perspective, one certainly cannot conclude that a normative power residual balanced in favor of staff produces involuntary consents by an institution's members.

Second, from an ethical (rather than legal) perspective, we may define involuntary consent as a product of inaccurate or insufficient information concerning sanctions (rewards or penalties) associated with refusal to consent. Rosen (1977) provides an example. Patients in the original consent condition were not blatantly threatened (e.g., "You must consent to data entry in the computer or we will not provide treatment"). Yet most of the applicants apparently assumed the presence of this sanction when they gave their consent. In a psychological sense, their presumption created a "coercive" condition, even without signs of malice by the staff (who merely failed to correct the misperception).

Even this definition of involuntariness, however, does not allow us to conclude that consent by institutional members can never be voluntary. It merely warns us that members may bring to the consent process various inaccurate expectancies about negative sanctions for refusal of research requests, which in turn may inappropriately influence their cost-benefit analyses during consent decision making. Members' consent within the institution may still be voluntary under this definition, if the inaccurate expectancy can be corrected in the informing process when consent is sought.

Third, again from an ethical perspective, we may define research consent as involuntary when, because of the status of the participant, it is highly likely that consent was the product of either acquiescence or inability to profit from information intended to correct the participant's expectancies about sanctions. The juveniles in Grisso's (1981) study, for example, were not blatantly coerced, and they were given accurate information concerning the *absence* of either positive or negative sanctions for research participation. Yet their youthfulness, as well as their expectancies associated with residence in a highly controlling setting, apparently rendered some of them resistant to modification of their inaccurate expectancies.

Appelbaum, Roth, Lidz, Benson, and Winslade (1986) have observed a similar effect in a research hospital among inpatients who consented to participation in medical research involving random, double-blind assignment to experimental and placebo medication groups. Queried after their consent, the great majority appeared to have made their decisions on the basis of a "therapeutic misconception." That is, despite explanations about the random assignment of medications, patients nevertheless believed the doctors would do what doctors typically are expected to do: deliver care that will provide the best available treatment for one's own malady. Appelbaum et al. (1986) went on to provide extra education to patients so as to disabuse them of this expectancy. Yet the investigators were only partially successful; about half of the patients still could not relinquish their expectancies about doctors' therapeutic roles and therefore they still could not comprehend the ways that the medical research differed from ordinary therapeutic care.

In this third definition, involuntariness is due to social expectancies that are highly resistant to correction and in which the participant's status pulls for acquiescence to the requests of authority figures even without overt coercion and inducements. Apparently these conditions are to be found in many institutional situations. Therefore, can we conclude that voluntariness, when defined in this way, is impossible in institutions?

INSTITUTIONAL VARIABILITY

The question of the institutional impossibility of voluntariness is difficult to answer because of variability among institutional settings themselves in the degrees of "totalness," the types of normative power residuals, and, therefore, the degrees to which they present a theoretical risk to voluntary consent.

It is tempting to propose that certain levels of risk to voluntariness may be associated with particular types of institutions conventionally labeled according to their objectives. For example, we might perceive educational institutions as having less threatening normative power residuals and greater permeability than mental hospitals, followed by correctional settings, where the degree of autonomy and power for members might be expected to be lowest. Thus, most discussions of ethics in research consent (e.g., American Psychological Association, 1981) emphasize increasing caution as one moves from schools to hospitals to prisons.

This typological presumption, however, is simplistic. Correctional institutions range from relatively open residential farms to super-maximum security facilities. Schools range from open universities to the military academies. And mental hospitals range from the day-patient unit to secure forensic units. Even in the latter there is much variation. At Wyoming State Hospital a forensic unit features steel-barred sliding doors, while 50 miles away at the Utah State Hospital a unit for similar patients has nothing but conventional window screens to inhibit the inmate from a one-story jump to freedom.

This diversity within institutions grouped by social function suggests that their within-group variance may rival their between-group variance on institutional variables associated with members' autonomy and sense of personal control. We are thus cautioned against drawing easy conclusions about the relative risks to voluntariness based merely on our stereotypes of institutions.

Studying the Normative Power Residual

I have proposed a construct, normative power residual, representing the institutionally shared "image" of particular power arrangements characterizing officials' and members' interactions. Further, earlier discussion indicated how the expectancies embodied in an institution's normative power residual might threaten self-determination in research-consent situations. We currently have little empirical knowledge about the specific nature of these expectancies, their degrees of threat to self-determination by institutional members, or the types of institutions characterized by more troubling normative power residuals. Several methods are available, however, for beginning to examine these variables more closely.

A considerable methodology has developed for describing institutions as they are perceived by their inhabitants. Many of these methods have focused on officials' and members' perceptions of typical or expected social interactions within the institution. Often these methods have used dimensional or typological structures for organizing this information.

For example, several research projects in the past two decades have examined the perceptions and beliefs of hospital personnel concerning mental-hospital patients and their proper treatment. Gilbert and Levinson (Gilbert, 1954; Gilbert & Levinson, 1956; Levinson, 1962) examined the "custodial" and "humanistic" ideological orientations of mental hospital staff. Their Custodial Mental Illness Ideology Scale was useful in identifying theoretically consistent differences between hospitals. Their definitions of custodial and humanistic ideologies in hospitals include presumptions about the degree of control exercised by staff in interactions with patients.

Similarly, Cohen and Struening (1962) developed a research tool, Opinions about Mental Illness, using five attitudinal dimensions with conceptual implications for power and influence in interactions between staff and patients. Their administration of the instrument to personnel in a large number of mental-hospital units revealed two major types of units, one having far higher Authoritarian and Social Restrictiveness mean scores than the other. (Interestingly, the two types were not so dissimilar on the dimensions of Benevolence and Mental Hygiene Ideology.)

Golding, Becker, Sherman, and Rappaport (1975) developed a Behavioral Expectations Scale based on Ellsworth's (1965) concept of "nontraditionalism" in attitudinal approaches to mental illness (i.e., attitudinal rejection of the notion that mental patients are fundamentally different from nonpatients in patterns of social behavior). Scores on the instrument were related as expected to the Cohen and Struening dimensions of opinions about mental illness, to some personality variables of hospital staff, and to staff members' ratings of vignettes regarding the behavior of hypothetical patients.

Other studies have focused on patients' perceptions of mental-hospital staff. For example, factor-analytic research with the Patient Perception of the Ward Scale (Ellsworth, Foster, Childers, Arthur, & Kroeker, 1968; Ellsworth, Maroney, Klett, Gordon, & Gunn, 1971) has produced several item groupings with content focusing on perceived staff characteristics (e.g., involved, dedicated staff, dominant staff, and imperceptive, disrespectful staff). Some of these variables could have implications for patients' perception of staff members' power and influence.

Finally, Price and Moos (1975) used the Ward Atmosphere Scale (Moos, 1974) in a cluster-analytic procedure to produce a taxonomy of inpatient treatment programs, based on the responses of staff and patients in 144 mental-hospital units. Their descriptions of these clusters, based on mean scores on the scale's 10 dimensions, could help identify typical power orientations in interactions between staff and patients associated with the various types of hospitals. For example, one cluster, therapeutic community type programs, was characterized by high scores on scale dimensions emphasizing openness of expression of feelings and patient involvement in making program decisions and low scores on dimensions of staff enforcement of rules. One might expect that patients on these wards would experience some greater degree of self-determination and autonomy than, for example, patients on wards in another cluster, control oriented programs (characterized by very high scores in areas of order, organization, strict rules, and carefully planned and structured activities).

Similar studies exist in educational institutions (e.g., Pace & Stern, 1958) and correctional institutions (e.g., Moos, 1968). The purpose of this brief review, however, has not been to summarize the literature on any of these institutions. Instead, it has merely offered examples of methods that might be used to characterize or make inferences about institutions' normative power residuals, as they may be related to our concerns about threats to self-determination in research-consent situations.

The research examples have several limitations for characterizing normative power residuals in institutions. First, the practice of characterizing an institution according to its global, perceived degree of staff control does not necessarily signify the degree of residents' power and self-determination. Even in institutions with relatively high degrees of official control, some residents may nevertheless adapt to the institution in ways that maintain a sense of personal control by making certain adaptations to the institution. For example, Braginsky, Braginsky, and Ring (1969) described subgroups of mental-hospital patients who learned to "use" the hospital as a respite from difficult life circumstances. Their power rested in their ability to control their entrance into the hospital, their activities while there, and the time of their discharge from the hospital, primarily by providing responses that would elicit predictable decisions from the staff. Similarly, a considerable literature (see, e.g., Toch, 1979) describes how a prisoner may adapt to institutional life in a "dignified" manner, thus "denying the custodians' power to strip him of his ability to control himself" (Sykes, 1958, p. 102).

The precise implications of these strategies of institutional adaptation for consent to research is unknown. They do suggest, however, that greater staff control on global indices such as those reviewed earlier does not necessarily translate into greater compliance to requests for all institutional members. Second, global measures of staff control tell us little about *how* the institution's officials maintain control and influence over its members. For example, Rosenberg and Pearlin (1962) described five methods of influence employed by mental-hospital staff:

- *coercive power*, involving overt compulsion, sanctions, and threats of sanctions
- *legitimate authority*, involving use of status (without specification of sanctions) as leverage for requiring compliance
- *persuasion*, based on the ability to convince a patient to comply by using logic or other persuasive arguments
- *benevolent manipulation*, including methods to gain compliance with-

out the patient's awareness (e.g., enlisting the help of other patients)

• *contractual power,* involving influence by development of reciprocal
obligations (e.g., token economy, or "If you do this, I will give you
that")

Institutions differing in their use of these approaches may have equivalent degrees of power over residents. Yet knowledge of an institution's predominant mode of influence has certain additional implications for considering special threats to autonomy in research consent. For example, we
might be more concerned about the effects of an institution's normative
power residual on research consent in an institution that employs "coercive power" in routine functions, compared with institutions with less extreme normative modes of influence. This may be true even if the institutions manifest equally high degrees of staff control on more global
measures of institutional milieu.

Knowledge of an institution's specific power strategies also may be used
to counteract the normative power residual in the research-consent situation. For example, imagine that in an institution in which "coercive power"
predominates, the researcher decides to take extra pains to explain the lack
of any negative consequences of refusal to consent to the research, then
employs logical "persuasion" regarding the potential benefits. Or in another institution in which "legitimate authority" or "persuasion" are the
primary tactics, the researcher employs "contractual power": that is, the
resident is offered something of modest value in return for research participation.

In both examples, the researchers chose modes of influencing research
participation that were different from the predominant mode with which
the institution's officials maintain control in interactions with residents.
There are two reasons this strategy could counteract the compliance effects
produced by an institution's normative power residual.

First, using modes of influence that are different from the institution's
dominant one may distance the researcher from the institution's staff and
their usual methods of control. In other words, it contradicts the usual
power orientation between the institution's officials and its members, thus
placing the research-consent interaction outside the parameters of residents' expectancies concerning interactions with authority figures in the
institution.

Second, it may serve to "empower" the resident. For example, in an institution in which "coercive power" is the predominant expectancy, the re-

searcher's use of "contractual power" (offering to provide the resident something of modest value in return for participation) places the resident in a power position (to consent or refuse) that is not allowed in systems that use overt compulsion to obtain compliance. (This is the case, of course, only if the contractual offer provides something that does not exploit deprivations experienced by residents in the institution.)

From the perspective of role theory (Shaw & Costanzo, 1970), therefore, the researchers use of a social-influence mechanism that is not typical in interactions between officials and members in the institution may produce role conflict for the institutional resident. It might offer to residents—and potentially induce them to assume—a greater degree of self-determination and sense of autonomy than that to which they have been socialized.

The intended effects described for these counteractive strategies, of course, are merely hypothetical. Furthermore, they may have their own undesirable effects on consent decision making. For example, a researcher's attempt to empower an institution's residents by treating them as individuals with rights of self-determination may itself create a compliance effect. Law-enforcement officers use this effect to their own advantage when they employ a "friendly" demeanor in interrogation of felony suspects; combined with the suspect's fearful expectancies in such circumstances, this approach often produces greater cooperation in securing confessions than would be obtained by strong-arm tactics (Inbau & Reid, 1967). Medical researchers' approaches to the consent procedure have been known to produce similar effects, intentional or otherwise (Appelbaum et al., 1986).

The point here, however, is not to recommend particular strategies in consent situations (see Kelman, 1972, for several possible strategies not considered here). This discussion merely suggests that an understanding of the ways officials maintain their power and influence in institutions—not merely the degree of staff control—may be important when considering the potential effects of normative power residuals for research-consent situations.

Recommendations

This discussion of the potential effects of an institution's "normative power residual" on residents' self-determination in research-consent situations has not produced information that allows confident recommendations for future consent procedures. It points out, however, the need for several kinds of research to inform us about the potential threats to voluntary consent in institutions.

First, we need to know far more about residents' expectancies regarding compliance and refusal. Available evidence suggests that institutional residents bring these expectancies to consent situations as a result of their socialization to norms of interaction with authority figures. Studies by Rosen, Grisso, and Appelbaum et al. suggest that these expectancies may be pervasive, somewhat different in various institutional settings, and subtle yet powerful in their effects on research-consent decisions. Further, as noted earlier, such expectancies might vary for different types of residents within a given institution.

A descriptive understanding of these expectancies should be the first order of business. Once they are documented, we may be able to determine further their relation to the global measures of perceived staff control or to the dominant modes of power and influence employed by staff, described in the review of research on institutional milieus.

One way to acquire this database concerning the expectancies of institutional residents in research situations would be to ask all researchers employing institutional samples to obtain information about the participants' expectations in the course of their research. That is, regardless of their studies' main purpose, researchers could be asked to include some procedure for discovering participants' presumptions regarding the conditions of their research participation. As in the study by Grisso, this might involve no more than a few standardized questions asked of each participant at the close of a research session, when it will not interfere with the main procedures of the study. Inquiry could solicit the recall of information about participation that was provided before the study. It could also explore any number of potential presumptions or misunderstandings that participants might have regarding institutional sanctions for research participation or refusal.

The researcher's agreement to include a procedure of this type could be made a part of IRB criteria for approval of the research protocol. Researchers have a commitment to employ research-consent procedures that promote informed and voluntary consent by participants. The proposed request would create this obligation in research situations in which the variables that might influence autonomy are not clear.

This proposal extends the researcher's obligations beyond the current requirement to use consent procedures that mitigate known threats; researchers would be further required to contribute to a database that would warn future researchers of as yet *unknown* threats to ethical obligations in research with institutional samples. Situations requiring fulfillment of this latter obligation might involve studies in any institution, as well as research involving noninstitutionalized individuals whose status renders them especially vulnerable to the decisions of others (e.g., children, persons with mental retardation).

A second, more experimental type of research would test the relation of various consent conditions to residents' decisions to consent to or refuse research participation. Rosen's study offers a general example. This type of research would compare compliance rates in two or more informational conditions, some of which would be designed to disconfirm faulty expectancies regarding institutional sanctions for consent or refusal to participate in research. Differences between groups in compliance rates would suggest both the existence and potency of the expectancy. In turn, this would inform researchers when disconfirmation of the expectancy may be important in future consent procedures, in order to mitigate the compliance effects of the institution's normative power residual.

Finally, research is needed to determine whether various strategies of influence in obtaining research consent in institutions (e.g., "persuasion," "contractual incentives") offer more or less protection from the influence of an institution's normative power residuals. A role theory perspective would suggest that residents' consent decisions might be more autonomous if the researcher were to adopt certain strategies of influence that are not typical of the institution's interactions between officials and members. Yet the earlier discussion also constructed competing hypotheses about these outcomes based on other considerations. Specific strategies should not be implemented until we have sufficient research to guide our use of the options available.

In conclusion, this chapter has offered theoretical and empirical reasons, a heuristic concept, suggestions for research methods, and a research agenda, all of which call for the study of effects of subtle residual sources of institutional influence that may threaten choice in consent to research participation. What is also needed to implement these studies is our own motivation, which should be fueled by our concern for ethical procedures in research involving institutionalized and therefore vulnerable individuals.

References

American Psychological Association (1981). *Ethical principles of psychologists*. Washington DC: American Psychological Association.

Andrews, L. (1984). Informed consent statutes and the decisionmaking process. *Journal of Legal Medicine, 5*, 163–217.

Appelbaum, P., & Roth, L. (1982). Competency to consent to research: A psychiatric overview. *Archives of General Psychiatry, 39*, 951–958.

Appelbaum, P., Roth, L., Lidz, C., Benson, P., & Winslade, W. (1986). Consent to research and the therapeutic misconception. *Hastings Center Report, 17*, 20–24.

Asch, S. (1956). Studies of independence and conformity: A minority of one against a unanimous majority. *Psychological Monographs, 70* (Whole No. 416).

Barton, R. (1959). *Institutional neurosis*. Bristol: Wright.

Braginsky, B., Braginsky, D., & Ring, K. (1969). *Methods of madness: The mental hospital as a last resort*. New York: Holt, Rinehart, & Winston.

Capron, A. (1973). Medical research in prisons. *Hastings Center Report, 3*, 4–6.

Carson, R. (1969). *Interaction concepts or personality*. Chicago: Aldine.

Cohen, J., & Struening, E. (1962). Opinions about mental illness in the personnel of two large mental hospitals. *Journal of Abnormal and Social Psychology, 64*, 349–360.

Ellsworth, R. (1965). A behavioral study of staff attitudes toward mental illness. *Journal of Abnormal Psychology, 70*, 194–200.

Ellsworth, R., Foster, L., Childers, B., Arthur, G., & Kroeker, D. (1968). Hospital and community adjustment as perceived by psychiatric patients, their families, and staff. *Journal of Consulting and Clinical Psychology, 32*, 1–41.

Ellsworth, R., Maroney, R., Klett, W., Gordon, H., & Gunn, R. (1971). Milieu characteristics of successful psychiatric treatment programs. *American Journal of Orthopsychiatry, 41*, 427–441.

Freedman, J., & Fraser, S. (1966). Compliance without pressure: The foot-in-the-door technique. *Journal of Personality and Social Psychology, 4*, 196–202.

Gilbert, D. (1954). *Ideologies concerning mental illness: A sociopsychological study of mental hospital personnel*. Unpublished doctoral dissertation, Radcliffe College, Cambridge MA.

Gilbert, D., & Levinson, D. J. (1956). Ideology, personality, and institutional policy in the mental hospital. *Journal of Abnormal and Social Psychology, 53*, 263–271.

Goffman, E. (1961). *Asylums: Essays on the social situation of mental patients and other inmates*. Garden City NY: Doubleday.

Golding, S., Becker, E., Sherman, S., & Rappaport, J. (1975). The Behavioral Expectations Scale: Assessment of expectations for interaction with the mentally ill. *Journal of Consulting and Clinical Psychology, 43*, 109–118.

Grisso, T. (1981). *Juveniles' waiver of rights: Legal and psychological competence*. New York: Plenum.

Grisso, T. (1986). *Evaluating competencies: Forensic assessments and instruments*. New York: Plenum.

Inbau, F., & Reid, J. (1967). *Criminal interrogation and confessions.* Baltimore: Williams & Wilkins.

Isen, A., & Levin, H. (1972). The effect of feeling good on helping: Cookies and kindness. *Journal of Personality and Social Psychology, 21,* 384–394.

Keith-Spiegel, P., & Koocher, G. (1985). *Ethics in psychology.* New York: Random House.

Kelman, H. (1972). The rights of the subject in social research: An analysis in terms of relative power and legitimacy. *American Psychologist, 27,* 989–1016.

Levinson, H. (1962). *Men, management, and mental health.* Cambridge MA: Harvard University Press.

Lidz, C., Meisel, A., Zerubavel, E., Carter, M., Sestak, R., & Roth, L. (1984). *Informed consent: A study of decisionmaking in psychiatry.* New York: Guilford.

Milgram, S. (1963). Behavioral study of obedience. *Journal of Abnormal and Social Psychology, 67,* 371–378.

Moos, R. (1968). The assessment of the social climates of correctional institutions. *Journal of Research in Crime and Delinquency, 5,* 174–188.

Moos, R. (1974). *Evaluating treatment environments.* New York: Wiley.

Pace, C., & Stern, G. (1958). An approach to the measurement of psychological characteristics of college environments. *Journal of Educational Psychology, 49,* 269–277.

Paul, G. (1969). The chronic mental patient: Current status—future directions. *Psychological Bulletin, 71,* 81–94.

Price, R., & Moos, R. (1975). Toward a taxonomy of inpatient treatment environments. *Journal of Abnormal Psychology, 84,* 181–188.

Protection of Human Subjects, 45 CFR §§46.101–46.124 (1992) (originally promulgated in 1981).

Relf v. Weinberger, 372 F. Supp. 1196 (D.C. 1974).

Rosen, C. (1977). Why clients relinquish their rights to privacy under sign-away pressures. *Professional Psychology, 8,* 17–24.

Rosenberg, M., & Pearlin, L. (1962). Power-orientations in the mental hospital. *Human Relations, 15,* 335–349.

Shaw, M., & Costanzo, P. (1970). *Theories in social psychology.* New York: McGraw-Hill.

Sommer, R., & Whitney, G. (1961). The chain of chronicity. *American Journal of Psychiatry, 118,* 111–117.

Swan, L. (1979). Research and experimentation in prisons. *Journal of Black Psychology, 6,* 47–51.

Sykes, G. (1958). *The society of captives: A study of a maximum security prison.* Princeton NJ: Princeton University Press.

Thompson, W. (1983). Psychological issues in informed consent. In President's Commission for the Study of Ethical Problems in Medicine and Biomedical and Behavioral Research (Eds.), *Making health care decisions: Vol. 3: Appendices: Studies on the foundations of informed consent* (pp. 83–115). Washington DC: U.S. Government Printing Office.

Toch, H. (1979). *Psychology of crime and criminal justice.* New York: Holt, Rinehart, & Winston.

Wexler, D. (1975). Reflections on the legal regulation of behavior modification in institutional settings. *Arizona Law Review, 17,* 132–143.

Wexler, D. (1981). *Mental health law.* New York: Plenum.

Wing, J. (1962). Institutionalism in mental hospitals. *British Journal of Social and Clinical Psychology, 1,* 38–51.

Conclusion / Is It Possible to Legislate Morality? Encouraging Psychological Research Contributions to Problems of Research Ethics

MICHAEL J. SAKS
University of Iowa
and
GARY B. MELTON
Institute for Families in Society
University of South Carolina

Does psychology have any special contribution to make to the problem of improving the quality of ethical thought and conduct among biomedical and behavioral-science researchers? When the question is framed so as to emphasize its empirical components, it begins to be easier to answer that question affirmatively. The purpose of this chapter is to identify some of those empirical questions and to point to existing theoretical and empirical work that may provide answers. Where no useful work has been done, we can at least point to empirical research possibilities that can eventually help provide answers.

At the outset, we should acknowledge that psychologists have been part of the problem. In part it was behavioral science research that attracted the attention of lawmakers and ethicists and aroused them to think about what it is we do, what of that activity creates ethical problems, and what regulations might restrain our conduct. In such a climate of public concern, behavioral scientists have been the most hostile researchers to regulation, at least by institutional review boards (IRBS) (see Gray & Cooke, 1980; Gray, Cooke, & Tannenbaum, 1978). That creates the potential for diminishing public faith in the enterprise of psychological research and consequent loss of support for scientific work in the public interest. For these reasons alone, we ought to be contributing to solutions.

Although lawyers and philosophers have dominated this preserve, it is not theirs exclusively because the questions are not exclusively normative. Even if the questions were completely normative, those norms are arguably to be sought not only in the analyses of scholars and the arguments of policymakers but also in the attitudes and values of citizens and "subjects" (see, e.g., Melton, 1988, 1990). For this and other reasons, even the debate over norms is partly empirical in nature. In any event, once those norms are agreed on and are promulgated, the problems of educating researchers about them, inviting them to accept those norms as their own, ensuring compliance with those norms, and so on raise a host of behavioral questions. Those questions are not new to psychologists and other social scientists; indeed, they parallel related interest in legal socialization, social change, and compliance with society's norms.

What is somewhat new in this realm is that the delinquents are not hyperactive children or teenage hoodlums or members of organized crime. The incorrigibles are scientists and scholars and teachers. They are us.

A concrete illustration of the difficulty of persuading scholars to obey the norms of their profession and the laws of the land serves as a useful way to begin. More general data will then be cited on the point. Finally we will discuss the possibilities for psychological research to help improve what some regard as a dreadful state of ethical affairs.

AN ILLUSTRATION

Several years ago the psychology department where one of the authors once held his primary academic appointment decided to revive the "subject pool" that had lay dormant for some time.[1] A committee was formed (of course) and several meetings were held to plan the renewed institution. Though not on the committee, we shared with them the American Psychological Association (APA) guidelines on the ethical use of subject pools (Committee for the Protection of Human Participants in Research [CPHPR], 1982). The members of that committee had been unaware of the APA guidelines; some individuals seemed surprised to learn of their existence.

The subject-pool procedures that were adopted by the department consisted, among other things, of mandatory participation for all students in the introductory psychology sequence. Prior notice of that requirement was not given. Students were informed on the first day of class that participation would be required of them. No alternatives to participation were provided. Any student not wanting to participate was instructed to report to a faculty member who oversees the pool, who would excuse the student if he or she offered an "acceptable reason." Acceptableness went undefined and was left to the complete discretion of the faculty member. Successful completion of participation was recorded on a form by the experimenters and that information was conveyed to instructors. Failure to participate, the students were told, would result in the withholding of the course grade, which in time would translate into failure in the course. Since these courses are taken primarily by psychology majors, that could translate into blocking graduation for failure to fulfill the research participation requirement. This would never come to pass, however, because of a secret understanding among the faculty that no student would ever be failed for not being a research participant. But a show of enforcement was made so that the great majority of students would be afraid of not participating. This is the velvet fist in the iron glove.

The adopted procedures anachronistically violated the APA Ethical Principles (Principle 9; APA, 1990) as well as the university's code of research ethics and federal regulation for the protection of human subjects ("Protection of Human Subjects," 1992). Compare the adopted practices to the language of the law and the university's own regulations (which, like a number of institutions, adopted the federal regulations as its own local code to ensure federal satisfaction with the university's assurances of ethical treatment of research participants):

> [N]o investigator may involve a human being as a subject in research . . . unless the investigator has obtained the legally effective consent of the subject. . . . An investigator shall seek such consent only under circumstances that provide the prospective subject . . . sufficient opportunity to consider whether or not to participate and that minimize the possibility of coercion or undue influence. ("Protection," 1992, §46.116)

> [P]articipation is voluntary, refusal to participate will involve no penalty or loss of benefits to which the subject is otherwise entitled. ("Protection," 1992, §46.116(a)(8))

The gap between ethical principle (in this instance incorporated into law) and departmental practice may be of interest to lawyers and ethicists. Even more interesting from our behavioral perspective were the reactions and actions of colleagues and others whose attention was directed toward that gap. First, the department chairman was asked why the APA guidelines were not followed. He answered that they created too many problems. For example, including notice in the course description would be troublesome. Also, if the principle of informed consent were honored, they might not get enough students for the department's experiments.

For three consecutive years the matter was brought before faculty meetings in an effort to persuade the faculty to modify the departmental policy in a way that would be more consistent with the ethical principles and more respectful of students' rights. The vote upholding the existing policy was invariably lopsided in the extreme, but the process of getting to that lopsided endorsement is instructive.

First, the central concern expressed was the anticipated loss of participants from experiments. Second, the reaction to the suggestion that this loss (if it materialized) should be endured in the interest of respect for ethical principles was as animated as any ever witnessed at faculty meetings. Third, no discussion about the content of the principles in question was ever undertaken. To borrow some language from the Vietnam War era, people seemed to have a need not to know. The last time the matter was brought before the department, typed handouts listing some of the most important provisions of the ethical principles of psychologists were distributed. When one colleague spied the words "informed consent," he announced to the crowd that such a practice would complicate our lives insufferably and we should have nothing to do with it. Instead of being passed around, examined, and discussed, the handouts were thrown aside.

Arguments that seemed to win the day against compliance with ethical principle were these: students themselves had not complained about the subject-pool requirement, the worst harm done to the students was boring them for an hour or two, this subject pool was no different from those used in the institutions where the present-day faculty members had been graduate students, an all-volunteer subject pool would be unrepresentative, the best if not the only way to get students to show up for experiments was in fact to coerce them, and these ethical principles came from outsiders, trouble-making busybodies as it were, be they federal bureaucrats, the APA, or university officials. Accordingly, the suggestion that we invite someone from the university's Office of Research Administration or its IRB to meet with us and work out a mutually acceptable plan was judged to constitute unwarranted intrusion into the affairs of the department. The debate, in short, had nothing to do with ethics and a great deal to do with meeting researchers' needs for participants and with departmental autonomy.

Worth noting are some comments made by some of the better-informed faculty, who had nevertheless remained silent during the meetings. Observing that there was no point in joining so hopeless a cause, one professor apologized for not dissenting. Another commented that he understood the ethical position being urged. He suggested that, when our version of the Nuremburg trials are held, a dissenting vote would qualify one as a member of the resistance. A third colleague, who had been a member of an IRB at a Boston research hospital as well as for the commonwealth's Department of Mental Health and who had also remained silent during the meetings, later commented that it would only be a matter of time before the feathers would fly. He proposed we start a betting pool on when that would be. Thus, while many members of this department did not know and did not want to know, others knew and understood and, for reasons worth trying to make sense of, remained silent.

The next step was to speak with someone in the university's Office of Research Administration. In an earlier, more casual conversation with the office's deputy, she remarked that she had attended a conference on research ethics and had learned, with considerable dismay, that at some universities professors compelled students to participate as research subjects. On the present occasion, after informing her that we were one of those universities, she showed clear signs of not wanting to believe what she was hearing, but she eventually promised to take the matter to the director. In a later telephone call she reported that her boss agreed that the practices complained of simply could not be allowed to go on and that the director would promptly speak to the department chairman and put a stop to it.[2] That was a long time ago. The subject pool continues as ever.

This story is full of hints about some of the forces at work among those who choose not to abide by ethical standards and among those who are asked to become involved in correcting those violations. We will extract some of those possibilities shortly and try to examine them through the eyes of a student of human behavior. In following the trail of some of those hints, we may be in a better position to figure out what can productively be done to improve the ethical conduct of researchers and scholars. But first we want to establish the generality of the problem by mentioning some of the findings of descriptive research on ethics-relevant behavior.

RESEARCH ON ETHICS-RELEVANT BEHAVIOR
Research attempting to measure the amount of researchers' behavior that conforms with major aspects of the ethical principles can be stated simply. There is little research or compliance.

The use of deception by social psychologists has increased steadily (Adair, Dushenko, & Lindsay, 1985; Gross & Fleming, 1982), seemingly in defiance but more likely in obliviousness to serious objections to the practice raised in the literature (e.g., Baumrind, 1964; Kelman, 1967) in the 1960s and the subsequent promulgation of ethical regulations admonishing it. According to the data of Adair et al. (1985), use of deception rose from 16.3% in 1961 to 58.5% in 1979. More than half of the published field experiments, once seen as a way to obviate the need for deception in laboratory experiments, reported the use of deception as part of their protocol.

Informed consent appears to present a problem not only for the psychology department described earlier. By 1983, reports of the use of that practice reached a high of 9.6% of published articles in social psychology (Adair et al., 1985). A recent survey of all U.S. psychology departments with subject pools and graduate programs found that only 12% complied fully with the APA ethical guidelines, and about half did not meet minimal ethical standards in their use of subject pools. However, 86% report that they advise students of their right to withdraw from participation in an experiment without penalty (Sieber & Saks, 1989).

We can attribute the failure of ethical conduct to many causes, but we may begin with simple ignorance. Ignorant people often assume that solutions to problems in those areas are intuitively obvious. At least this is the case for many lawyers' views of methodological and statistical problems and many researchers' views of ethical and legal problems. The less one knows about something, the less one can reason about or even notice the problem. Few graduate departments have courses on ethical dilemmas in research and their solution, and few standard research-methods courses or textbooks include the topic of ethics.

One might think that knowledge of the law and ethical principles relevant to one's area of activity would be among an informed researcher's problem-solving tools, much as design and analysis skills are. In short, while Boruch and Cecil (1982), Sieber (1982), and others labor at inventing methodologically ingenious solutions to ethical dilemmas, most researchers are unaware that dilemmas exist.

WHAT DO ETHICAL PRINCIPLES AND REGULATIONS TRY TO ACCOMPLISH?

The promulgation of a code of ethics by a professional organization is an attempt by a central authority, usually an organizational elite (Abbott, 1983), to place some limits on and create some aspirations for the behavior of members at large. The promulgation of more or less parallel government regulations is at least in part a reflection that the professional and scientific organizations have not succeeded and that the public or political interests now demand something more. In either case, the goal is to alter existing behavior patterns among people whose existing organizations, traditions, reward structures, and/or needs have led them to behave differently from what their own elites or government now desire.

What is the basis of such efforts at large-scale behavior change? Some efforts to impose change violate existing moral standards by trying to substitute a bureaucratically created regulatory regime. Those efforts to "legislate morality" confront formidable odds. In the instance of researchers' ethics, however, it seems that ethical codes and regulations try to clarify and enforce a widely accepted moral code that is sometimes violated by researchers pursuing their largely pragmatic need to collect data. This is not to say that the quest for knowledge is not a moral good (cf. Bermant, 1982) and one to which researchers quite rightly subscribe. But the notions that people (research participants) are to be treated as autonomous and self-determining and ought not be deceived or harmed for the benefit of others (researchers) are not exactly foreign to Western cultural traditions. Thus, the norms embodied in ethical codes and federal regulations for the most part reflect values familiar to society's moral traditions.

PSYCHOLOGICAL AND SOCIAL ANALYSIS OF THE CURRENT APPROACH

One might view the promulgation of ethical codes and regulations as an effort to bring about behavior change by announcing these norms and reminding researchers that in their pursuit of knowledge their behavior should not be inconsistent with other deeply held values. Thus, they serve an educational or symbolic function (Andenaes, 1977; Macaulay, 1987; Melton, 1988; Melton & Saks, 1986). They remind people about values they already share. Moreover, the announcing agencies—major professional associations and the federal government—are among the most legitimate sources of such announcements. Thus, the ethical codes and regulations rely on moral and institutional legitimacy. This would not be a bad start, but it should be apparent that it is not always enough.

Let us ask ourselves what constitutes opposition to these announcements of norms. This is another way of asking what maintains the old behavior. For some time we have held a pet theory that an ethical code contains a list of what members of a profession characteristically do that they ought not to do. By *characteristically*, we mean that the behaviors mentioned in the code define or reflect what is unique to that field. A good picture of the conduct of a field's members can be obtained by inverting the "shalt nots" of ethical codes and translating them into descriptive statements. By reading ethical codes we can discern, for example, that lawyers sometimes misuse clients' funds and miss filing dates, while psychologists sometimes become sexually involved with their patients. Such misbehavior is disturbingly common (see, e.g., Holroyd & Brodsky, 1977; Pope, Levenson, & Schover, 1979). However, it is also true that most lawyers do not pilfer their clients' accounts and most psychologists do not sexually exploit their clients and students. A successful regulatory strategy must both alter the contingencies that induce unethical behavior and sustain those that guide the behavior of moral professionals. The fact that members of different professions tend to do characteristic things may be an important clue that something in the structure of their activities maintains that behavior.

NEEDS FULFILLED

Our anecdote began by noting that the subject pool was being resurrected after years of disuse. Members of the department were going to a fair amount of trouble to set up and enforce a subject pool. Going to such lengths would be unnecessary if the subject pool did not meet an important need, namely, to facilitate their research. As the department changed and people joined the faculty whose research depended on human participants in laboratory settings, the ubiquitous sophomore was not to be passed up. Their work, with its intrinsic satisfactions as well as the rewards that come from publishing one's research, was made possible by the subject pool. In addition, they believed that without coercion students would not show up for experiments.

The reward structure of academic and entrepreneurial research supports getting research done. How likely is it that procedures that fulfill important needs for the faculty will be abandoned or seriously altered merely because someone in faraway Washington prints on paper that the procedures violate norms of the profession and the society?

LACK OF AWARENESS

As was hinted by the anecdote, ignorance may in part serve as insulation from the dissonance of knowing that what one is doing is frowned on. In this realm, ignorance of the law *is* an excuse. That is, ignorance is an escape from administrative liability. It surely appears to be an escape from personal responsibility. And if and when one is caught, it is far better to plead ignorance than to try to justify willful and knowing violation. Researchers who are made aware of the mere existence of ethical principles have a vague sense that whatever is in them is going to create problems, and it is better not to know their contents. From this comes, if not a need not to know, then at least a benefit from not knowing.

We already have alluded to researchers simply not knowing the content of ethical norms. The APA Ethical Principles are low on most scholars' list of reading material. What would motivate someone to want to know what they contain, much less to advert to them? The Code of Federal Regulations is even more obscure. Most researchers do not know their contents, and many do not even know of their existence. Although APA is working to change that—by requiring instruction in ethics as part of the curriculum in APA-approved (i.e., professional) graduate programs—it will not affect most researchers. Moreover, we fear that psychology students may hold such courses in the same low regard that law students hold required courses in professional responsibility.

Research on the process of socialization into the legal profession may be particularly instructive to would-be regulators of psychological research. Scholarship on research ethics has been part of the tradition of the ethics of health care; indeed, leading lights in the field are prominent in studies of ethics of both research and treatment (see, e.g., Beauchamp & Childress, 1983; Beauchamp, Faden, Wallace, & Waters, 1982). Within that tradition, the emphasis has been on informed consent, as reflected, for example, in the federal regulations. By contrast, legal ethicists have tended to be most concerned with problems of conflicts of interest. As suggested in the anecdote we have described, such an analysis is certainly applicable to research (see, e.g., Melton & Gray, 1988). Although rigorous ethics is often consistent with rigorous research, flashy, "quick and dirty" studies are apt to provide relatively prompt and sometimes substantial reinforcement. In fact, many of the classic studies in social psychology—the sort that are standard in introductory psychology textbooks—are ones that now are regarded as ethically problematic.

Where "crime" *does* pay, as is often the case in research, efforts to make the social significance of such behavior salient are particularly important. The legal profession is again analogous, even though the underlying social causation may differ. It is only slightly caricatured to say that the legal profession systematically socializes law students away from concern for the public interest (Stover & Erlanger, 1989). In that context, the conflicts be-

tween legal practice and legal values necessitate an elaborate system of regulation to ensure that lawyers do not exploit their clients and that arbiters
not "bend the rules" to protect self-interest. The resulting norms are sustained by a common culture even though they are not immediately advan-
tageous.

The significance of such an ethical culture is illustrated by research suggesting that the most important effect of deterrence may be to neutralize
bad examples. More generally, dramatic social change through law seems
to occur when the state guides the citizenry toward a new view of morality
(e.g., cigarette smoking is socially undesirable). The law and quasi-legal
systems operate then as complex systems of social cues in which the influence of the community is internalized (for research on the law as a media-
tor of social influence, see, e.g., Bank, 1985; Paternoster, Saltzman, Waldo,
& Chiricos, 1983; Williams, 1985; see also the research reviewed in Melton
& Saks, 1986).

Existing Norms, Beliefs, Attitudes, and Habits: Socialization

Researchers have been socialized by their training and other experiences.
Norms that run throughout the profession—as well as the local enclaves
we call academic departments and research firms—support the activity of
research, not the creation of barriers to getting research done. In assessing
the propriety of their current behavior, people recall how things were done
at other places they have been. They share beliefs that what they are doing
is right, or at least that it is all right. Or that, even if it is wrong, it is only a
little bit wrong (e.g., if we violate the principle of informed consent, the resulting harm is still minor), it is being done for a good cause (there is no
higher calling than the quest for knowledge), everyone else is doing it, or it
is an unavoidable necessity.

If nothing else, the old practices enjoy a certain familiarity and endure
through social inertia. What was perfectly all right when we were students
cannot have become wrong now that we are professors. And we can comfort ourselves that we are not alone in our belief that these things are, if not
good, then at least acceptable. Other departments model the behavior for
us, we for them, and within a department we model acceptance of those
practices for each other. Researchers also share the belief that others would
not understand these matters as well as they do, and, therefore, others

ought not to be invited to participate in the local policy-making. That brings us to the problem of small and relatively cohesive organizations being resistant to change from without.

GROUP COHESION VERSUS ALIEN AUTHORITY

A number of group processes work to enforce the existing practices. The attitudes, beliefs, and norms mentioned above are largely the product of group processes. Individuals' most immediate group connections teach and then support the attitudes and beliefs they hold. (See chaps. 5 and 10 in Saks & Krupat, 1988.) Outsiders not only have less opportunity to influence the group but are viewed as lacking sufficient understanding or legitimacy. We suggest that those who propose a change of norms are outsiders whose reference groups are not the local membership group. That explains why a member of the group is dissenting·("He is not really one of us," "He is not a 'good citizen'") and helps the group discount the suggestion of change even if it is being made from within the group.

The power of the group to enforce its norms is familiar to us all, even though we ignore it in devising means of advancing ethical conduct. Most people feel great discomfort disagreeing with colleagues, especially over something that might affect the single most important feature of a researcher's work life: the ability to do research. Most of us prefer to avoid conflict with our colleagues.[3] But more palpable sanctions exist in work groups. The colleague who served on hospital and state IRBs may have held his tongue at the faculty meeting because he hoped to win tenure in that department. And those who did have tenure and also understood what was being talked about saw nothing to gain, and perhaps a few things to lose, by opposing an overwhelming majority that preferred the status quo.

Discussions of ethics may draw an affective response similar to reactance motivation (see Brehm, 1966). When behavior that has not been perceived as objectionable among one's peers is challenged (as happens, e.g., when deceptive research is criticized), the individual whose work is the brunt of the critique is apt to perceive a threat to personal integrity and freedom (indeed, behavior that is societally defined as within the realm of academic freedom).

Even if individuals involved in such discussions are not defensive, "seeing" the ethical issues in psychological research is often difficult, because the issues are generally more subtle than in professional ethics. When no discernible harm results from a particular practice, it is hard to see how a participant may be wronged by it. Similarly, the fact that research generally is not for participants' own benefit has enormous significance for the ethics of research involving minors (see Melton & Stanley, in this volume), but that meaning is unlikely to be intuitively obvious.

Given such a context, it seems unlikely that ethical decision making in research will be mastered simply through modeling. When the problems are as abstract and the social influences as intense as they are in research ethics, simple "mentoring" is unlikely to be sufficient. In that regard, both trained and student psychologists typically regard their preparation in ethics as inadequate, and they particularly rue the lack of practice in formal ethical problem solving (Tymchuk, 1985).

Against such forces—cognitive, motivational, and social—what chance do toothless pronouncements from Washington have? To violate legal and professional norms entails no apparent serious consequences, and probably no consequences at all. To violate the local group norms, or even to challenge them, results in immediate psychological costs and potential social and material costs. The traditional modes of regulation by professions and by government are weak and diffuse influences against the panoply of forces arrayed against them.

WHAT OTHER STRATEGIES MIGHT CHANGE THE BEHAVIOR?

Development of a comprehensive strategy to promote the ethical conduct of psychological research could be informed by consideration of data and theories developed in other contexts to explain the efficacy (or lack thereof) of legal and quasi-legal regulation. Zimring and Hawkins (1977) have offered a particularly rich, if often commonsensical, set of hypotheses about the relevant factors. For example, they have suggested that the greater the moral and cultural significance of a given custom, the more force that will be necessary if authorities are to succeed in changing it. Similarly, the force necessary to change a custom increases with the organization level of those who adhere to the custom. By contrast, if legal regulation inherently reduces the motivation for following a particular practice (e.g., if prohibition of segregation in public accommodations substantially reduces or altogether removes the competitive advantage of segregationist restaurant owners), then less force will be required.

As Zimring and Hawkins's analysis implies, the forces that determine the efficacy of a particular legal strategy typically are complex and variable. With that caveat, however, we will consider alternative strategies that often come to mind when people discuss what might replace or supplement weak regulatory devices that have failed predictably to create behavior change—the situation that we believe applies to current modes of research regulation.

MORE AGGRESSIVE REGULATION

If the federally mandated creation of IRBs on every university campus and the compulsory adoption of codes of ethics and assurances of local enforcement have accomplished as little as they appear to have, one is hard-pressed to think of a feasible way of doing better through more regulations. Nevertheless, in the face of such an imbalance of forces, one is quick to think of trying to change the regulatory practices—increasing surveillance, intrusiveness, and the ability to impose sanctions. It seems likely, however, that the resources necessary to accomplish all of that would neither be nor should ever be forthcoming. The likely benefits of such intrusive regulation seem not to warrant either the cost of deploying them or the damage they may do to the research enterprise.

CRIMINAL SANCTIONS

Our concern about the hidden costs of aggressive enforcement exceeding the expected benefits is made clearer in the area of criminal penalties. One could, out of frustration, ask a legislature to proscribe undesirable researcher conduct through the use of criminal penalties. Researchers who, for example, failed to obtain informed consent or deceived participants could be subjected to fines and perhaps imprisonment or simply be prosecuted—because, as one political scientist has put it, the process is the punishment (Feeley, 1979)

First, behavioral science research is an unlikely candidate for criminal legislation. As researchers keep noting, the material harm is small. The offenders are engaged in what is essentially a productive social activity. And they do not come from the socioeconomic class legislatures are inclined to sanction criminally. The social and economic costs of such laws, if enforced even occasionally, would exceed any good they would accomplish. The problem here is that such penalties may tend to inhibit the productive activity at the same time they inhibit the illegal activity. Highly risk-averse researchers may be so frightened by the possibility of erroneous enforcement that they would decide to get out of the empirical research business altogether, which is assuredly not the goal of law or ethics in this area. This reasoning is well explained in Block and Sidak's (1980) "The Cost of Antitrust Deterrence: Why Not Hang a Price Fixer Now and Then?" Deterrence that is not optimal is likely to stop socially useful activity along with the harmful activity.

The drafters of the federal regulations appeared to recognize the potential for unintended negative side effects by their prohibition of IRBS' consideration of potential social consequences ("Protection," 1992, §46.111(2)), presumably because of the chilling effect such government-sanctioned review might have on unconventional ideas (cf. Askin, 1972). In any event, the "goal" of research regulation might be characterized as *positive side effects*, even more than the express purposes.

This idea can be illustrated by the finding that the legal requirement for bottle deposits—intended to reduce litter—results in a striking reduction in glass-related lacerations of children (Baker, Moore, & Wise, 1986). Thus, a manipulation of the market to reduce roadside bottles not only results in less litter but also structures a world in which glass, as a general matter, is used more wisely. In the same vein, research regulation is ultimately aimed not at increasing or decreasing particular practices. Instead, it is intended to facilitate the development of an ethical climate for the conduct of research, in which scientists can be trusted to undertake considered, informed judgments about the ethics of their work.

One still might be tempted, though, to suggest that if we occasionally imprison a violator, we will finally get the attention of the rest of the research community. An interesting illustration comes from the practice of dueling in the American South during the first half of the 19th century. Cultural norms and, it is argued, important considerations of efficiency in social control supported the custom. The same class of people who felt compelled by the cultural norms to support the duel were also hard at work in legislatures passing laws calculated to deter dueling. Although it might not be manly to back off from a duel or to violate the expectations of one's colleagues, deference to the law would be tolerable. In order for the law to serve as such a catalyst of cultural change, enforcement would have to be vigorous and prompt. Thus, some practioners, caught in the transition from one set of cultural norms to another, would have to bear the cost of that transition (Schwartz, Baxter, & Ryan, 1984).

Even if such laws were passed, another problem still remains. Unlike laws to prohibit dueling, these laws would be so widely perceived as inappropriate to the crime that the few reported offenses would be unlikely to be prosecuted. The few that were prosecuted would be unlikely to result in convictions. Each actor in the legal process might exercise his or her discretion to nullify the law.

TORT ACTIONS

In the mixed society, lying somewhere between regulation by the invisible hand of the free market and regulation by the government, the private enforcement of tort litigation has grown. Tort law has some apparent successes to its credit, among them the creation of safer products and practices. Surely it has succeeded in catching the attention of the nation's physicians and manufacturers (Saks, 1986a, 1986b). If nothing else, tort law helps spread the cost of unavoidable injuries among many of us instead of allowing the cost to fall entirely on the innocent victim. Could we, in accord with tort law, leave enforcement of ethical standards and regulations to the participants themselves?[4]

On the positive side, the existence of standards (both governmental and professional) makes it easier for the plaintiff participant to prove that the defendant researcher breached his or her duty of care and performed the research negligently. Moreover, although they are exceedingly rare, lawsuits by research participants against psychologists for violating participants' rights are not altogether unheard of (Ruback & Greenberg, 1986). If such suits became more common and successful, researchers might begin to practice defensive research, assumed to consist of conducting research in a safe and ethical manner. (Indeed, if researchers had any conception of what a marvelous protection against liability informed consent is, they would welcome the opportunity to obtain and document it.)

But few plaintiffs' lawyers will be seen leaving their business cards around psychology departments, now or in the future. Although liability could probably be shown, rarely is there a palpable injury worth compensating. For that reason potential plaintiffs as well as their lawyers are unlikely to bring suits. While the harm in the aggregate may actually amount to something compensable (say, just compensation for their time), the injury is so diffuse that it would take a class action to make a worthwhile case. But unlike the usual class action, the defendants are again spread far and wide. The expected value of the case may be judged by counsel not to be worth its cost. Thus, psychologists seem safe from any specter of a subject-pool malpractice crisis. Those engaged in applied and evaluation research may run somewhat greater risks, but they are probably more sensitive to the rights and dignity of their participants (if only because they are not students and the distribution of power is often far different).

PROFESSIONAL SELF-REGULATION

For reasons that have been explored often elsewhere (Hogan, 1983; Keith-Spiegel & Koocher, 1985), formal attempts at professional self-regulation through continuing education and through ethics and disciplinary bodies are, despite the most sincere efforts of those officials directly involved, renowned for their lack of success. This has been found in professions such as law (e.g., Burbank & Duboff, 1974; Carlin, 1966) and medicine (e.g., Derbyshire, 1983; Freidson, 1975) and in the forensic sciences (e.g., Saks, 1989; Saks & Van Duizend, 1983). Reasons for the limited success of professional disciplinary bodies are numerous; they are not self-starting investigatory or enforcement bodies, but they react to complaints. The focus on individuals and the careful privacy that is maintained through most of the process works against having much educative or general deterrent impact on the larger group. Ethics committees are habitually maintained at resource levels too low to allow them much impact. Because they are creatures of the professional organizations of the "defendants," they are necessarily sensitive to the members' rights and interests. Organizations must balance the tension between needing to police their members (whether out of the purest or most pragmatic of motives) and the need not to ruffle too many of the members' feathers. Thus, ironically, the more widespread the ethical violations, the more unlikely are those practices to become candidates for aggressive enforcement.

Fear of its own liability will also cause the rational organization to prefer to err in its members' direction. A sanctioned member, whose livelihood may be threatened, has both a strong economic motive and a colorable suit against the association. An outsider complainant who feels a whitewash was carried out has less of both. Finally, their jurisdiction (acting only against members and individuals) and their sanctions (the most Draconian being dismissal from the association) amount to nothing for many researchers. Even where possible, expulsion is probably more costly in many respects to the professional association than to the ethical offender (cf. Keith-Spiegel & Koocher, 1985).

One interesting and hopeful, if small, attempt at professional self-regulation is the requirement that editors of APA and division journals exact from authors certification that the data reported in their study were gathered within the ambit of the ethical standards. Unethically gathered data are not to be accepted for review, much less for publication. Here the profession shows itself so concerned about the problem of research ethics that it is willing to accept the potential price of losing some substantive knowledge as the cost of encouraging more ethical research practices. What makes this a potentially effective device is that it applies to all researchers, not only those against whom complaints are filed. And the policy's posture as a routine requirement for manuscript submission gives it educative power. Certification of ethical conduct will be a permanent gate through which every researcher's work must pass if it is to be published by an APA-affiliated journal.

In the experience of one of the authors as a journal editor enforcing this policy, researchers have complied cheerfully and promptly with the certification requirement. We note with a mixture of pride and skepticism that not a single submitter to the journal reported that the research was conducted in any way less than in full accord with APA's ethical standards and the federal regulations. This high level of compliance is a bit puzzling in light of the research showing widespread questionable practices. Perhaps only the more scrupulous researchers submit their work to *Law and Human Behavior*. Perhaps someone who will violate ethical standards also has no scruples against lying to editors, both acts serving to get the research published. Or perhaps the puzzle is explained by widespread ignorance of the content of the Ethical Principles. If one does not know the principles, it becomes easier to assume that one has not acted in violation of them. The loopholes or ambiguity (real or perceived) may also account for the unanimous self-perception of ethical compliance. Or perhaps researchers delude themselves that *their* research is ethical, given the "obvious" benefits of their work to society.

FURTHER SOCIAL AND PSYCHOLOGICAL ANALYSIS OF THE
TRADITIONAL STRATEGIES

Are we, then, faced with the impossibility of developing ways of changing the behavior of researchers and the inevitability of devising solutions that do not work? We think not. After all, it has been possible to get police to give *Miranda* warnings (even though they may dislike them) and real-estate brokers to offer a right of first refusal to tenants in condominium conversions (though they might prefer not to). Surely it cannot be harder to get social and behavioral scientists to behave ethically even though they may not want to. Furthermore, we would like to think that, if anyone has the empirical knowledge and analytical tools to figure out how to accomplish this little bit of social change, psychologists and other social scientists do.

In response to the title of this chapter, we believe that we can "legislate morality." But the most effective way to do so is indirectly. That is, a legislature cannot pass a statute commanding people to adopt certain attitudes and beliefs, but it can use its power to structure social arrangements that will in turn eventually bring about new attitudes and beliefs. The law, for example, operates as a social architect not so much when it uses carrots and sticks to enforce norms of conduct but when it structures a world that quietly and sometimes imperceptibly encourages or compels one kind of behavior rather than another. Under such circumstances, attitudes form to justify and maintain the behavior being omitted. Examples that have been discussed in the psychology-and-law or policy literature range from the constitutional structuring of relations among parts of the government, through choosing school-desegregation strategies, licensing, and common-law liability rules, to regulating which side of the road cars will drive on. (See Bem, 1970; Kelman, 1958; Melton & Saks, 1986).

With this in mind, let us examine some additional reasons why past attempts might have failed, and then see whether, in this analytic light, we can devise some strategies that might be more successful.

DISTRIBUTION OF POWER

The language of the APA ethical principles reveals its sensitivity to the pernicious consequences that tend to result when researcher and participant differ sharply in their power. "The investigator respects the individual's freedom to withdraw from the research at any time. The obligation to protect this freedom requires careful thought and consideration when the investigator is in a position of authority or influence over the participant. Such positions of authority include, but are not limited to, situations in which . . . the participant is a student, client, or employee of the investigator" (Principle 9f; APA, 1990).

Similarly, the federal regulations contain special sections seeking to provide "additional protection" to fetuses, pregnant women, and others ("Additional Protections," 1992). The special vulnerability of some populations is not inherent but flows from their limited social power relative to the researcher. It is no mere coincidence that psychological knowledge is much more likely to be built on data obtained from college students rather than staff, children rather than parents, clients rather than professionals, soldiers rather than officers, and workers rather than managers. Studies of hospital patients, child abuse, treatment of children in schools, and treatment of the elderly lead to similar conclusions (see Sieber, 1989, for an analysis of ethical issues in studying powerful people).

Similarly, the contrast between the failure to win the acquiescence of departmental colleagues and the response of authors who submitted their manuscripts to *Law and Human Behavior* is not a result of the editor suddenly learning the art of persuasion. Only one departmental colleague among two dozen voted in favor of ethical treatment of research participants. At the journal the editor owns the only vote that counts. Not surprisingly, the ability to bring about behavior change in researchers is also conditioned on the distribution of power.

In at least a small way, the policy of journal editors "reminding" would-be contributors about their ethical responsibilities capitalizes on this principle. An even more direct application is in the current procedure for review of grant applications by the federal Alcohol, Drug Abuse, and Mental Health Administration (ADAMHA). Study sections are charged with reviewing procedures for protecting human participants, even though proposals will generally have already passed IRB review. Moreover, as a response to several well-publicized incidents involving research fraud and academic misconduct by ADAMHA grantees and plagiarism by the former director of the National Institute of Mental Health, a branch of ADAMHA (see Hunt, 1989), applicants for research training grants now must specify the means by which they conduct training in research ethics. In turn, such plans are a part of the merit review by the study section. Whether these relatively new procedures are being taken seriously by reviewers is unknown, but they clearly present the opportunity for both self-scrutiny and external review, with proximal reinforcement contingencies.

Although these insights are not particularly novel, they are important. Any informed attempt to bring about social change cannot be oblivious to the distribution of power.

THE FUNCTIONING OF BUREAUCRATIC INSTITUTIONS
Bureaucratic organizations are defined by the compartmentalization of responsibilities and are characterized by inertia. Academic bureaucracies work to preserve the narrow autonomies of departments and scholars. For many purposes these are desirable characteristics, and in any event they are unlikely to be changed—and certainly not so that more ethical research practices can be enforced. But again, these characteristics of institutions must be considered by the architects of reform if reform is to be made more likely.

The provisions of the federal regulations seem to have failed in this regard, at least where academic institutions are concerned. First, no real monitoring or enforcement, even in traditional terms, is put into place by them. As the President's Commission (1981) observes, enforcement "relies largely on a promise of faithful execution of certain regulatory responsibilities by those at local institutions" (p. 37). The design of the federal regulations was to create IRBS as the major ethics enforcement device. In government agencies or private research firms, or perhaps even in some research hospitals, with their more centralized control over the choice of projects and procedures, an administrative body has some chance of succeeding, particularly where income from budgeted or contract research is the fiscal life blood of those organizations.

In universities, however, IRBS are altogether alien creatures. They were created to perform a centralized monitoring function in institutions that are structured as semiautonomous units. Their advent did not involve plugging them into existing lines of authority but creating new and unfamiliar lines. Thus, to make prospects for success even more unlikely, academic researchers, unaccustomed to being told what they may or may not do, are now to be restrained by unfamiliar bodies that previously had no power over any aspect of their lives. Researchers resent the requirement of IRB approval of their research proposals and actively resist suggestions that IRBS fulfill their obligation to engage in continuing oversight (President's Commission, 1981). The researchers need not worry about that. One study of IRB activity found that 63% of them made no effort at all to go beyond initial proposal reviews and few of the rest did much more (National Commission, 1978; President's Commission, 1981, p. 46).

Further, IRBS are placed in the middle of a transaction in which the federal regulations concerning ethical conduct are made applicable to individual researchers through their institutions. Although this seems convenient from a federal bureaucratic perspective, it means that individual researchers feel little responsibility for honoring the regulations (assuming they know about them). The institutional officials who made the promises to the government are not assigned the responsibility for monitoring and enforcement and certainly have no direct control over the researchers. The IRB, which is required to monitor the research, has little ability or inclination to do so. To whom can one turn but the university official to report a violation? Yet, what can one do when it is the IRB that has the legal and intellectual authority to act? If the IRB did investigate and agreed that a violation existed, who is it, within the institutional structure, to tell colleagues in another department what to do? The federal regulations direct the IRB, instead, to report serious or continuing violations to the appropriate federal agency, but IRBS rarely do so. And if they did, even though the federal regulations provide for debarment or suspension of institutions and researchers (see "Misconduct in Science and Engineering," 1992; "Governmentwide Debarment and Suspension," 1992), most agencies respond to such reporting with confusion and unevenness (President's Commission, 1981, p. 53).

Thus, the architecture for enforcement of the federal regulations seems calculated to blunt the effort at every turn. A simple way to view the result is through the concept of diffusion of responsibility (Latane & Darley, 1970). The regulations break up the responsibility into so many fragments that no one with the authority to act feels the responsibility to do so. The architects of reform need to focus on the existing units of control and harness their influence within organizations. These may vary among types of institution, based on their own characteristic structures. What the President's Commission (1981, p. 39) has to say about the negotiation of assurances between local institutions and the federal government could also be said about much of the process of regulating research: it "may discourage thoughtful self-scrutiny and actual compliance."

For example, some IRBs have been diligent in specifying what informed-consent forms should look like, down to such details as the type of headings to use. But they have declined to become interested in the process by which people are meaningfully informed and whether or not their consent is more than a formality. No useful purpose is served by the perfunctory filling out of papers, except providing researchers with evidence of their superficial compliance.

GROUP DYNAMICS AND REFERENCE GROUPS

We will not try to repeat here the vast literature on organizational and group dynamics (see Chaps. 12 and 13 in Saks & Krupat, 1988). We will do little more than to suggest that it has to be relevant to understanding the failure of legislated changes to bring about behavioral modification. Reformed regulations need to be aimed at the correct parts of an organization and call into play the proper group processes.

That our colleagues regarded the values of their government and their professional association and the authority of their university as illegitimate or deserving resistance is significant. It should not surprise a social psychologist to find that obedience to the norms of the group that is immediately present, whose day-to-day interactions make up our work lives, is deemed more vital than obedience to the contrary norms of one's university, profession, and nation. To think that we can institute norms and regulations from above and expect the researchers in the trenches to fall into line as soon as word reaches them is to ignore the power of the small group.

At the same time, this is not to say that anything outside the small group is alien. These same people have as reference groups certain researchers, certain other parts of the university, and opinion leaders in their field, among others. They aspire to be like and to be accepted by those other groups. What is done and valued by those reference groups is likely to be learned by and adopted by those for whom those groups are references. Thus, another challenge for research in this area might be to figure out who are viewed as reference groups for most or many researchers, and how those reference groups might be employed to bring about changed attitudes and behavior. Individuals and groups who are outsiders have the power both to facilitate and to inhibit change. We have relied on them in ways that add barriers to change and have failed to exploit their strengths. We have tried to bring about change by ignoring what we know and are able to find out about the processes of change in groups.

SOCIAL INFLUENCE ANALYSIS

The final area of psychological knowledge to be discussed is social influence. A thorough review of this enormous and relevant area will not be attempted. The literature on social influence embraces the determinants of conformity, normative and informational influence, modeling of behavior, social and material incentives, deterrence, the consequences of nonoptimal deterrence, the possibilities for and even the benefits of minority influence, authority, the multiple bases of social power, internalization of new values versus mere compliance, and the need for perceived freedom (and the accompanying danger that excessive external control invites violation) (see Saks & Krupat, 1988). This research clearly suggests the potential for social change. By combining it with knowledge of group processes and knowledge of how organizations and people within them behave, more effective social change ought to be possible.

APPLIED RESEARCH THAT MIGHT LEAD US TO THE PROMISED LAND

We have been suggesting that more knowledge of the principles and processes of behavior will assist the architects of change in bringing more change about. The lack of success in improving ethical thought and conduct among researchers and their institutions results in part from the architects' not knowing much more than their intuitions about behavior change and few psychologists and other social scientists turning their attention to the problem. For example, most psychologists would say that, in order to change behavior, the forces maintaining the old behavior must be understood and considered in the change strategy. The architects of bureaucratic change have overlooked altogether what is axiomatic for most psychologists.

One of the major aims of this chapter has been to demonstrate that a base of knowledge exists on which new and more effective strategies could be built. That base of knowledge includes building blocks ranking from the cognitive levels of belief and attitude change through the dynamics of groups, reward structures, and optimal deterrence and the structure and functioning of organizations.

Another aim has been to try to suggest lines of research that might be undertaken by social scientists and others interested either in the problem of ethical conduct for itself or as one instance of behavior change (or lack of change) through law. The research might begin with the development of better and more regular measures of the behavior of interest, so that change over time can be assessed. A prerequisite to knowing whether anything has worked is measuring the conduct the reforms are supposed to be working on. A second major line of work might involve measurement of researchers' knowledge of ethical principles and their beliefs and attitudes about ethics-relevant issues. To discover that they know nothing of the content of ethical norms suggests quite a different starting place than to discover they understand them well but have no intention of complying with them. The latter implies the third line of research, which is to try to identify, with empirical and theoretical guidance, the forces maintaining the current behavior. The fourth theme is the creation of change strategies that are better informed by theory and by the findings of the research that have been outlined. The fifth step has been implied by all of the others: empirical evaluations of the effectiveness, side effects, and so on of the strategies that have been put in place.

VISITATION

We conclude by offering one illustration of a strategy that shows the possibility for somewhat-novel solutions that can be informed by existing knowledge of behavior and might be both more effective and cost-effective. We call this plan "visitation."

Imagine that a large number of psychology departments around the country received a call from a neighboring psychologist, saying that, in accord with a program sponsored by the APA or American Psychological Society (APS), several psychologists from a neighboring institution would like to visit with them and discuss their research activities and particularly how they have solved ethical issues in their research. The visitors would then come, sit down with the chairperson and several other members of the visited department, and talk. The visitors themselves had been contacted by a psychologist from APA or APS whose job it was to organize such visitors' groups.

The visitors themselves would be inclined to accept the assignment since such a "site visit" is a relatively prestigious thing to be asked to do. It would not take long, and a visit with a neighboring department is often enjoyable. When one is singled out and personally asked, it is fairly hard to decline. Because the visitors themselves may not know much about research ethics, the person at APA or APS would provide them with reading materials. And because they want to be prepared for their visit, lest they look foolish to their neighboring colleagues and to themselves, they will read and think about the material. Thus, we will have educated a substantial number of psychologists at the outset. Similarly, those who are to be visited will prepare themselves by figuring out what they are doing by way of research ethics and will themselves obtain and read some material because they do not want to look bad.

The fact of being visited by someone—anyone—who wants to know what one is up to in the realm of ethics is unheard of. Yet any occasion for meeting people and having to say things to them compels most of us to do some preparation. Even if the visit did not take place, some education and soul searching would have been accomplished. The visit itself provides an occasion for neighboring colleagues to talk about research ethics—friendly enough and, without institutional power, nonthreatening—but with outsiders, so those visited will want to look good, knowledgeable, perhaps even ethical, another rare event that the visitation program would set into motion. The visitors' assignment would be to discuss and to solve problems. They are not there to formally evaluate or to file charges if violations are seen. At the same time, they are to state frankly their views of how well the department is doing. They would be expected to send a letter to the APA or APS reporting on their visit. Although the report should carry no sanctions, it implies further scrutiny. The possibility of follow-up visits, which would be held open, again suggests further scrutiny and the desirability of looking even better next time.

Such a program would cost a salary and support for someone at the APA or APS, but it is highly decentralized and nonbureaucratic. It uses social influence aimed by friendly strangers at the people who are in the business of doing research. The visitors cannot be rejected as an elite from Washington, because they are from a nearby university or just as ignorant about psychological research. The visitation strategy subtly sets in motion a need to know that was previously absent, and perhaps a felt need to reform. We would, of course, need to evaluate the effectiveness of such a program.

This is only one strategy among a potentially large number. It is offered as an illustration that, with some knowledge of principles of behavior change, we may be able to design quiet strategies that are more effective in promoting more ethical behavior and more knowledge of ethical issues and begin to create an ethos in which ethical concerns are an inherent part of the research enterprise.

Notes

1. To remove any doubt, the department referred to is not in Iowa, Nebraska, or South Carolina.

2. Considering that one department's flagrant conduct places the entire university's eligibility for federal research funding at risk, it is surprising that any university-level official would tolerate the violations. On the other hand, as a practical matter, the risk of being caught is small and the sanctions are not likely to be severe.

3. One study of psychiatrists found that 41% believed they had observed a colleague incorrectly administer electroconvulsive therapy. Of those, only 2% reported the apparent error to an appropriate authority and only 17% spoke to the colleague of their concern (Benedict & Saks, 1987).

4. The potential utility of the tort system for shaping socially desirable behavior through deterrence was illustrated to the second author during a sabbatical in Norway. Although snow seemed to fall daily in the wintertime, no one shoveled their walks—a fact reflected in Norway's high accidental injury rate. Colleagues explained the behavior (more precisely, *lack* of behavior) on the basis of the minimal risk of a tort action for negligence if one's property is not kept safe. Meanwhile, because of the collectivization housing developments as well as the cost of street and sidewalk maintenance, social responsibility (not just legal responsibility) is diffuse. A senior official in the national public health programs confided a half-serious wish that every person who fell and broke a hip would be brought to the highway department before being taken to the hospital. Although wintertime accidents in Norway may seem far from the topic, the example illustrates the necessity of structures to sustain socially desirable behavior.

References

Abbott, A. (1983). Professional ethics. *American Journal of Sociology, 88*, 855–885.

Adair, J. G., Dushenko, T. W., & Lindsay, R. C. L. (1985). Ethical regulations and their impact on research practice. *American Psychologist, 40*, 59–72.

Additional Protections Pertaining to Research, Development, and Related Activities Involving Fetuses, Pregnant Women, and Human *in vitro* Fertilization, 45 C.F.R. §§46.201–46.211 (1992).

American Psychological Association (1990). Ethical principles of psychologists (amended June 2, 1989). *American Psychologist, 45,* 390–395.

Andenaes, J. (1977). The moral or educative influence of criminal law. In J. L. Tapp & F. J. Levine (Eds.), *Law, justice and the individual in society: Psychological and legal issues* (pp. 50–59). New York: Holt, Rinehart, & Winston.

Askin, F. (1972). Chilling effect: A view from the social sciences. *Columbia Human Rights Law Review, 4,* 59–88.

Baker, M. D., Moore, S. E., & Wise, P. H. (1986). The impact of "bottle bill" legislation on the incidence of lacerations in childhood. *American Journal of Public Health, 76,* 1243–1244.

Bank, B. J. (1985). Comparative research on the social determinants of adolescent drinking. *Social Psychology Quarterly, 48,* 164–177.

Baumrind, D. (1964). Some thoughts on the ethics of research: On reading Milgram's "Behavioral study of obedience." *American Psychologist, 19,* 421–423.

Beauchamp, T. L., & Childress, J. F. (1983). *Principles of biomedical ethics* (2nd ed.). New York: Oxford University Press.

Beauchamp, T. L., Faden, R. R., Wallace, R. J., & Waters, L. R. (Eds.). (1982). *Ethical issues in social science research.* Baltimore: Johns Hopkins University Press.

Bem, D. J. (1970). *Beliefs, attitudes, and human affairs.* Belmont CA: Brooks/Cole.

Benedict, A. R., & Saks, M. J. (1987). The regulation of professional behavior: Electroconvulsive therapy in Massachusetts. *Journal of Psychiatry and Law, 1987,* 247–275.

Bermant, G. (1982). Justifying social science research in terms of social benefit. In T. L. Beauchamp, R. R. Faden, R. J. Wallace, & L. R. Waters (Eds.), *Ethical issues in social science research* (pp. 87–103). Baltimore: Johns Hopkins University Press.

Block, M. K., & Sidak, J. G. (1980). The cost of antitrust deterrence: Why not hang a price-fixer now and then? *Georgetown Law Journal, 68,* 1131–1139.

Boruch, R., & Cecil, J. S. (1982). Statistical strategies for preserving privacy in direct inquiry. In J. E. Sieber (Ed.), *The ethics of social research: Surveys and experiments* (pp. 167–189). New York: Springer.

Brehm, J. W. (1966). *A theory of psychological reactance.* New York: Academic Press.

Burbank, D. O., & Duboff, R. S. (1974). Ethics and the legal profession: A survey of Boston lawyers. *Suffolk University Law Review, 9,* 66–117.

Carlin, J. (1966). *Lawyers' ethics: A survey of the New York City bar.* New York: Sage.

Committee for the Protection of Human Participants in Research. (1982). *Ethical principles in the conduct of research with human participants.* Washington DC: American Psychological Association.

Derbyshire, R. C. (1983). How effective is medical self-regulation? *Law and Human Behavior, 7,* 183–202.

Feeley, M. (1979). *The process is the punishment: Handling cases in a lower criminal court.* New York: Sage.

Freidson, E. (1975). *Doctoring together: A study of professional social control.* Chicago: University of Chicago Press.

Governmentwide Debarment and Suspension, 45 CFR §§76.100–76.635 (1992).

Gray, B. H., & Cooke, R. A. (1980). Ethics and regulation: Impact of Institutional Review Boards on research. *Hastings Center Report, 10,* 36–41.

Gray, B. H., Cooke, R. A., & Tannenbaum, A. S. (1978). Research involving human subjects. *Science, 201,* 1094–1101.

Gross, A. E., & Fleming, I. (1982). Twenty years of deception in social psychology. *Personality and Social Psychology Bulletin, 8,* 402–408.

Hogan, D. B. (1983). Professional regulation (Special issue). *Law & Human Behavior, 7,* 99–305

Holroyd, J. C., & Brodsky, A. (1977). Psychologists' attitudes and practices regarding erotic and nonerotic physical contact with patients. *American Psychologist, 32,* 843–849.

Hunt, M. (1989, May 14). Did the penalty fit the crime? *New York Times Magazine.*

Kelman, H. C. (1958). Compliance, identification, and internalization: Three processes of attitude change. *Journal of Conflict Resolution, 2,* 51–60.

Kelman, H. C. (1967). Human use of human subjects: The problem of deception in social psychological experiments. *Psychological Bulletin, 7,* 1–11.

Keith-Spiegel, P., & Koocher, G. P. (Eds.). (1985). *Ethics in psychology: Professional standards and cases.* New York: Random House.

Latane, B., & Darley, J. (1970). *The unresponsive bystander: Why doesn't he help?* New York: Appleton-Century-Crofts.

Macaulay, S. (1987). Images of law in everyday life: The lessons of school, entertainment, and spectator sports. *Law and Society Review, 21,* 185–218.

Melton, G. B. (1988). The significance of law in the everyday lives of children and families. *Georgia Law Review, 22,* 851–895.

Melton, G. B. (1990). Law, science, and humanity: The normative foundation of social science in law. *Law and Human Behavior, 14,* 315–332.

Melton, G. B., & Gray, J. N. (1988). Ethical dilemmas in AIDS research: Individual privacy and public health. *American Psychologist, 43,* 60–64.

Melton, G. B., & Saks, M. J. (1986). The law as an instrument of socialization and social structure. In G. B. Melton (Ed.), *The law as a behavioral instrument* (pp. 235–277). Lincoln: University of Nebraska Press.

Misconduct in Science and Engineering, 45 CFR §§689.1–689.9 (1992).

National Commission for the Protection of Human Subjects of Biomedical and Behavioral Research. (1978). *The Belmont report: Ethical Principles and guidelines for the protection of human subjects of research* (DHEW Pub. No. OS 78–0012). Washington DC: U.S. Government Printing Office.

Paternoster, R., Saltzman, L. E., Waldo, G. P., & Chiricos, T. G. (1983). Perceived risk and social control: Do sanctions really deter? *Law and Society Review, 17,* 457–479.

Pope, K. S., Levenson, H., & Schover, L. R. (1979). Sexual intimacy in psychology training. *American Psychologist, 34,* 682–689.

President's Commission for the Study of Ethical Problems in Medicine and Biomedical and Behavioral Research. (1981). *Report.* Washington DC: President's Commission for the Study of Ethical Problems in Medicine and Biomedical and Behavioral Research.

Protection of Human Subjects, 45 CFR §§46.101–46.124 (1992).

Ruback, R. B., & Greenberg, M. S. (1986). Ethical and legal aspects of applied social psychological research in field settings. In M. J. Saks & L. Saxe (Eds.), *Advances in applied social psychology, Volume 3* (pp. 207–229). Hillsdale NJ: Erlbaum.

Saks, M. J. (1986a). In search of the "lawsuit crisis." *Law, Medicine & Health Care, 14,* 77–82.

Saks, M. J. (1986b). If there be a crisis, how shall we know it? *Maryland Law Review, 46,* 63–77.

Saks, M. J. (1989). Prevalence and impact of ethical problems in the forensic sciences. *Journal of Forensic Sciences, 34,* 772–793.

Saks, M. J., & Krupat, E. (1988). *Social psychology and its applications.* New York: Harper & Row.

Saks, M. J., & Van Duizend, R. (1983). *The uses of scientific evidence in litigation.* Williamsburg VA: National Center for State Courts.

Schwartz, W. F., Baxter, K., & Ryan, D. (1984). The duel: Can these gentlemen be acting efficiently? *Journal of Legal Studies, 13,* 321–355.

Sieber, J. E. (1982). *The ethics of social research: Surveys and experiments.* New York: Springer.

Sieber, J. E. (1989). On studying the powerful (or fearing to do so): A vital role for IRBs. *IRB: A Review of Human Subjects Research, 11*(5), 1–6.

Sieber, J. E., & Saks, M. J. (1989). A census of subject pool characteristics and policies. *American Psychologist, 44,* 1053–1061.

Stover, R. V., & Erlanger, H. S. (1989). *Making it and breaking it: The fate of public interest commitment during law school*. Urbana: University of Illinois Press.

Tymchuk, A. J. (1985). Ethical decision-making and psychology students' attitudes toward training in ethics. *Professional Practice of Psychology, 6*, 219–232.

Williams, P. P. (1985). Deterrence and social control: Rethinking the relationship. *Journal of Criminal Justice, 13*, 141–151.

Zimring, F., & Hawkins, G. (1977). The legal threat as an instrument of social change. In J. L. Tapp & F. J. Levine (Eds.), *Law, justice, and the individual in society: Psychological and legal issues* (pp. 60–68). New York: Holt, Rinehart, & Winston.

Contributors

Robert F. Boruch is University Trustee Chair professor of education and statistics at the University of Pennsylvania. His work in the United States and other countries bears on generating evidence in difficult settings about social problems and their possible resolution. He and his collaborators have a special interest in how ethical standards can be met in generating good evidence.

Joe S. Cecil is a project director in the Division of Research at the Federal Judicial Center. He is currently directing the center's Program on Scientific and Technical Evidence and served as principal editor of the center's *Reference Manual on Scientific Evidence*.

Michael Dennis is a senior research psychologist at the Research Triangle Institute. He specializes in conducting randomized field experiments related to substance-abuse health services research.

Thomas Grisso is professor of psychiatry (clinical psychology) at the University of Massachusetts Medical School, where he is director of the Forensic Training and Research in the Law Program. He is author of *Evaluating Competencies*.

Jeannine R. Guido has a master's degree in psychology from the University of Detroit. She has worked as a research scientist at the New York State Psychiatric Institute in New York City, where she researched ethical issues in psychiatry, on suicide, and on the psychological consequences of AIDS.

Gary B. Melton is professor of neuropsychiatry, law, and psychology and director of the Institute for Families in Society at the University of South Carolina. The author of more than 200 publications, he is a past president of the American Psychology-Law Society and the American Psychological Association Division of Child, Youth, and Family Services.

Michael J. Saks, a social psychologist, is professor of law at the University of Iowa, where he also holds an appointment in the psychology department. His research interests include the behavior of the litigation system, the law's use of forensic science, and the psychological bases of the rules of evidence.

Joan E. Sieber, an applied social and industrial psychologist, is professor of psychology at California State University, Hayward. She is a fellow of the American Psychological Association and has been a senior visiting research scholar at the Kennedy Institute of Ethics. Her recent books include *Planning Ethically Responsible Research* and *The Ethics of Social Research,* volumes 1 and 2.

Barbara H. Stanley is a full professor in the Department of Psychology at City University of New York–John Jay College, a member of the doctoral faculty of the Criminal Justice Program at City University of New York, and a lecturer in the Department of Psychiatry at Columbia University's College of Physicians and Surgeons. She has authored many articles on research ethics and has edited books on the ethics of research with children and adolescents and geriatric psychiatry.

William C. Thompson, a lawyer and social psychologist, is associate professor of criminology, law, and society and the University of California, Irvine. He is interested in the ability of laypersons to draw appropriate conclusions from scientific and statistical evidence and has published a number of academic articles about the standards that should control the admissibility of such evidence in jury trials. He occasionally represents criminal defendants in cases involving novel scientific and statistical issues. His interest in the law and informed consent stems from his work in 1981 as a staff member for the President's Commission for the Study of Ethical Problems in Medicine and Biomedical and Behavioral Research.

Author Index

Subject Index

DATE DUE

MAY 0 1 2006		
DEC 0 1 2007		